P9-DWJ-458

The Art
of Policy Making

Tools, Techniques, and Processes in the Modern Executive Branch

George E. Shambaugh IV
*Edmund A. Walsh School of Foreign Science
and Department of Government
Georgetown University*

Paul J. Weinstein Jr.
*Progressive Policy Institute
and Former Senior White House Policy Adviser*

Longman

New York   San Francisco   Boston
London   Toronto   Sydney   Tokyo   Singapore   Madrid
Mexico City   Munich   Paris   Cape Town   Hong Kong   Montreal

Vice President/Publisher: Priscilla McGeehon
Executive Editor: Eric Stano
Senior-Marketing Manager: Megan Galvin-Fak
Production Manager: Charles Annis
Project Coordination, Text Design, and Electronic Page Makeup: Pre-Press Co., Inc.
Cover Design Manager: Wendy Fredericks
Cover Designer: Nancy Sabato
Manufacturing Manager: Al Dorsey
Printer and Binder: The Maple Vail Book Manufacturing Group
Cover Printer: Coral Graphic Services

Library of Congress Cataloging-in-Publication Data

Shambaugh, George E., 1963–
    The art of policy making: tools, techniques, and processes in the modern executive
branch / George E. Shambaugh IV, Paul J. Weinstein, Jr.
    p. cm.
Includes bibliographical references and index.
ISBN 0-321-08103-X (alk. paper)
1. Political planning —United States. I. Weinstein, Paul J. II. Title.

JK468.P64 S47 2002
352.3'4'0973—dc21   2002069454

Copyright © 2003 by Addison Wesley Longman, Inc.

All rights reserved. No part of this publication may be reproduced, stored in a retrieval system, or transmitted, in any form or by any means, electronic, mechanical, photocopying,
recording, or otherwise, without the prior written permission of the publisher. Printed in
the United States.

Please visit our website at http://www.ablongman.com

ISBN 0-321-08103-X

3 4 5 6 7 8 9 10—MA—05 04 03

Contents

Part I. The Policy Makers

Part III. Case Studies

Preface

This book is designed to introduce students and practitioners to the tools, techniques, and processes needed to master the art of policy making in the Executive branch, and to explain how and why these tools, techniques, and processes affect policy development. To accomplish these objectives, we identify key individuals in the executive branch and the roles they play in the policy-making process, we introduce the tools that enable policy makers to communicate with one another, and we analyze a series of case studies based on real-world situations to demonstrate how tools are used and how individuals interact throughout the policy-making process. Our book is heavily informed by the insights and experiences of policy makers in the George H. W. Bush, William J. Clinton, and George W. Bush administrations. While presidential management styles differ and the organizational structure of policy making evolves over time, lessons learned from these administrations can shed light on the problems and successes of past administrations and help current and future policy makers succeed.

Understanding the tools, techniques, and processes of policymaking is critical because, all else equal, policy makers with competing interests or views are more likely to support the formulation, adoption, and implementation of a particular policy if they believe that a designated body is responsible and accountable for policy development, and the tools, techniques, and processes used enable them to voice their policy ideas and concerns. Although it is certainly true that the existence of an accountable and representative policy-making process does not guarantee that the final policy decision will be the best of all possible decisions, it increases the probability that the decisions made will reflect the input and evaluation of people with a variety of competing values and objectives.

The goal of this book is, thus, to complement existing studies and theories of the policy-making process by providing students and practitioners with the tools, techniques, and processes necessary to make the policy-making process function effectively. By doing so, it also seeks to demonstrate the impact of procedural legitimacy on the policy-making process and the corresponding fruitfulness of incorporating the tools, techniques, and processes of policy making into extant theories of the policy-making process.

We could not have written this book without the insights and contributions made by many individuals within the Administrations of George H. W. Bush, William J. Clinton and George W. Bush. Paul Weinstein would particularly like to thank former Vice President Albert Gore, Jr.—who gave him his first opportunity to work in government and politics—and former President William J. Clinton for giving him the opportunity to serve his country and to hone the skills that are presented in this book. In addition, the authors would like to thank all those who helped make this book possible. While it is not possible to list all those who contributed to this project, a few people deserve special recognition: Anthony Arend, Michael Bailey, Kris Balderston, Kenneth Baer, Andrew Bennett, Eric Berman, John Bruce, Brian Burke, Jose Cerda, Victor Cha, Alan Cohen, Steve Cohen, Paul

Dimond, George Edwards, Bill Eimicke, Tom Freedman, Al From, John Harris, Mark Jacobsen, Andrea Kane, Jim Kennedy, Jim Kestler, Karin Kullman, Alan Lamborn, Jacquie Lawing, Joseph Lepgold, Bruce Lindsey, Gene Ludwig, Will Marshall, Thurgood Marshall, Jr., Sylvia Mathews, Mark Mazur, Dana Milbank, Warren Mitofsky, Steven J. Nider, Norm Ornstein, John Orszag, Bruce Reed, Douglas Reed, Cynthia Rice, Anna Richter, Leanne Shimabukuro, Gene Sperling, Alan Stone, Sue Thomas, and Stephen Wayne. We also would like to thank Eric Stano, the editors and staff at Longman, and the following outside reviewers for their insights: Scott Adler, University of Colorado; J. Theodore Anagnoson, California State University, Los Angeles; Thomas J. Boldino, Wilkes University; Thomas A. Birkland, University of Albany; Ross E. Cheit, Brown University; Michael Coulter, Grove City College; Matt Lindstrom, Siena College; R. Philip Loy, Taylor University; F. Glenn McNitt, SUNY, New Paltz; Don Ostdiek, Rice University; Kent J. Rissmiller, Worcester Polytechnic Institute; Michael J. Scicchitano, University of Florida; and Jonathan P. West, University of Miami. We are indebted to Kelly Miller for her editorial assistance. In addition, we would like to offer special thanks to Jacquelyn Shambaugh, George Shambaugh III, Elaine Jaeger, Lynne Weinstein, and Paul Weinstein Sr. for their tireless support throughout this endeavor.

George E. Shambaugh IV
Paul J. Weinstein Jr.

About the Authors

George E. Shambaugh IV is Assistant Professor of International Affairs in the Edmund A. Walsh School of Foreign Service and Department of Government at Georgetown University. He is the author of *States, Firms, and Power: Successful Sanctions in US Foreign Policy*, and coeditor of *Anarchy and the Environment: The International Politics of Common Pool Resources*. He has written on additional topics of international politics, international political economy, and the environment. He is currently working on a book on the politics of global capital flows in newly emerging market economies. Dr. Shambaugh received a Bachelor of Arts in Government and Physics from Oberlin College, and a Master of International Affairs and a Master of Philosophy and Doctor of Philosophy in Political Science from Columbia University.

Paul J. Weinstein Jr. is currently a senior fellow at the Progressive Policy Institute, a chief analyst with the Promontory Financial Group, and adjunct professor at Johns Hopkins University. He is the author of numerous articles and papers that have appeared in major newspapers and policy journals. Mr. Weinstein previously served as Senior Advisor for Policy Planning and Coordination to former Vice President Albert Gore, Jr. Prior to joining the vice president's staff, he worked at the White House as Special Assistant to the President for Domestic Policy and Chief of Staff of the Domestic Policy Council, advising President William J. Clinton on tax, economic development, banking, and political and government reform issues. Before joining the White House, Mr. Weinstein served as a Legislative Assistant to former Representative C. Thomas McMillen (D-MD) and then-Senator Albert Gore, Jr. (D-TN). Mr. Weinstein was born and raised in New York City. He received a Bachelor of Science degree from the School of Foreign Service at Georgetown University, and a Master of International Affairs from Columbia University.

Acronyms

AFDC	Aid to Families with Dependent Children
APA	Administrative Procedure Act
BTU	British Thermal Unit
CBO	Congressional Budget Office
CEA	Council of Economic Advisers
CENTCOM	Centralized Joint Command of the U.S. Military with jurisdiction in the Middle East
CEQ	Council on Environmental Quality
CIA	Central Intelligence Agency
COLA	Cost of Living Adjustment
CRA	Community Reinvestment Act
DNC	Democratic National Committee
DOD	Department of Defense
DPC	Domestic Policy Council
DPP	Democratic Progressive Party of Taiwan
DSCC	Democratic Senatorial Campaign Committee
EEZ	Exclusive Economic Zone
EOP	Executive Office of the President
EPA	Environmental Protection Agency
EU	European Union
FEMA	Federal Emergency Management Agency
GAO	General Accounting Office
GSA	General Services Administration
HHS	U.S. Department of Health and Human Services
HUD	U.S. Department of Housing and Urban Development
INS	Immigration and Naturalization Service
JCS	Joint Chiefs of Staff
KMT	Kuomintang Party of Taiwan
LRM	Legislative Referral Memorandum
NAFTA	North American Free Trade Agreement
NEC	National Economic Council
NEPA	National Environmental Policy Act
NGA	National Governors' Association
NSC	National Security Council
NSTC	National Science and Technology Council
OC	Office of Communications

OIRA	Office of Information and Regulatory Review
OIA	Office of Intergovernmental Affairs
OLA	Office of Legislative Affairs
OMB	Office of Management and Budget
ONDCP	Office of National Drug Control Policy
OPA	Office of Political Affairs
OPD	Office of Policy Development
OPEC	Organization of Petroleum Exporting Countries
OPL	Office of Public Liaison
OSTP	Office of Science and Technology Policy
PCAST	President's Committee of Advisers on Science and Technology
PO	Press Office
PRC	People's Republic of China
Q&As	Question and Answer Sheets
RNC	Republican National Committee
ROC	Republic of China on Taiwan
SAP	Statement of Administrative Policy
SBA	Small Business Administration
SSA	Social Security Administration
SSI	Supplemental Security Income
UN	United Nations
UNSC	United Nations Security Council
WTO	World Trade Organization

CHAPTER 1

Introduction: Why the Policy-making Process Matters

Overview of This Book

During the first six months of the Clinton administration in 1993, disorganization, disarray, confusion, and general chaos were the rules, not the exceptions. For 12 years Democrats had been absent from the halls of power in the executive branch. A young president and an even younger staff were unfamiliar with the decision procedures and systems within the Executive Office of the President. Faced with a large agenda—which included an economic stimulus package, universal healthcare coverage, welfare reform, anticrime legislation, and national service—the White House became bogged down, incapable of setting priorities and developing coherent policies. It took almost a year for the president's staff to become proficient in using the tools, techniques, and processes available to decision makers within the administration. In 2001 and 2002, the George W. Bush administration was trying to master the same tools, techniques, and processes in order to successfully promote its tax, energy, education, and security policies in the face of opposition from within and outside of the executive branch. The tragic events of September 11, 2001 gave the George W. Bush administration a unifying purpose and wide support for its counter-terrorism policies. The experiences of his father's administration, however, suggest that this support could be fleeting and unlikely to transfer to his other policy agendas. Consequently, President George W. Bush will need to master the art of policy making.

The primary objective of this book is to provide students and practitioners with an introduction to the tools, techniques, and processes used to make policy in the executive branch of the U.S. government. On a pragmatic level, a basic understanding of the policy-making trade—including how to write and when to use decision memoranda, how and when to use polling during the policy-making process, how to place an issue on the legislative agenda, how to get policies through the legislative clearance and coordination processes, and how and when to communicate and market policies—is necessary to function effectively within the executive

1

branch. These tools, techniques, and processes are the primary means through which the policy-making process is initiated, the ideas and concerns of policy **stake holders** are expressed and debated, and policy options are presented, made, and implemented. Policy stake holders include individuals, agencies, departments, and interest groups in the policy-making community with vested interests in the issues or policies at hand. Given time and experience, practitioners and students of policy making who have an opportunity to work in the White House will become familiar with these groups and the tools, techniques, and processes they use. This book is intended to facilitate that process and accelerate the learning curve of those who are entering the executive branch from other arenas.[1] It is also intended to further understanding of how stake holders in the executive branch interact throughout the policy-making process and the impact that their behavior has on the process itself.

To accomplish the objective of explaining how various tools, techniques, and processes affect policy development, we

- Identify key individuals in the executive branch and the roles they play in the policy-making process
- Introduce the tools that enable policy makers to communicate with one another
- Analyze a series of case studies based on real-world situations to demonstrate how these tools are used and how these individuals interact throughout the policy-making process

Our book is heavily informed by the insights and experiences of policy makers in the George H. W. Bush (1989–1993), William J. Clinton (1993–2001) and George W. Bush (2001–present) administrations. Although presidential management styles differ and the organizational structure of policy making evolves over time, lessons learned from these administrations can shed light on the problems and successes they experienced and help current and future policy makers avoid pitfalls.

The book is divided into four parts following this introductory chapter. Part I (Chapters 2–4) focuses on key actors in the policy-making apparatus. Chapter 2 focuses on the policy councils. Over the years, control of policy development has become increasingly centered in the White House and in the policy councils in particular. We will discuss the role of the three White House policy councils—the National Security, National Economic, and Domestic Policy councils—and describe their chief responsibilities: (1) honest broker, (2) protector of the president's agenda, and (3) incubator for new ideas. Chapter 3 focuses on the White House staff and describes the roles of the various offices in the White House and their relationship to one another. It also explains the flow and control of information within the White House. Chapter 4 focuses on the roles and responsibilities of agencies in the policy-making process. It also discusses the role of agencies and the White House in implementing policy decisions—by drafting regulations, filling in the details on legislation submitted by the president to Congress, carrying out presidential decisions presented in Executive Orders, and other means.

---

[1] This is particularly important in the White House because few, if any, of the core staff or records from the previous administration remain when a new president enters office. For a discussion of the difficulties of organizing the White House in a new administration, see Martha Joynt Kumar, "The White House as City Hall: A Tough Place to Organize," *Political Studies Quarterly* 31, no. 1 (March 2001): 44–55.

Part II (Chapters 5–8) provides the fundamental tools needed to create policy. Chapter 5 presents the decision memorandum. Readers will learn how to write decision and other types of memoranda for senior government officials. Using the formats developed by the Office of the White House Staff Secretary, we will guide readers through the memo-writing process and the distinctions between decision memoranda, briefing memoranda, and information memoranda. Actual presidential memoranda are provided to help the reader learn to differentiate between a well written and a poorly written memorandum. Chapter 6 analyzes the role of polling in policy making. Successful pollsters use poll data not only to identify popular ideas but also to learn how to market proposals that an administration wants to pursue. Good polling data helps policy makers refine ideas they have already developed and build a consensus. Inaccurate or incomplete polling data can doom a good proposal. Readers will learn how to prepare polling questions to ensure they capture accurate information.

Chapter 7 discusses SAPs, LRMs, and other policy acronyms. We discuss how administration policy is cleared through the executive branch. The chapter discusses the role of the Office of Management and Budget (OMB) in circulating proposals to be adopted as administration policy. A discussion of controlling the executive branch would be incomplete without discussing the role of OMB. This is where the day-to-day activities of the entire government can be routinely monitored and rendered reasonably accountable. In addition, OMB has the power to clear legislation and major regulations, and it issues administration positions on various policy matters. You will learn the relevance and uses of Statements of Administration Policy (SAPs), Legislative Referral Memorandums (LRMs), and other policy-making facilitators. We will demonstrate how to draft these documents, and we provide official formats to help guide the reader through the process.

Chapter 8 analyzes the art of communicating and marketing policy. We analyze the role of the press and communications office in the policy-making process. We also discuss how to draft press statements, Question and Answer sheets (Q&As), and backgrounders the press office can use to sell a policy agenda to the general public.

Part III (Chapters 9–11) examines three case studies based on real-world situations, decision-making events, and policy memoranda. Each case is a step-by-step analysis of an actual executive branch decision as seen through the eyes of a practitioner involved in the policy-making process. The case studies demonstrate how the tools and techniques presented in the first part of the book are used in the policy-making process. The cases include the following:

- **A pressing domestic policy issue:** Welfare Reform during the Clinton administration
- **An important economic issue:** The development of President Clinton's Economic Plan in 1993
- **A vital national security crisis:** The transition from Desert Shield to Desert Storm under the first Bush administration in 1991

Part IV (Chapter 12) develops a ten-step policy-making checklist that summarizes the lessons presented in this book. It also presents series of sample policy scenarios. This unique and special feature enables you to rehearse the tools and techniques provided in the book to hone your policy skills. Each scenario includes suggestions about the policy-making process that you can use to check understanding and application of the tools and techniques you have learned. The fictitious scenarios include the following:

- **An international political/military scenario:** A crisis in the Taiwan Straits
- **An important economic issue:** A U.S. economic recession
- **An important domestic political issue:** Congressional pressure to address campaign finance reform
- **An important multilateral issue:** A multilateral environmental initiative

Situating the Tools, Techniques, and Processes in the Existing Literature

By focusing on the basic tools of the trade of policy making, this book provides a unique complement and supplement to the plethora of textbooks and scholarly studies of policy making in the executive branch.[2] Political scientists and policy analysts have developed a variety of useful frameworks to help practitioners and scholars alike understand the policy-making process. One of the most prominent among them divides the policy-making process into a series of sequential stages—including problem identification, formulation, adoption, implementation, and evaluation—and categorizes policy actions as they vary from stage to stage.[3]

There is also a growing and increasingly sophisticated body of literature about policy makers,[4] preferences,[5] and the dynamics of individual and collective decision

---

[2] Prominent texts in the field include: George C. Edwards III and Stephen J. Wayne, *Presidential Leadership: Politics and Policymaking*, 5th ed. (New York: Worth/St. Martin's Press, 1999); Erwin C. Hargrove and Michael Nelson, *Presidents Politics and Policy* (New York: Knopf, 1984); Samuel Kernell, *Going Public*, 3d ed. (Washington, D.C.: The Congressional Quarterly, 1997); Michael Nelson, *The Presidency and the Political System* (Washington, D.C.: Congressional Quarterly, 1997); and Richard E. Neustadt, *Presidential Power and the Modern Presidents* (New York: Free Press, 1990).

[3] The *sequential approach*, also known as the "stages heuristic," or "the textbook approach," was developed by James Anderson, Charles Jones, Gary Brewer, and Peter deLeon. See James E. Anderson, *Public Policymaking: An Introduction* (Boston: Houghton Mifflin, 1990), and Peter deLeon, "The Stages Approach to the Policy Process: What Has it Done? Where is it Going?" in Paul Sabatier, ed. *Theories of the Policy Process* (Boulder: Westview Press, 1999), 19–32. For a critique of this approach, see Charles Lindblom and Edward J. Woodhouse, *The Policy-Making Process* (Englewood Cliffs, N.J.: Prentice Hall, 1993), and John Kingdon, *Agendas Alternatives, and Public Policy* (Boston: Little Brown, 1984).

[4] Classics in this tradition include I. M. Destler, *Presidents, Bureaucrats, and Foreign Policy* (Princeton: Princeton University Press, 1972), and Richard E. Neustadt, *Presidential Power and the Modern Presidents* (New York: Free Press, 1990).

[5] This includes theories about the source of policy-maker preferences as well as rational choice and institutional rational choice theories about how individuals pursue act to maximize their preferences within a set of institutional constraints. On the former, see Graham Allison and Philip Zelikow, *Essence of Decision: Explaining the Cuban Missile Crisis* (New York: Longman, 1999), and Roger Hilsman with Laura Gaughran and Patricia A. Weitsman, *The Politics of Policymaking in Defense and Foreign Affairs: Conceptual Models and Bureaucratic Politics*, 3d ed. (Englewood Cliffs, N.J.: Prentice Hall, 1993). On the latter, see Kenneth Shepsle, *Analyzing Politics* (New York: W. W. Norton, 1997), and John Kingdon, *Agendas, Alternatives, and Public Policies* (New York: Harper Collins, 1995). For a critique of rational choice approaches to policy analysis, see Deborah Stone, *Policy Paradox and Political Reason* (Glenview, Ill.: Scott, Foresman and Company, 1988).

making in an institutional context.[6] These include studies focusing on the impact of the organizational process, bureaucratic politics, and presidential management styles on the policy-making process. For example, the presidential management model analyzes the impact that different management strategies and decision-making styles have on the ability of presidents to manage individuals and agencies competing to dominate the policy-making process.[7]

In addition, other scholars are dedicated to informing these theoretical debates with insights and perceptions of policy makers regarding the role and structure of important organizational units within the executive branch. Prominent among these are recent publications by the Presidency Research Group (PRG), which provide insights and detailed information about particular executive branch units based on extensive interviews with practitioners in recent administrations.[8]

Combined, these literatures provide useful analyses of how legal, institutional, historical, organizational, psychological, and political factors affect the policy making in the executive branch.[9] They are, however, relatively silent about the tools and techniques that policy makers in the executive branch use to achieve their ends and the impact that these practices have on the process of policy making. By highlighting tools and techniques, we do not suggest that the factors emphasized by other writers in this diverse literature are unimportant; indeed, many of them rely on and influence those tools, techniques, and processes.

One of the most broadly recognized characteristics of the modern executive branch noted in the existing literature is the existence of a gap between the high demands and expectations that the public place on the president and the president's

---

[6] For example, the Advocacy Coalition Framework developed by Sabatier and Jenkin-Smith focuses on the interaction between advocacy coalitions in the policy-making process. See Paul Sabatier and Hank Jenkin's Smith, *Policy Change and Learning: An Advocacy Coalition Approach* (Boulder: Westview Press, 1993). In addition, Jeffrey Pressman and Aaron Wildavsky analyze the problems that arise as a result of having multiple participants and perspective involved in the policy implementation. See Jeffrey Pressman and Aaron Wildavsky, *Implementation*, 2d ed. (Berkeley: University of California Press, 1979).

[7] The *organizational process model* evaluates policy making in terms of executive efforts to manage a conglomeration of semi-independent agencies and departments, each promoting a policy that reflects its own interests and perspectives. The *bureaucratic politics model* emphasizes bargaining among individuals and coalitions whose perceptions, interests, and ambitions reflect, at least in part, their organizational affiliations. For a review of these approaches, see William Newmann, "Causes of Change in National Security Processes: Carter, Reagan, and Bush Decision Making on Arms Control," *Presidential Studies Quarterly* 31, no. 1 (March 2001): 69–103.

[8] Professor Martha Kumar is the research director of the Presidency Research Group, which includes the White House Interview Program. The program's objective was to provide a detailed job description of some of the most important positions in the White House. Beginning in December of 2001 with the publication of guidelines for planning a transition to power for the new president, its findings have been published in *Presidential Studies Quarterly*. Citations to PRG articles are included throughout the text for those readers interested in additional information about specific executive branch organizations and the views of practitioners within them. The *Presidential Studies Quarterly* is published by the Center for the Study of the Presidency in Washington, D.C. Other publications sponsored by the Center include David Abshire, ed., *Triumphs and Tragedies of the Modern Presidency: Sixty-Six Case Studies in Presidential Leadership* (Westport, Conn.: Preager, 2001).

[9] For a summary of this literature see George C. Edwards III and Stephen J. Wayne, "Appendix A: Studying the Presidency," in George C. Edwards III and Stephen J. Wayne, *Presidential Leadership: Politics and Policy Making*, 5th ed. (New York: St. Martin's/Worth Publishing, 1999), 503–516.

comparatively limited legal, political, and institutional capabilities to meet them.[10] We argue that understanding the tools, techniques, and processes can help policy makers reduce this problem and bridge the performance-expectations gap. This is because, all else being equal, policy stake holders are more likely to support the formulation, adoption, and implementation of a particular policy if they feel that the tools, techniques, and processes used by the president (or designated decision maker accountable for policy development) enable them to voice their policy ideas and concerns.

The Importance of Procedural Legitimacy in Building Policy Support

The process of molding an idea into a policy within the executive branch involves the collective action of a wide range of individuals, policy councils, agencies, and departments who have a stake in its outcome. The majority of these executive branch stake holders share some common policy goals most of the time; indeed, in terms of their goals, the degree of compatibility among executive branch members is likely to be much greater than the degree of compatibility between those in the executive branch and those in the legislative and judicial branches.[11] Nevertheless, the individuals, policy councils, agencies, and departments within the executive branch often disagree about the relative importance of bringing one issue versus another to the president's attention. Even if there is agreement that something must be done on a particular issue, there often is disagreement about precisely what the

---

[10] See Richard E. Neustadt, *Presidential Power and the Modern Presidents* (New York: Free Press, 1990); Joseph A. Pika and Norman C. Thomas, "The Presidency since Mid-Century," *Congress and the Presidency* 19, no. 1 (Spring 1992): 29–46; Karen M. Hult, "Strengthening Presidential Decision-Making Capacity," *Presidential Studies Quarterly* 30, no. 1 (March 2000): 27–46. Recent critics of this viewpoint, including Terry Moe and William Howell, argue that modern presidents have a great institutional capacity to act unilaterally and make law on their own. See Terry M. Moe and William G. Howell, "Unilateral Action and Presidential Power: A Theory," *Presidential Studies Quarterly* 29, no. 4 (1999): 850–872. Others, including Charles Jones, argue that presidents may be able to take advantage of the competition among different units in the federal government to assert influence over the policy agenda. See Charles O. Jones, "Reinventing Leeway: The President and Agenda Certification," *Presidential Studies Quarterly* 30, no. 1 (March 2000): 6–26. For some of the potential problems resulting from this gap, see Colin Campbell, *The US Presidency in Crisis: A Comparative Perspective* (New York: Oxford University Press, 1998); Larry M. Lane, "The Public Administration and the Problem of the Presidency," In *Refounding Democratic Public Administration: Modern Paradoxes, Postmodern Challenges*, eds. Gary L. Wamsley and James F. Wolf. (Thousand Oaks, Calif.: Sage, 1996); and Paul C. Light, *Thickening Government: Federal Hierarchy and the Diffusion of Accountability* (Washington, D.C.: Brookings Institution, 1995). Stephen J. Wayne, G. Calvin MacKenzie, David M. O'Brien, and Richard L. Cole, *The Politics of American Government*, 3d ed. (New York: St. Martin's/Worth Publishing, 1999), 498. See also Karen Hult, "Strengthening Presidential Decision-Making Capacity," *Presidential Studies Quarterly* 30, no.1 (March 2000): 27–46, and Terry N. Moe, "The Politicized Presidency," in John Chudd and Paul Peterson, eds. *The New Directions in American Politics* (Washington, D.C.: Brookings, 1985); Bert A. Rockman, *The Leadership Question* (New York: Preager, 1984).

[11] The division of powers and preferences into the executive, legislative, and judicial branches were, of course, part of the system of checks and balances established by the Framers of the Constitution to keep any one group from gaining pervasive influence over another. For a discussion of policy makers and the policy environment, see James Anderson, *Public Policymaking: An Introduction* (Boston: Houghton Mifflin, 1990), 41–76.

specific objectives of the administration's policy response should be or how best to achieve those objectives. For example, prior to the inauguration in 1993 President-elect Clinton's policy-making team did not agree on the relative merits of pursuing welfare versus healthcare reform and, even when welfare reform eventually was given priority, the Domestic Policy Council and the Department of Health and Human Services did not concur on the structure welfare reform policy should take.

The policy-making environment is, thus, often characterized by multiple groups with both common and competing viewpoints vying to influence the form and content of policy ideas. Power and responsibility are distributed unevenly and tend to shift among these groups over time and across issues.[12] At the same time, however, there are powerful incentives for these groups to **strain toward agreement** and reach a collective solution to the problems at hand.[13] Because policy makers have shared ideas, especially about the importance and role of the executive branch in policy making, they recognize that their integrity as policy makers and the integrity of the system as a whole lies in the ability to function and respond to specific problems.

In such a complex environment, it is often difficult to achieve a consensus about a policy goal or the best means to reach that goal. Stake holders are, however, often more readily able to agree on the fairness and effectiveness of the procedures for policy making. As a consequence, they often evaluate the practices of other policy makers in terms of the tools, techniques, and processes or procedures by which they function in addition to the outcomes they produce.[14] Sociological, legal, and policy studies suggest that the perceived legitimacy of the tools, techniques, and procedures of complex decision-making processes have a significant impact on the willingness of people to take part in that process. It also affects willingness to implement or comply with the resulting policy. For example, in a 1984–1985 survey of 2379 people who were involved with the U.S. legal system, Tom Tyler found that perceptions of **procedural legitimacy** had a significant impact on how people evaluated the decisions made and the decision-making processes used by politicians, the courts, and the police.[15] He found that the more "fair" and "appropriate" the procedures were perceived to be, the more people were willing to accept and comply with a particular interpretation of the law, even when the outcome was undesirable. The perception of procedural legitimacy mattered more when the issues were contentious and less when they were not,

---

[12] For a discussion of different aspects of fragmentation within the executive branch, see Roger Porter, *Presidential Decision Making* (Cambridge, England: Cambridge University Press, 1980), 11–25.

[13] Roger Hilsman with Laura Gaughran and Patricia A. Weitsman, *The Politics of Policymaking in Defense and Foreign Affairs: Conceptual Models and Bureaucratic Politics*, 3d ed. (Englewood Cliffs, N.J.: Prentice Hall, 1993), 80–81, Warner Schilling, "The Politics of National Defense: Fiscal 1960," in *Strategy, Politics and Defense Budgets*, eds. Warner R. Schilling, Paul Y. Hammond, and Glenn H. Snyder (New York: Columbia University Press, 1962), 23, and Deborah Stone, *Policy Paradox and Political Reason* (Glenview, Ill.: Scott, Foresman and Company, 1988), 7.

[14] Tom Tyler, *Why People Obey the Law* (New Haven: Yale University Press, 1990), 109.

[15] Ibid., 105.

more when compliance with a given set of procedures or rules was voluntary than when it was enforced, and far more when the participants valued a particular outcome highly than when they did not (regardless of whether or not the decision was favorable). Consistent with this finding, studies of international law suggest that even in the absence of a central authority or viable enforcement mechanism in international politics, nation-states are likely to accept and conform to international rules and norms when they perceive them to have a high degree of legitimacy.[16] Conversely, when international rules and norms are not considered to be legitimate, compliance decreases substantially.

Political scientists have argued, further, that the political significance of legitimacy is one of the most fundamental components of political interaction. For example, Alan Lamborn argues that how people react to a particular set of policy outcomes in a political context will vary depending on the importance they attach to creating or sustaining legitimate relationships, their beliefs about legitimate procedures and outcomes, and their perceptions of how legitimate their existing relationships are.[17] Consistent with the individuals in Taylor's study of the legal system discussed above, Lamborn argues that the political importance of the legitimacy of a specific policy outcome and the legitimacy of the policy process from which it evolved are inversely related. In other words, the lower the legitimacy of policy outcome, the greater the political significance of procedural legitimacy.[18] If people place a high value on sustaining legitimate relationships (as competing policy makers in the executive branch do when they "strain toward agreement" on collective decisions) and their relationships are perceived to be legitimate, then they are more likely to accept outcomes that adversely affect their short-term policy preferences.[19]

Given the central role of legitimacy in the policy-making process, it is important to understand how policy makers define fair or legitimate procedures. Some take an *instrumental* view and argue that fairness may be defined in terms of the policy outcome and the degree to which the outcome reflects the specific interests of particular policy makers. The ends, thus, justify and motivate the means. Others take an *institutional* perspective and argue that legitimacy may be explained in terms of the rules about how laws are made, how decision makers are chosen, and how public participation is achieved.[20] In support of the second of these two viewpoints,

[16] International legal scholars emphasize the importance of legitimacy as a property of a rule or rule-making institution which itself exerts a pull towards compliance. See Thomas Franck, *The Power of Legitimacy Among Nations* (Oxford, England: Oxford University Press, 1990), 25.

[17] Alan Lamborn, "Theory and the Politics of World Politics," *International Studies Quarterly* 41 (1997): 187–214.

[18] The converse is also true.

[19] Alan Lamborn, "Theory and the Politics of World Politics," *International Studies Quarterly* 41 (1997): 193.

[20] This view builds on Max Weber's conception of legitimacy in terms of a specific process. See Thomas Franck, *The Power of Legitimacy Among Nations* (Oxford: Oxford University Press, 1990), 17. Some scholars have expressed a concern that constitutional, institutional, and procedural constraints have created obstacles to policy development and change. See, for example, David Robertson and Dennis Judd, *The Development of American Public Policy: The Structure of Policy Constraint* (Boston: Scott, Foresman and Company, 1989).

Tyler's statistical study suggests that people actually value the ability to obtain a specific outcome less than the opportunity to present their arguments, being listened to, and having their views considered by those responsible for policy development.[21] Individuals who felt that they played a role in the decision-making process were more accepting of the outcome, regardless of its nature. The study also found that perceptions of legitimacy and fairness were linked to judgments about the neutrality of the chief decision maker and the unbiased nature of the decision-making process. Those who felt that the process was biased, or that their views were not being considered by those responsible for policy development were more apt to exit the formal decision-making process and evade its decisions.

These findings have important implications for policy making in the executive branch. In particular, policy makers in the executive branch often negotiate over highly contentious and politically volatile issues, they generally act voluntarily rather than being compelled to do so, and they often have a high stake in particular outcomes. Consequently, based on the survey results, one would expect procedural legitimacy to matter greatly to policy makers in the executive branch. The policy-making process is, thus, likely to be evaluated as much in terms of how it operates as by what it produces. As Deborah Stone argues, the policy-making process is largely a struggle over ideas; ideas serve both as the medium of exchange among policy makers and the source of influence over the policy-making process.[22] Given the importance of ideas to the policy-making process, we argue that the process of developing a policy, establishing a policy proposal, securing passage of the proposal, and implementing it will work most smoothly when all relevant policy makers perceive the policy-making process as an effective and legitimate means of voicing their policy ideas to the chief decision maker.

We join prominent scholars and practitioners in defining legitimacy in terms of how things are done (that is, whether proper procedures are used) as well as what is actually being done.[23] As noted by Thomas Franck, for example, the fairness of any legal system will be judged, "first by the degree to which the rules satisfy the participant's expectations of justifiable distribution of costs and benefits [substance], and secondly, by the extent to which the rules are made and applied in accordance with what the participants perceive as the right process [procedure]."[24] Belief that the right process has been followed will be greatest when policy makers believe that "decisions about the distributive and other entitlements will be made by those duly authorized and in accordance with procedures which protect against corrupt, arbitrary, or idiosyncratic decision-making or decision-executing."[25]

---

[21] Tom Tyler, *Why People Obey the Law* (New Haven: Yale University Press, 1990), 163.

[22] Deborah Stone, *Policy Paradox and Political Reason* (Glenview, Ill.: Scott, Foresman and Company, 1988), 7.

[23] James Anderson, *Public Policymaking: An Introduction* (Boston: Houghton Mifflin, 1990), 110.

[24] Thomas M. Franck, *Fairness in International Law and Institutions* (Oxford, England: Clarendon Press, 1995), 7.

[25] Ibid., 7.

Some of the rules and procedures of the policy-making process are codified in the Constitution, determined by Congress, or specified in Executive Orders or other legal processes. As we have noted, when policy making is conducted outside of established rules and procedures, its legitimacy is likely to be questioned. At the same time, however, acting within the bounds of one's legal authority is not sufficient to guarantee that the process will be perceived as legitimate. Indeed, as James Anderson argues, "Some actions of government, even when within the legal or constitutional authority of officials, may not be regarded as legitimate because they depart too far from prevailing notions of what is acceptable."[26] Consequently, we evaluate the legitimacy of the policy-making process within the executive branch in terms of the extent to which the relevant members of the policy-making community believe that the procedures and tools used in formulating and adopting policy provide an effective means of adding their ideas and concerns to the policy debate. Learning to write and use tools like decision-making memoranda effectively are important precisely because when they are used appropriately, they can make the policy-making process work smoothly and thereby increase the level of support the resulting policy is likely to receive.

The degree to which members of the policy-making community believe that the process of policy making is legitimate may be as important a factor in gaining their support for a particular policy proposal as the potential distributional consequences of the final policy decision. When accountability is unclear, or when the tools utilized fail to provide an effective means for those with opposing viewpoints to participate in policy development, disgruntled stake holders tend to circumvent the process and use other means—such as leaking information to the media, circumventing or ignoring bureaucratic hierarchies, and attempting to contact the president (or the decision makers responsible for policy development) directly—to promote their objectives.[27] Such activity undermines the policy-making process because it tends to present the president (or the decision makers responsible for policy development) with a biased view of the issue at hand, and it often sparks similar retaliatory action by others who do not share that view.[28] This wastes time and sends a signal of uncertainty to Congress; in addition, the public's willingness to support executive actions may be reduced.[29] The end result may be an ill-considered policy or, more likely, political deadlock and a decline in the president's reputation in

---

[26] James Anderson, *Public Policymaking: An Introduction* (Boston: Houghton Mifflin Company, 1990), 110.

[27] In the words of Albert O. Hirschman, the ability to voice one's concerns tends to be associated with increased loyalty, while the inability to do so is associated with a tendency to exit. Albert O. Hirschman, *Exit, Voice, and Loyalty: Responses to Decline in Firms, Organizations, and States* (Cambridge, Mass.: Harvard University Press, 1970).

[28] In political science jargon, the failure of the chief decision maker to weigh all options in an unbiased manner reduces his or her ability to act in a fully rational manner.

[29] Richard Neustadt, one of the most influential scholars of the presidency, argues that the president's power to lead is greatly affected by his reputation for competency in Washington and his prestige with the general public. In support of this contention, George Edwards found that popular presidents received more congressional support regardless of party affiliation. George C. Edwards III, *At the Margins* (New Haven, Conn.: Yale University Press, 1989), 124; Richard E. Neustadt, *Presidential Power and the Modern Presidents* (New York: Free Press, 1990).

Washington as well as in his prestige with the general public. Although it is certainly true that the existence of an accountable and representative policy-making process does not guarantee that the final policy decision will be the best of all possible decisions, it increases the probability that the decisions made will reflect the input and evaluation of a variety of competing values and objectives; this, in turn, increases the likelihood that the policy will be supported and adopted.[30]

As we noted, one of the most prominent techniques scholars have used to conceptualize and evaluate the policy-making process is to divide it into a series of sequential stages—including problem identification, formulation, adoption, implementation, and evaluation—and categorize policy actions as they vary from stage to stage. We argue that the development of pertinent and acceptable courses of action for dealing with **action-forcing events** in the policy *formulation* stage, and the development of support for a specific proposal so that it gains broad enough acceptance to be authorized in the policy *adoption* stage, are more likely to take place when the participants perceive the process itself to be a legitimate and effective means of voicing their positions and concerns to the chief decision maker. In essence, support for a particular policy is likely to be higher when the process—as well as the president or the decision-making unit responsible and accountable for policy development—is considered to be an honest and effective broker of competing policy proposals.

Presidential Management and Procedural Legitimacy

The way in which the president organizes and manages the executive branch may have significant implications for the level of procedural legitimacy that stake holders are likely to grant to the policy-making process and, hence, the level of support they will give the resulting policy proposal. In particular, one of the primary lessons learned from the policy-making experiences of the George H. W. Bush, William J. Clinton, and George W. Bush administrations is that stake holders in the executive branch are more likely to consider the process to be legitimate when the authority and responsibility for policy development is centralized in a designated unit and the tools, techniques, and processes used by that unit facilitates stake holder participation. Thus, policy making is likely to be considered legitimate when the tools, techniques, and processes used provide accountability and access to those who wish to have their views represented.

The process used by the National Economic Council (NEC) when it developed the Clinton economic plan in 1993 was accountable and representative (see Chapter 10). As a consequence, the level of procedural legitimacy and support by stake holders in the executive branch was high. In contrast, when the responsibility and accountability for policy development are not centralized, as was true with

---

[30] Roger Porter, *Presidential Decision Making* (Cambridge, England: Cambridge University Press, 1980), 1.

Clinton's welfare reform policy issue before 1994, or when the process is centralized but key policy makers are excluded or unable to express their views and concerns as the policy develops, as was true during Desert Storm and Desert Shield (discussed in Chapter 11), the amount of support among stake holders in the executive branch will decline and the likelihood that people will bypass the process increases.

Much of the recent work on presidential decision making has emphasized the importance of institutional arrangements and organizational characteristics on policy choices.[31] As mentioned above, prominent among these is the presidential management model which posits that the organizational strategies and decision-making styles presidents use can have a significant impact on their ability to lead and maintain control over individuals and agencies competing to dominate the policy-making process.

The organizational strategies and decision-making styles used by presidents vary on a variety of dimensions. For example, differences in management style include the extent to which the president is involved in the intricacies and details of policy making. Presidents Franklin Roosevelt, Lyndon Johnson, Jimmy Carter, and Bill Clinton preferred greater involvement; President Reagan preferred to delegate. They also include the president's preference for

- Establishing hierarchies of authority versus more informal, ad hoc systems of policy making—Presidents Harry Truman, Dwight Eisenhower, Richard Nixon, and Ronald Reagan preferred the former, Presidents Franklin Roosevelt, Harry Truman, and John Kennedy preferred the latter
- Verbal debate versus a preference carrying out debates and briefings in writing—Presidents Franklin Roosevelt and Harry Truman preferred the former, presidents Richard Nixon and Jimmy Carter the latter
- Involvement in negotiations—Franklin Roosevelt and Lyndon Johnson preferred to negotiate, while John Kennedy, Richard Nixon, and Jimmy Carter preferred to let others negotiate on their behalf [32]

---

[31] See for example John P. Burke, *The Institutional Presidency* (Baltimore: Johns Hopkins University Press, 1992); Colin Campbell, *Managing the Presidency* (Pittsburgh: University of Pittsburgh Press, 1983); Alexander George, *Presidential Decisions in Foreign Policy* (Boulder: Westview Press, 1980); John Hart, *The Presidential Branch: From Washington to Clinton*, 2d ed. (Chatham, N.J.: Chatham House, 1995); Stephen Hess, *Organizing the Presidency*, 2d ed. (Washington, D.C.: Brookings Institution, 1998); Margaret G. Hermann and Thomas Preston, "Presidents, Advisors and Foreign Policy: The Effects of Leadership Style on Executive Arrangements," *Political Psychology* 15, no. 1 (1995): 75–96; Terry M. Moe and William G. Howell, "Unilateral Action and Presidential Power: A Theory," *Presidential Studies Quarterly* 29, no. 4 (1999): 850–872; William Newmann, "Causes of Change in National Security Processes: Carter, Reagan, and Bush Decision Making on Arms Control," *Presidential Studies Quarterly* 31, no. 1 (March 2001): 69–103; and Roger Porter, *Presidential Decision Making: The Economic Policy Board* (Cambridge, England: Cambridge University Press, 1980); Robert J. Thompson, "Contrasting Models of White House Staff Organization: The Eisenhower, Ford and Carter Experiences," *Congress and the Presidency* 19 (Autumn 1992): 113–136; Shirley Anne Warshaw, *The Domestic Presidency: Policymaking in the White House* (Boston: Allyn and Bacon, 1997).

[32] Jack H. Watson, Jr. "The Clinton White House," *Presidential Studies Quarterly* 23 (Summer 1993): 429. Written approaches require that options that go to the president be throughly reviewed by all relevant officials beforehand. Consequently, they may provide a conduit to the president for those who find it difficult to express themselves to him directly. As noted by George C. Edwards and Stephen J. Wayne, this may be especially true if presidents, like Lyndon Johnson, Nixon, and Clinton gain a reputation for being unreceptive or react strongly against those aides who present options or information they dislike. George C. Edwards III and Stephen J. Wayne, *Presidential Leadership: Politics and Policymaking*, 5th ed. (New York: Worth/St. Martin's Press, 1999), 232.

Roger Porter, a noted political scientist, recently synthesized these characteristics into three general types of presidential management: **centralized management** characterized by a hierarchical and formal staff structure; **adhocracy** in which decision making is flexible and informal; and **multiple advocacy** in which key staff members are responsible for managing the system and making sure that all competing groups and individuals are represented in the policy-making process.[33]

The organization of the policy-making process within the executive branch tends to vary across issues and over time throughout any given administration.[34] Like Franklin Roosevelt and other twentieth-century presidents, President Clinton at first played an active but unsystematic role in policy making. Consistent with the **adhocracy model** of policy management, President Clinton initially distributed assignments and selected whom to seek advice from and when, without making much use of regularized meetings or institutionalized patterns of providing policy advice.[35] This organizational strategy does not rely heavily on institutionalized or regularized patterns of policy input; instead it relies much more on the direct, though unsystematic involvement of the president in determining how he receives advice. This strategy has the advantage of being highly flexible and quickly responsive, while enabling the president to maintain confidentiality regarding new policy initiatives by limiting the number of personally selected advisors involved in the process.[36]

Despite its attractiveness and prevalence in the early phases of new administrations, the adhocracy management model has several drawbacks.[37] One of them is that it promotes the creation of interagency groups to address particular aspects of broad policy initiatives without providing a clear view of, or mandate to address, the policy in its entirety. In such cases, responsibility for policy development is often

---

[33] Roger Porter, *Presidential Decision Making* (Cambridge, England: Cambridge University Press, 1980). Other scholars emphasize the distinction between competitive management styles, hierarchical management styles, and collegial or "spoke of the wheel" management styles. See for example Bruce Buchanan, "Constrained Diversity: The Organizational Demands of the Presidency," *Presidential Studies Quarterly* 20 (1991): 791–822; Alexander George, *Presidential Decision Making in Foreign Policy* (Boulder: Westview Press, 1980); Richard Johnson, *Managing the White House* (New York: Harper & Row, 1974); Robert J. Thompson, "Contrasting Models of White House Staff Organization: The Eisenhower, Ford and Carter Experiences," *Congress and the Presidency* 19, no. 2 (1992): 113–136. In his study of the Carter and Reagan presidencies, Professor Colin Campbell evaluates the impact of a variety of additional characteristics including the president's preference for centralized versus decentralized management, the president's relationships with his advisors, and the relationships among the president's advisors. See Colin Campbell, *Managing the Presidency: Carter, Reagan, and the Search for Executive Harmony* (Pittsburgh: University of Pittsburgh Press, 1986). For a review of this literature, see William Newmann, "Causes of Change in National Security Processes: Carter, Reagan, and Bush Decision Making on Arms Control," *Presidential Studies Quarterly* 31, no. 1 (March 2001): 71–72.

[34] See Robert J. Thompson, "Contrasting Models of White House Staff Organization: The Eisenhower, Ford and Carter Experiences," *Congress and the Presidency* 19, no. 2 (1992): 113–136.

[35] The turning point away from an adhocracy approach to a more centralized organization of policy making came with a confluence of events after two years in office, including the Republican takeover of Congress and the appointment of Leon Panetta to the position of Chief of Staff. Elizabeth Drew, *On the Edge: The Clinton Presidency* (New York: Touchstone, 1994), 347–349. For a discussion of the adhocracy approach, see Roger Porter, *Presidential Decision Making* (Cambridge, England: Cambridge University Press, 1980), 25, 231–235.

[36] Roger Porter, *Presidential Decision Making* (Cambridge, England: Cambridge University Press, 1980), 233.

[37] Ibid., 235.

diffuse or unclear, and access to the president is uncertain. Under such circumstances, the president's limited time is often wasted on resolving internal disputes and clarifying or defending his organization rather than developing and promoting a particular policy. For example, during the adhocracy period of the early Clinton administration, an interagency committee including the Domestic Policy Council, the Department of Health and Human Services, and the Department of Labor was established to analyze welfare reform. No clear mandate was given to the group, nor were the responsibility and leadership roles within the group well defined. As a result, Bruce Reed, who jointly directed the working group with David Ellwood and Mary Jo Bane, sent memoranda directly to the president on several occasions merely to inform him of internal conflicts and seek his help in resolving disputes within the working committee; rather than to propose policy options or promote welfare reform itself. As a result, the group was frustrated and the welfare reform policy process stagnated. This wastes time and is a misuse of an otherwise powerful policy-making tool.

As his administration evolved, President Clinton changed his organizational strategy to a hybrid of a **centralized management model** and a **multiple advocacy model**.[38] A centralized management model is characterized by heavy reliance on the White House and the president's staff to filter ideas, policy proposals, and recommendations coming to the president from executive departments and agencies.[39] It emphasizes systematic evaluation of policy questions with control vested in individuals solely responsible to the president; they are often advocates of his views. While executive branch departments and agencies have input into the policy-making process, their role is managed and mediated by the Executive Office and the president's personal staff. This organizational strategy has the benefits of clearly specifying who has the authority and responsibility for the development of specific policies and enabling the president to manage a wide variety of issues, respond to change quickly, and minimize leaks by filtering actions through a personal staff.

One of the most important dangers of the centralized management model is that it tends to focus responsibility for a particular policy in the hands of an individual or small group which is given preferential and often exclusive access to the president. At worst this can promote a tendency known as **groupthink,** in which individuals in small, insulated, and cohesive decision-making groups lack the procedures to guarantee an outside appraisal of their actions. Under such circumstances, decision makers in the group tend to evaluate and rationalize problems collectively, develop illusions of invulnerability and unanimity, view other groups and opponents as less capable, tolerate only self-censorship, and pressure internal dissenters to conform.[40] The group's assumptions and concerns are self-confirmed, and

[38] Roger Porter, *Presidential Decision Making* (Cambridge, England: Cambridge University Press, 1980), 214–223, 235–252. See also Alexander George, "The Case for Multiple Advocacy in Making Foreign Policy," *American Political Science Review* 66 (September 1972): 751–785, and "The Devil's Advocate: Uses and Limitations," in U.S. Commission on the Organization of the Government for the Conduct of Foreign Policy, *Appendices* (Washington, D.C.: GPO, June 1975), vol. 2, 83–85; and George Edwards and Stephen Wayne, *Presidential Leadership: Politics and Policy Making*, 5th ed. (New York: St. Martin's/Worth Publishing, 1999), 226–229.

[39] Roger Porter, *Presidential Decision Making* (Cambridge, England: Cambridge University Press, 1980), 235.

[40] Irvin Janis, *Victims of Groupthink* (Boston: Houghton Mifflin, 1972), 42.

a desire for unanimity and support for the group's leader override the motivation for realistically appraising potentially challenging alternative actions. This dynamic may be exacerbated by presidents—like Richard Nixon and apparently George W. Bush—who discourage public dissent and emphasize loyalty among their staff.

Even if the worst aspects of groupthink dynamics do not appear, if other policy makers, departments, or agencies feel that this arrangement prevents them from voicing their concerns and having their policy proposal considered by the president, they are likely to become frustrated and attempt to influence the president by other means. As we discuss in Chapter 11, even though public and congressional support for military action was high, President George H. W. Bush's heavy reliance on a very small group of decision makers led a variety of senior officials to try influencing policy by operating outside of existing procedures and processes during Desert Storm and Desert Shield in 1991. Although policy makers without access to the president or a chief decision maker are not likely to be able to bring an alternative policy to fruition, they often are capable of stalling or disrupting the policy-making process. This pattern of policy making played itself out vividly on the issue of healthcare reform in the first Clinton administration. President Clinton centered control and responsibility over healthcare reform in the First Lady's office. Doing so alienated a large number of individuals, agencies, and departments in the executive branch. Contrary to some media stories, many of these policy makers stated that they were not alienated because of the policy itself or the intensive involvement of Hillary Clinton; rather, the process broke down because many policy makers who had a vested concern in healthcare reform felt that their concerns and policy suggestions were not being voiced or considered by the president while others were being given preferential access.

In contrast, a system of multiple advocacy is designed specifically to expose the president to stake holders who represent different viewpoints and concerns.[41] The president's role in this system is to be an honest broker between departments and agencies competing to promote their policy proposals. This competition exposes the president to a wide range of ideas and promotes quality control by guaranteeing that no single viewpoint dominates the decision-making process. This organizational strategy has the benefit of promoting participation and, therefore, helping to create an opportunity for all parties to express their views about a given policy. Participation tends to enhance the perception of legitimacy and helps to build support for a particular outcome. In its ideal form, the final stages of the decision-making process in this system involve a meeting between the president and multiple advisors in which each is able to present and debate the trade-offs of a final policy proposal.

The process of welfare reform policy formation during the second half of the Clinton administration represented a combination of centralized management and multiple advocacy. In contrast to the jointly-directed-multiple-agency working group set up in 1992, Bruce Reed and the Domestic Policy Council were given a mandate and specific responsibility for managing and developing a welfare reform

---

[41] Alexander George, "The Case for Multiple Advocacy in Making Foreign Policy," *American Political Science Review* 66 (September 1972): 751–785, and Roger Porter, *Presidential Decision Making* (Cambridge, England: Cambridge University Press, 1980), 243–247.

policy beginning in 1994. From that point on, consistent with a centralized management model of organization, the DPC managed the process and acted as a conduit and advocate of presidential initiatives on welfare reform. In addition, however, the president and the DPC made an effort to address the concerns of key policy makers in the Department of Health and Human Services (HHS) and other agencies and departments. For example, in the spirit of the multiple advocacy model, the final decision to sign the welfare reform legislation in 1996 was taken after a meeting between President Clinton and senior advisers representing various positions in the welfare reform debate. His advisors disagreed, and the president made his decision to sign the legislation after listening to each person in the room express his or her position regarding the proposed welfare reform.

As the very term *centralized management model of policy management* suggests, the Executive Office of the President (EOP) has played a central role in both the Bill Clinton and George W. Bush administrations as the conduit through which policy proposals must pass before reaching the president. Despite public comments that he would decentralize the role of the White House and raise the profile of the cabinet, President George W. Bush continued President Clinton's efforts to strengthen the role of the Executive Office of the President in coordinating and leading policy making. For example, he kept both the National Economic Council and the Domestic Policy Council that President Clinton created. This means that both councils will likely become institutionalized much as their exemplar, the National Security Council, did. Bush has also created a cabinet-level Office of Homeland Security, which centralizes and coordinates intelligence and relief activities of a variety of federal agencies in the White House. During the first year of the George W. Bush administration, the president relied on highly centralized and relatively closed policy-making processes to develop policies related to the budget, taxation, education, energy, missile defense, and anti-terrorism efforts.

Lessons from the successes and failures of policy making during the George H. W. Bush and William J. Clinton administrations suggest that while centralized management and the clear designation of authority and accountability for policy development in a designated unit can increase the perception of procedural legitimacy, this is contingent upon the decision-making unit's ability to act as an honest broker and create a process that enables all stake holders to express their voices in the policy-making process. Increased centralization of policy making in the policy councils during the Clinton administration enhanced the perceived effectiveness of the policy-making process as a means of promoting policy ideas. In addition, the policy councils have been considered by many in the executive branch to be less affected by a particular set of constituents and less biased toward a particular institutional position than are the various executive agencies or departments and the political appointees who lead them. As a result, during the Clinton administration, the policy councils were often able to act as honest brokers between competing viewpoints and concerns. Consequently, increasing centralization tended to enhance (rather than diminish) the perception among others in the executive branch that the process was legitimate. When the two strategies of centralization and multiple advocacy worked in tandem, they increased the administration's capability to develop, promote, and implement its policy ideas.

Conclusion

The ability of executive branch policy makers to navigate and manage the policy-making process is complicated by the fact that ideas for a particular policy may come from virtually any source—including members of the President's staff, executive agencies and departments, Congress, the media, academic scholars, or special interest groups. All of these groups provide inputs and compete to influence the ideas, information, and proposals for the policy at hand. Paradoxically, the president has little direct influence over many of these people, yet he will likely need their support and expertise to formulate and implement executive branch policy initiatives effectively.

When used appropriately, the tools, techniques, and processes of policy making can facilitate the formulation, adoption, and implementation of policy in the executive branch by enabling these stake holders to communicate with one another and voice their ideas and concerns to those responsible for policy development. This, in turn, will increase the perceived legitimacy of the process, and create an incentive for stake holders in the executive branch to comply with its rules and practices. As a result, the process will be more likely to produce an outcome that the participants are willing to accept and support throughout its development.

Key Terms

Action-Forcing Event: A potential or existing situation that necessitates presidential action or review. Examples of action-forcing events include military conflict, an upcoming vote on important legislation, or the issuing of an Executive Order by the President.

Adhocracy Model:[42] A model of policy making that emphasizes the central role of the president in distributing assignments and selecting whom he listens to and when, with little use of regularized and systematic patters of providing advice.

Centralized Management Model:[43] A model of policy making that emphasizes heavy reliance of the president on White House staff and entities within the Executive Office of the President.

Groupthink: A situation where decision makers in the group begin to evaluate and rationalize problems collectively, develop illusions of invulnerability and unanimity, view other groups and opponents as less capable, tolerate only self-censorship, and pressure internal dissenters to conform.

Multiple Advocacy Model:[44] A model of policy making that is designed to expose the president to competing arguments and viewpoints made by the advocates themselves in a systematic manner. The president or chief decision maker

---

[42] Roger Porter, *Presidential Decision Making* (Cambridge, England: Cambridge University Press, 1980), 25.

[43] Ibid., 26.

[44] Ibid.

manages the process by acting as an honest broker among competing ideas and viewpoints.

Procedural Legitimacy:[45] A quality associated with the policy-making process that promotes acceptance of policy. It is enhanced when policy makers perceive that decisions are made by those duly authorized, in accordance with procedures which protect against corrupt, arbitrary, or idiosyncratic decision making or decision executing, and provide a reliable means of contributing to the decision-making or decision-executing process.

Sequential Approach: An approach to policy making that divides the policy-making process into a series of sequential stages—including problem identification, formulation, adoption, implementation, and evaluation—and categorizes policy actions as they vary from stage to stage.

Strain Toward Agreement: The motivation of policy makers with common as well as competing interests to reach a collective solution to the problems at hand.

Stake Holders: The individuals, agencies, departments, and interest groups in the policy-making community with vested interests in the issues or policies at hand.

Review Questions

1. What is procedural legitimacy?

2. Which presidential management styles are most likely to enhance procedural legitimacy? Why?

3. Discuss three ways in which the tools and techniques of policy making affect the policy-making process.

4. At what stages in the sequential approach to the policy-making process do the tools and techniques discussed in this book apply?

---

[45] Thomas M. Franck, *Fairness in International Law and Institutions* (Oxford, England: Clarendon Press, 1995), p. 7

CHAPTER 2

The Policy Councils

The Policy Councils and the
Structure of the Executive Branch

Since the 1960s, control over policy development has become increasingly centered in the White House.[1] This trend was driven by domestic pressure to:

- Enhance presidential accountability
- Increase responsiveness of the executive to public demands
- Reduce the resistance to change that characterizes many bureaucracies
- Promote policies in the context of divided government and, generally, an effort to manage an increasingly large federal bureaucracy[2]

Presidents Ronald Reagan, George H. W. Bush, Bill Clinton, and George W. Bush continued this trend by centralizing management of the policy-making process in the **Executive Office of the President (EOP)**.[3] The two largest and most influential offices in the EOP are the **Office of Management and Budget (OMB)** and the **White House Office (WHO)**. As we will discuss in Chapter 7, the OMB plays a critical role in executive branch policy-making process by monitoring executive agencies and departments and functioning as the clearinghouse for all new legisla-

---

[1] See Hugh Helco, *A Government of Strangers: Executive Politics in Washington* (Washington, D.C.: The Brookings Institutions, 1977), Samuel Kernell, "The Evolution of the White House Staff," in ed. John Chubb and Paul Peterson, *Can the Government Govern?* (Washington, D.C.: The Brookings Institution, 1989), Margaret Jane Wyszomirski, "The Deinstitionalization of Presidential Staff Agencies," *Public Administration Review* 42 (1982): 448–458.

[2] Terry M. More, "The Politicized Presidency," in ed. John Chubb and Paul Peterson, *The New Direction in American Politics* (Washington, D.C.: Brookings Institution, 1985), and Thomas Weko, *The Politicizing Presidency* (Lawrence, TN: University of Tennessee Press, 1989).

[3] The Executive Office of the President was established in 1939. It was composed of the Bureau of the Budget (which became the Office of Management and Budget in 1970), and the White House Office. See Stephen J. Wayne, G. Calvin MacKenzie, David M. O'Brien and Richard L. Cole, *The Politics of American Government*, 3d ed. (New York: St. Martin's/Worth Publishing, 1999), chap. 14.

tion, positions on existing legislation, and congressional testimony. The WHO, in turn, houses the White House **policy councils,** which are the principal units responsible for policy development and the management and coordination of input from departments and agencies into the policy-making process.[4]

The most prominent among the policy councils are the National Security Council, the National Economic Council, and the Domestic Policy Council. These councils play three primary roles: they are honest brokers between other actors in the policy-making process, think tanks for policy development, and protectors of the president's agenda. Unlike other agencies and departments, the policy councils have no programmatic or specific constituencies beyond the president. The lack of a program bias helps to increase the perceived legitimacy of their role in the process, which in turn increases support for the process and the policy outcome. In addition, they collectively provide conduits and filters for ideas, policy proposals, and recommendations that travel from executive agencies and departments to the president. This helps to increase the efficiency of the policy-making process by centralizing responsibility for action.

Reflecting the central roles they play in the policy-making process, the White House councils are situated at the inner core of the policy-making apparatus. The organizational structure of the executive branch can be pictured as an egg (see also "The Structure of the Executive Branch," page 21).[5] The president sits at the center and is surrounded by the White House Office, which includes the policy councils and several other offices (which we discuss in the next chapter). Together these make up the egg yoke. The yoke is surrounded by egg white, which contains the Executive Office of the President (EOP). The EOP consists of agencies of differing size and importance. Agencies in the EOP are congressionally mandated, their top political appointees are confirmed by the Senate, they are required to testify before Congress on policy matters, and they have regulatory and/or programmatic responsibilities. In contrast to agencies within the EOP, policy councils within the White House Office are presidentially appointed, they are not confirmed by the Senate, they run no programs, set no regulations, and there is a long-standing tradition based in the doctrine of "separation of powers" that staff members do not have to testify on policy issues (though they can be subpoenaed by Congress when there is evidence of illegal or unethical behavior). Unlike the agencies, the policy councils are thus not beholden to Congress and do not have specific programmatic interests. Indeed, presidents have often bolstered this independence by protecting internal communications with the policy councils under the claim of executive privilege.[6]

---

[4] The policy councils developed by President Clinton evolved from issue-based cabinet councils created by President Reagan and President George H. W. Bush. For a discussion of the evolution of the staffing, organization, and roles of players within the executive branch, see George C. Edwards III and Stephen J. Wayne, *Presidential Leadership: Politics and Policy Making,* 5th ed. (New York: St. Martin's/Worth Publishing, 1999), pp. 184–217.

[5] For a review of the relationship between senior staff and the president in the several recent administrations, see Robert J. Thompson, "Contrasting Models of White House Staff Organization: The Eisenhower, Ford and Carter Experiences," *Congress and the Presidency* 19, no. 2 (1992): 113–136.

[6] Stephen J. Wayne, G. Calvin MacKenzie, David M. O'Brien, and Richard L. Cole, *The Politics of American Government,* 3rd ed. (New York: St. Martin's / Worth Publishing, 1999), 519–521.

The Structure of the Executive Branch

The White House Office

Office of the Chief of Staff

Office of the Vice President

Office of the First Lady

Public Liaison

Legislative Affairs

Intergovernmental Affairs

Scheduling

Advance

Cabinet Affairs

Political Affairs

Staff Secretary

Administration

Counsel

Communications/Speechwriting

Press

Domestic Policy Council

National Security Council

National Economic Council

Executive Office of the President

Office of Management and Budget

Council on Environmental Quality

Office of National Drug Policy Control

Council of Economic Advisers

Office of Science and Technology Policy

President's Foreign Intelligence Advisory
Board

United States Trade Representative

The Cabinet

Department of State

Department of Treasury

Department of Defense

Department of Justice

Department of Interior

Department of Agriculture

Department of Commerce

Department of Labor

Department of Health and Human Services

Department of Housing and Urban
Development

Department of Transportation

Department of Education

Department of Energy

Department of Veteran Affairs

These distinctions are important because they enable the policy councils to act in a relatively unfettered manner. This freedom enhances their capability to shape and defend the president's position and to act as honest brokers between other actors in the policy-making process.

The shell of the egg includes all the cabinet departments and agencies not under the authority of the president, with the exception of fully independent agencies such as the Federal Reserve. In the past the secretary of the cabinet was responsible for coordinating cabinet policy making. But as the cabinet has grown in size—it is now too large for regular meetings and has become unwieldy and is often disjointed—the role of the secretary of the cabinet has shifted to one of scheduling. The role of coordinating policy development and the decision-making process within the cabinet has shifted to the policy councils within the White House Office. Indeed, the growth of policy councils was in part a response to the increased number of issues and of cabinet agencies with interest in a large range of policy matters.

How the Policy Councils Operate
and Why They Are Important

Lyndon Johnson was the first president to begin concentrating policy-making control within the White House.[7] This shift was reflected in the rise of Joseph Califano, who became known as a freewheeling, all-purpose domestic policy tsar within the Johnson White House.[8] Following the Johnson administration, however, the shift toward more centralized policy making was slow and uneven. It was not until the early 1970s that the Office of Policy Development (OPD) became an institutional entity within the White House.[9] And, despite being institutionalized, the OPD lacked a clear mandate from the president, its role was unclear, and its influence was minimal. It did not play a major role during the Ford administration. And, although it gained in importance during the Carter administration under the leadership of Stuart Eizenstat, it declined in importance during the Reagan and George H. W. Bush administrations where it was overshadowed by the Office of Management and Budget.

The role and significance of the White House domestic policy-making staff increased dramatically after President Clinton took office in 1993. Clinton entered his office with a desire to create a more coordinated policy development and planning apparatus. He also sought to centralize control over policy making by placing primary responsibility for policy development and planning in the hands of political appointees rather than career civil servants. To do so, the president separated the OPD into two distinct offices: The National Economic Council (NEC) and the Domestic Policy Council (DPC). As discussed in Chapter 10, the NEC played a prominent role in the first half of the Clinton administration during which time it was responsible for the development of the 1993 economic plan. As discussed in Chapter 9, the DPC was initially overshadowed by the NEC, but it came to prominence in 1995 when the Clinton administration engaged the newly elected Republican Congress on welfare reform.

The Clinton administration used the National Security Council (NSC) as the model for the NEC and DPC. Consequently, the new policy councils were designed to serve three primary missions. First, the NEC and DPC serve as honest brokers on policy decisions that can not be resolved at lower levels. Since they do not manage any programs, they have none of the programmatic baggage that could hinder the ability of other cabinet agencies to mediate disputes. In particular, because the policy councils are made up of cabinet agencies and some of the smaller noncabinet departments, like the Small Business Administration, they can resolve disputes by coordinating a direct exchange among department heads and the chair of the relevant agencies. This increases the capacity for all parties to provide input to the policy-making process, thereby increasing the perceived legitimacy of the process itself and the likelihood that each party will buy into the process and the results it produces.

---

[7] I.M. Destler, *Presidents, Bureaucrats, and Foreign Policy* (Princeton, N.J.: Princeton University Press, 1972), and Richard Neustadt, *Presidential Power: The Politics of Leadership* (New York: Wiley, 1960).

[8] Charles L. Heatherly and Burton Yale Pines, eds. *Mandate For Leadership III: Policy Strategies for the 1990s* (Washington, D.C.: The Heritage Foundation, 1989).

[9] Ibid.

Second, the policy councils serve as think tanks and develop new ideas that fit the president's agenda. The policy councils are responsible for integrating executive agencies such as the Office of Management and Budget (OMB), Treasury, Health and Human Services (HHS), the Department of Labor, and the Environmental Protection Agency (EPA) into the policy development structure. They also work in conjunction with the Office of congressional Affairs (OCA) in developing a legislative strategy on initiatives which require congressional approval. Finally, the councils are responsible for overseeing the OMB to ensure that the president's agenda is being implemented by the agencies. These roles create a specific point of contact and responsibility for policy making. As such, they increase the efficiency and manageability of the policy-making process.

Not every issue facing the United States government comes before the policy councils. Although they have grown in power, the councils are simply not large enough to oversee every bit of bureaucratic minutia. The day-to-day running of government programs still largely resides with the various cabinet, noncabinet, and independent agencies, and outside analysis regarding the running of these programs is mainly the responsibility of the Office of Management and Budget. White House policy councils get involved in issues of vital national interest or security, such as an armed conflict or treaty negotiation, and issues that have been identified as presidential priorities, such as the welfare and healthcare reform legislation debate during the first term of the Clinton administration. Three individuals have the power to decide which issues merit the attention of the policy councils: the president, his chief of staff, or the head of the relevant policy council itself. Often a cabinet agency will seek policy council involvement because it brings the cachet of presidential interest. At other times, however—particularly if a president is unpopular with Congress—cabinet agencies will do everything they can to avoid policy council involvement.

One of the chief responsibilities of the policy councils is to develop new policy proposals for the president that are consistent with his or her political agenda.[10] This underscores the need for a council head who is ideologically in tune with the president. For example, avoiding ideological conflict was part of President Clinton's motivation for increasing the role that the policy councils play in the policy-making process. Lack of ideological conflict is important given the prominent role of the policy councils in establishing the policy-making agenda, preparing the State of the Union address, and submitting the president's proposed fiscal budget every year. The delivery of the State of the Union every January and the submission of the president's budget every February are critical events because they provide the president with highly visible and widely publicized platforms for presenting his or her policy agendas to the American people and the Congress. Controlling the policy agenda is a critical aspect of presidential power and can have a large impact on securing support

---

[10] For a review of the impact of the policy-making process and agenda setting, see Paul C. Light, "Domestic Policy Making," *Presidential Studies Quarterly* 30, no. 1 (March 2000): 109–132. Despite appearances to the contrary, the separation of powers and competition among political units vying to influence the policy agenda of the federal government may give the president an opportunity to shape the agenda as he sees fit. See Charles O. Jones, "Reinventing Leeway: The President and Agenda Certification," *Presidential Studies Quarterly* 30, no. 1 (March 2000): 6–26.

from Congress and the public for executive branch policy initiatives.[11] The president can, of course, propose new policies at White House conferences or through the presentation of government studies, and so on. However, the State of the Union address and the president's budget are the only two *annual* vehicles and they are widely recognized as the definitive declaration of presidential initiatives and priorities for the coming year. Indeed, recent studies have shown that increased presidential attention to particular policies—or even the mention of particular issues—in the State of the Union address increases public concern about them.[12]

The policy councils are intimately involved in the preparation of the State of the Union address and work in conjunction with the OMB to develop the president's proposed budget. (See "The Path to a U.S. Budget," page 25.) The policy councils begin their preparation by setting up a variety of **interagency working groups** in late August, usually after Congress leaves for its summer recess. These interagency groups are composed of all agencies with an interest in a potential policy initiative and are directed by a special assistant to the president serving on one of the policy councils. The working groups are often jointly run by two policy councils. For example, the National Economic Council (NEC) and the National Security Council (NSC) may jointly chair an interagency working group on trade, while the NEC and Domestic Policy Council (DPC) may chair jointly a working group on poverty or welfare. Typically, the policy councils ask each participating agency to develop and prioritize new policy proposals that require either legislative, executive (presidential action via **Executive Orders** or memoranda), legal (via the courts), or regulatory action. The policy councils will also independently develop a set of new proposals. The policy councils will then meet during August and September to forge a consensus regarding proposals that will be included in the State of the Union address.

Concurrently, the OMB runs its budget process, through which it evaluates all the other nonpresidential-level initiatives and the maintenance of existing programs. At the end of this process, the policy councils and the OMB merge their efforts and prepare a fiscal budget proposal. Although the policy councils and the OMB work together throughout this phase, it is the policy councils that are responsible for presenting any disagreements over how much to spend on any particular item in the budget to the president. With regards to proposals for the State of the Union, the councils try to resolve most of the issues at either the **deputy** or the **principal** (agency head) **level.** However, to insure a fair process, any agency can ask for an issue to be presented to the president for resolution. In these circumstances, a memo is prepared by the head of the relevant council and his or her staff and sent to the president for his decision (see Chapter 5). The decision regarding what policies will be included in the State of the Union or the president's budget are finalized in mid-January. All appeals to the president are submitted in late December or early January.

---

[11] On the importance of agenda setting and policy making, see Paul Light, *The President's Agenda*, rev. ed. (Baltimore: Johns Hopkins University Press, 1991), and Wayne Steger, "Presidential Policy Initiatives and the Politics of Agenda Control," *Congress and the Presidency* 24 (1997): 17–36.

[12] See for example Jeffry E. Cohen, "Presidential Rhetoric and the Public Agenda," *American Journal of Political Science* 39, no. 1 (February 1995): 87–107.

The Path to a U.S. Budget

July	Mid-session review is published, new ten-year budget projections released by OMB and CBO
August	Cabinet agencies submit programs and cost to OMB
September	Congress begins period of final passage of appropriations bills
October	Beginning of Fiscal Year
November	OMB "passbacks" White House decisions on budget to each agency
December	President hears any agency appeals regarding "passbacks"
January	President gives State of the Union, outlines priorities for coming year
February/March	President submits detailed budget plan to Congress

Source: Washington Post, April 7, 2000

After the State of the Union and the submission of the president's budget, the policy councils work with the relevant White House offices to secure passage of action on each policy item. Some councils have regular bimonthly principals' and deputies' meetings, while others prefer to meet on an as-needed basis. On some occasions, rather than have all the principals meet to discuss all issues, meetings will be broken down by issue, such as education or welfare. In either case, each special assistant to the president is responsible for maintaining contact and exchanging information with all relevant parties. Throughout the year, the chief of staff will ask for updates on each major policy initiative. If legislative action is required, the councils will work with the Legislative Affairs office and develop a congressional strategy. They will then brief members of Congress and their staffs throughout the winter. The councils will also work with the White House offices of Intergovernmental Affairs and Public Liaison to build support among state, local, and tribal governments and among interest groups. If the action requires a presidential directive, White House counsel becomes involved. Follow-up media events designed to build support for proposals are put together with the assistance of White House offices for communications, press, and speechwriting. In all cases, however, the councils serve as the linchpin.

Titles

In the White House, senior staffers are ranked as "officers to the president." The highest rank is that of assistant to the president. The White House chief of staff, press secretary, head of White House counsel, the chairs of the DPC and NEC, and the National Security Advisor are all "assistants." This rank places these individuals on roughly the same basis as cabinet secretaries. The next rank is that of deputy assistant to the president, followed by special assistant to the president. The term principal refers to the head of a council, agency, or department. The term deputy refers to an individual who is directly subordinate to a principal. Other staffers in the White House are not given a rank but are not necessarily junior staffers or administrative support. A commission from the president is a highly sought-after title and often leads to considerable tension within the White House.

Inside the White House Policy Councils

The National Security Council

The National Security Council is the president's principal forum for considering national security and foreign policy matters with his senior national security advisers and cabinet officials. The NSC also serves as the president's principal arm for coordinating policies among these various government agencies. It is the oldest and largest of all the policy councils. The NSC was established in the Truman administration by the National Security Act of 1947 (PL 235-61 Stat. 496; U.S.C. 402), amended by the National Security Act of 1949 (63 Stat. 579; 50 U.S.C. 401 et seq.). Later in 1949, as part of the Reorganization Act, the council was placed in the Executive Office of the President.[13]

Under President Eisenhower, the National Security Council system evolved into the principal arm of the president in formulating and executing policy on military, international, and internal security affairs.[14] While Truman was uncomfortable with the NSC system and only made regular use of it under the pressure of the Korean war, Eisenhower embraced the NSC concept and created a structured system of integrated policy review. President Kennedy, who was strongly influenced by critics of the Eisenhower NSC system, moved quickly at the beginning of his administration to reconfigure the NSC process and simplify the foreign policy-making process. In a very short period after taking office, President Kennedy reduced the NSC staff from 74 to 49, limited the substantive officers to 12; he also held NSC meetings much less frequently and sharply curtailed the number of officers attending. The Johnson administration did not change the formal role of the National Security Council. Like Kennedy, Johnson much preferred small, informal advisory meetings to large council meetings supported by an elaborately organized staff. In contrast, under Nixon the NSC grew in stature and size. It became the dominant actor in foreign policy decision making. NSC Advisor Henry Kissinger doubled the size of the NSC staff and had direct party-to-party contacts with the foreign ministers of several leading international powers. By 1973 Kissinger held both the positions of NSC director and secretary of state. Under President Ford, Brent Scowcroft focused the NSC on serving as an "honest broker" responsible for coordinating policy advice for the president and providing him with analysis rather than recommendations.

Although President Carter was originally committed to cutting the size of the NSC and reducing its influence, tensions between the NSC and the State Department arose again during his administration partly because of the differing agendas of NSC Director Zbigniew Brzezinski and Secretary of State Cyrus Vance.[15] An attempt to put into effect a more collegial approach to government decision

---

[13] The NSC home page is http://www.whitehouse.gov/nsc/

[14] Additional information is provided on the White House Web page, Office of the Historian, U.S. Department of State, http://www.whitehouse.gov/nsc.history.html

[15] Ibid.

making was emphasized in the Reagan administration. The national security adviser was downgraded, and the chief of staff to the president exercised a coordinating role in the White House. Unfortunately, the collegiality among powerful department heads was not successfully maintained, and conflicts became public. The NSC staff tended to emerge as a separate, contending party. In an attempt to resolve the conflict between the NSC and the State Department, a Special Situation Group (SSG) was established to coordinate responses to international crisis. The SSG however failed to meet more than once. Under Directors Clark, McFarlane, and Poindexter, the NSC continued to have an operational as well as coordination role. President George H. W. Bush brought his own considerable foreign policy experience to his leadership of the council and restored collegial relations among department heads. He reorganized the NSC organization to include a Principals Committee, Deputies Committee, and eight Policy Coordinating committees. The Clinton administration continued to emphasize a collegial approach within the NSC on national security matters. The NSC membership was expanded to include the secretary of the treasury, the U.S. Representative to the United Nations, the president's chief of staff, and the president's national security adviser. The NSC also placed a greater emphasis on economic issues in the formulation of national security policy.

The administration of George W. Bush has maintained the membership of the Clinton NSC with a few additions. Currently the president remains the chair of the council. Its regular attendees (both statutory and nonstatutory) are the vice president, the secretary of state, the secretary of the treasury, the secretary of defense, and the assistant to the president for national security affairs. The chairman of the joint chiefs of staff is the statutory military advisor to the council, and the director of the Central Intelligence Agency is the intelligence adviser.[16] The chief of staff to the president, counsel to the president, and the assistant to the president for economic policy are invited to attend any NSC meeting. In addition, the Bush administration now allows the attorney general and the director of the Office of Management and Budget to attend meetings pertaining to their responsibilities. The Bush administration also permits the heads of other executive departments and agencies, as well as other senior officials, to attend meetings of the NSC when appropriate.

The NSC staff serves as the president's national security and foreign policy staff within the White House. The staff receives its direction from the president, through the national security adviser (also known as the assistant to the president for national security affairs). The NSC staff performs a variety of activities in advising and assisting the president and the national security adviser. It is responsible for preparing briefing materials (including the preparation of meeting agendas and decision and discussion papers) for the president and the national security adviser to assist them in making decisions regarding national security policy and operations. The NSC staff also serves as an initial point of contact for departments and agencies who wish to bring a national security issue to the president's attention. Staff members

---

[16] Additional information is provided on the White House Web page, Office of the Historian, U.S. Department of State, http://www.whitehouse.gov

participate in interagency working groups organized to assess in a coordinated fashion policy issues among several agencies at an initial staff level; they prepare analysis
and recommendations for the deputy assistants to the president for national security
affairs, the assistant to the president for national security affairs, and the president.

The influence that the national security staff and national security adviser
have played in the policy arena has varied substantially over the past several administrations.[17] Henry Kissinger, for example, was able to act independently and exerted substantial influence on the policy-making process in the Nixon White
House. Similarly, Zbigniew Brzezinski exerted substantial influence in the Carter
White House. In contrast, Anthony Lake played a much less public role in the
Clinton administration.

The executive secretary of the NSC is its chief manager and administrative
officer, assisting in directing the activities of the NSC staff on the broad range of
defense, intelligence, and foreign policy matters, including the preparation necessary for meetings with foreign leaders in connection with the president's foreign
travel. He or she also assigns, reviews, and ensures proper coordination of all information and action memoranda submitted by the NSC staff to the national security
adviser and the president. The executive secretary is the principal point of contact
between the council and other government agencies and with the EOP.

Under President Bush, the NSC is divided into 15 different groups:

1. Office of the Director
2. Administration
3. African Affairs
4. Asian Affairs
5. Defense Policy and Arms Control
6. Democracy, Human Rights, and International Operations
7. European and Eurasian Affairs
8. Intelligence Programs
9. Legal Office
10. Legislative Affairs
11. Near East and North African Affairs
12. Non-Proliferation Strategy, Counterproliferation, and Homeland Defense
13. Press and Speechwriting
14. Transnational Threats
15. Western Hemisphere Affairs

The majority of each of these divisions is headed up by a special assistant to the
president/senior director. Like her predecessors in the Clinton administration, NSC
Adviser Condoleezza Rice has two deputies, although one serves as a general deputy
the other focuses solely on counterterrorism. Under President George W. Bush,
staffing levels have dropped to around 70 people. Under President Clinton and
President George H. W. Bush, staffing levels approximated 100 individuals. The

---

[17] Jean A. Garrison, *Games Advisors Play: Foreign Policy in the Nixon and Carter Administrations* (College
Station, Tex.: Texas A&M University, 1999).

current Bush administration has also eliminated or combined several of the divisions that existed in the Clinton administration. These include International Health Affairs, South East Europe Affairs, Russia, Ukrainian, and Eurasian Affairs, and Multilateral and Humanitarian Affairs.

The National Economic Council

The National Economic Council (NEC) was created by presidential executive order on January 25, 1993.[18] (See page 32.) The principal functions of the council are:

- To coordinate the economic policy-making process with respect to domestic and international economic issues
- To coordinate economic policy advice to the president
- To ensure that economic policy decisions and programs are consistent with the president's stated goals, and to ensure that those goals are being effectively pursued
- To monitor implementation of the president's economic policy agenda

The NEC is chaired by the president and consists of 18 members. Under Clinton the staff size was roughly 30 individuals (considerably smaller than the NSC, which has historically been staffed by some 100 people). Because it is smaller, and newer, the NEC is considerably less bureaucratic and somewhat more freewheeling than the NSC. This gives it some advantages, including a more innovative approach to policy making, but the smaller staff means it has fewer resources available than the NSC.

By creating the National Economic Council, President Clinton instituted the most significant broad purpose, policy-staff initiative since President Nixon mandated the transformation of the National Security Council under Henry Kissinger in 1969.[19] He used the NSC as a model and intended it to coordinate economic policy making in the same manner that the NSC coordinated foreign policy making. Under the initial leadership of Robert Rubin, the NEC quickly became a powerful force inside the White House. Its role was enhanced by the general power vacuum of the first year of the Clinton White House—at which time the offices of the chief of staff and White House communications were weak, and the Office of Legislative Affairs was largely ignored due to a lack of strategic thinking and overreliance on the Democrats in the Congress. In the context of day-to-day chaos inside the Clinton White House, Rubin followed a well-orchestrated, businesslike approach to policy making and systematically expanded the NEC's role beyond that of designing policy proposals on behalf of the president to include the creation and implementation of the legislative and communications strategies that accompanied these proposals.

---

[18] The NEC home page is http://www.whitehouse.gov/nec/

[19] I.M. Destler, "National Economic Council: A Work In Progress," *Policy Analyses in International Economics* #46 (Washington, D.C.: Institute for International Economics, 1996).

Terms

Cookies: The key to knowing who the players are at any meeting with the president is who eats the cookies. When a proposal is to be presented to the president, the White House mess staff—who cook for the president—bring out a tray of cookies. One goes in front of the president, and the other is for the staff. Most staffers won't touch the cookies, for fear that they will be caught with their mouth full right at the moment the president asks them a question. However, those staffers who are truly comfortable in the presence of the president have no qualms about stuffing a few chocolate chip macadamia nut cookies into their mouths. By the way, when the meeting with the president has concluded and he has left the room, the cookie tray is picked clean by famished staff.

Rubin created teams of NEC staffers who focused on core issues, including education and training, transportation, banking and finance, economic development and housing, energy and environment, defense conversion, international trade, etc. Each team consisted of three or four individuals who were directed by a special assistant to the president. Rubin also appointed two deputies: one focused on day-to-day management and the other focused on long-range strategic planning. Under Rubin, the NEC's power grew and it became the de facto channel through which decisions—even those with no economic impact—were forwarded to the president. For example, the meetings to discuss policy initiatives involving campaign finance reform were chaired by Rubin and the NEC, even though the majority of the discussion was led by then DPC Deputy Bruce Reed and the policy initiatives had been developed by members of the DPC.

Early on, the extension of the NEC's role often clashed with the Office of Management and Budget (OMB) and the Council of Economic Advisers (CEA), particularly over the issue of which body was to serve as the coordinator of economic policy for the President. The OMB had controlled economic policy development under the first Bush administration, and the CEA had a tradition of providing economic analysis to presidents, yet the NEC usurped the roles of both agencies under the Clinton administration. It succeeded in doing so for two reasons. First, many of the agencies outside the executive branch resented the influence that the career staff at OMB had over the president's agenda. These agencies preferred working directly with the political appointees of the NEC because they had some direct or independent connection to the president. Second, Rubin made it clear that the NEC would be an honest broker and would insure that all views were presented to the president. This was something OMB had a reputation for not doing, especially since the agency's mandate to fit programs within a budget (preferably a balanced one) sometimes conflicted with the president's policy agenda. Furthermore, the CEA had become increasingly marginalized since its congressional mandate conflicted with the Clinton administration's desire to center decision making within the White House.

The Domestic Policy Council

After establishing the NEC, President Clinton placed the remainder of the staff from the now defunct Office of Policy Development into the Domestic Policy Council (DPC).[20] Officially, the DPC was established by Executive Order on August 16, 1993, although it existed de facto shortly after President Clinton's inauguration in January of 1993. Like the NSC and NEC, the DPC is chaired by the president, but run by an assistant to the president—in this case the assistant to the president for domestic policy.

The DPC plays a role at every stage of the policy-making process to ensure policies reflect and carry out the goals of the president. The principal functions of the Domestic Policy Council are to coordinate the domestic policy-making process, to relay domestic policy advice to the president, to ensure that the president's stated goals are being effectively pursued, and to monitor implementation of the president's domestic policy agenda. The DPC consists of 24 agencies, more than either the NSC or the NEC. On the other hand, when it was first created, it only had approximately 10 staffers. Over time it grew to around 30 staffers under President Clinton, approximately the same size of the NEC. In part this was due to its increasing importance within the White House, as was reflected by its responsibility for managing Clinton's anticrime package and the welfare reform proposal late in his first term. Passage of both these bills, combined with the departure of Robert Rubin to the Treasury Department in 1995, put the DPC on par with the NEC in terms of its importance within the White House.

Under President Clinton, the DPC was divided into the following teams, each headed by a special assistant to the president: Education and Training; Welfare Reform; Policy Planning; Crime and Drug Policy; Children and Families; Healthcare, and Management. Policy Planning specifically focuses on new ideas and policy issues that do not fall within the structure of the other teams. The Management team supports the assistant to the president for domestic policy and is similar in purpose to the executive secretary of the NSC. Like the NSC and NEC, the DPC has two deputies who oversee the management of the policy process.

After taking over the DPC in 1997, Bruce Reed believed the office should concentrate on issues most important to the president and allow the agencies and OMB to concentrate on the implementation of policy matters *outside* the president's primary agenda. Recognizing that 30 staffers could never effectively oversee the development and implementation of every policy, and that any attempt to do so would only lead to slower, more bureaucratic decision making, Reed decided to empower the team and have a very small management staff supporting him directly. He chose the team structure intentionally to encourage individual creativity and to increase the effectiveness of team management. The goal was to eliminate the hierarchical structure of the old DPC and replace it with one that fostered a considerable amount of horizontal interaction between the teams involved with different problems or issues.

---

[20] The DPC home page is http://www.whitehouse.gov/dpc/

Establishment of the National Economic Council

January 25, 1993

EXECUTIVE ORDER

ESTABLISHMENT OF THE NATIONAL ECONOMIC COUNCIL

By the authority vested in me as President of the United States by the Constitution and the laws of the United States of America, including sections 105, 107, and 301 of title 3, United States Code, it is hereby ordered as follows:

Section 1. Establishment. There is established the National Economic Council ("the Council").

Sec. 2. Membership. The Council shall comprise the:

(a)   President, who shall serve as Chairman of the Council;

(b)   Vice President;

(c)   Secretary of State;

(d)   Secretary of the Treasury;

(e)   Secretary of Agriculture;

(f)   Secretary of Commerce;

(g)   Secretary of Labor;

(h)   Secretary of Housing and Urban Development;

(i)   Secretary of Transportation;

(j)   Secretary of Energy;

(k)   Administrator of the Environmental Protection Agency;

(l)   Chair of the Council of Economic Advisers;

(m)   Director of the Office of Management and Budget;

(n)   United States Trade Representative;

(o)   Assistant to the President for Economic Policy;

(p)   Assistant to the President for Domestic Policy;

(q)   National Security Adviser;

(r)   Assistant to the President for Science and Technology Policy; and

(s)   Such other officials of executive departments and agencies as the President may, from time to time, designate.

During the Clinton administration, the role of the NEC in the White House policy-making process diminished even as the NEC's directors—first Laura Tyson and later Gene Sperling—rose in individual prominence. One reason for this may have been a shift in limited staff resources away from policy matters toward the personal needs of the heads of the NEC. For example, when Robert Rubin directed the NEC, he did so with the aid of an assistant and a special assistant, Sylvia Mathews. Mathews, who later followed Rubin to Treasury as his chief of staff, acted as the de facto chief of staff of the NEC. Under the leadership of Tyson (between 1995 and

Sec. 3. Meetings of the Council. The President, or upon his direction, the Assistant to the President for Economic Policy ("the Assistant"), may convene meetings of the Council. The President shall preside over the meetings of the Council, provided that in his absence the Vice President, and in his absence the Assistant, will preside.

Sec. 4. Functions. (a) The principal functions of the Council are: (1) to coordinate the economic policy-making process with respect to domestic and international economic issues; (2) to coordinate economic policy advice to the President; (3) to ensure that economic policy decisions and programs are consistent with the President's stated goals, and to ensure that those goals are being effectively pursued; and (4) to monitor implementation of the President's economic policy agenda. The Assistant may take such actions, including drafting a Charter, as may be necessary or appropriate to implement such functions.

(b) All executive departments and agencies, whether or not represented on the Council, shall coordinate economic policy through the Council.

(c) In performing the foregoing functions, the Assistant will, when appropriate, work in conjunction with the Assistant to the President for Domestic Policy and the Assistant to the President for National Security.

(d) The Secretary of the Treasury will continue to be the senior economic official in the executive branch and the President's chief economic spokesperson. The Director of the Office of Management and Budget, as the President's principal budget spokesperson, will continue to be the senior budget official in the executive branch. The Council of Economic Advisers will continue its traditional analytic, forecasting and advisory functions.

Sec. 5. Administration. (a) The Council may function through established or ad hoc committees, task forces or interagency groups.

(b) The Council shall have a staff to be headed by the Assistant to the President for Economic Policy. The Council shall have such staff and other assistance as may be necessary to carry out the provisions of this order.

(c) All executive departments and agencies shall cooperate with the Council and provide such assistance, information, and advice to the Council as the Council may request, to the extent permitted by law.

WILLIAM J. CLINTON

THE WHITE HOUSE, January 25, 1993

1996) and Sperling (from 1997 onward), the director's staff was increased to two assistants, a press secretary, a chief of staff, and a deputy chief of staff. While the concentration of limited staff resources weakened the NEC's role in policy development, the prominence of its directors combined with the tradition of holding deputies' meetings enabled the NEC to build and maintain its role as an honest broker in the policy arena. In the meantime, the DPC rose as the main force within the White House and the administration behind the creation of "new ideas." The DPC developed policy initiatives regarding the hottest issues of President Clinton's second term—including the K–12 education reform and class size reduction initiative; healthcare reform, containing both Medicare and the Patient's Bill of Rights; and the tobacco legislation and litigation efforts.

The DPC also regained control over several issues that had been given to the NEC in the first term. Education and healthcare, which had been handed to the NEC after the failed healthcare reform effort of the First Lady Hillary Clinton, were placed under the control of the DPC in 1997. In addition, the DPC became the major proponent of using presidential authority (such as Executive Orders and memoranda, the publishing of studies, and the creation of task forces or holding of White House conferences) to promote issues such as Medicare, youth violence, child care, and the use of litigation in lieu of legislative remedies in the suit against the tobacco companies.

The George W. Bush Administration and the NEC and DPC

During the 2000 campaign, it was unclear whether George W. Bush would continue to keep the NEC and DPC or whether he would revert to the structure of the pre-Clinton White House and combine both councils into a single entity. Interestingly, President Bush chose to maintain the structure put in place by President Clinton rather than adopt the single policy entity used by his father. In addition, despite his rhetoric to raise the level of importance of his cabinet, early evidence suggests that the policy councils are more significant than the cabinet agencies.

This is not to say that President George W. Bush has not made his mark on the structure of the councils nor does it imply that their role will not continue to evolve as his presidency moves forward. At the time of this writing, both councils were about half the size of their peak in the Clinton administration, although there are still openings on both the DPC and NEC. The current chairman of the NEC, Larry Lindsey, is exerting the same level of influence as former directors Rubin, Tyson, and Sperling did. DPC Director Margaret Spellings and her Special Adviser Sandy Kress projected considerable input on President Bush's top domestic agenda item, education reform. The Bush DPC has also designated a staff slot to work on budget issues, something the Clinton DPC did not focus on to a great extent. However, the DPC, according to some observers, is not involving itself to the level of detail seen in the Clinton administration.[21] For example, the White House only sent up principles on education reform rather than actual bill language. Also, both councils have moved away from utilizing a team structure focused on a single policy area and have instead adopted a structure where one senior, individual policy staffer is assigned to one particular issue. In addition, under Bush the DPC has only a single deputy and the NEC shares one of its deputies with the NSC. Finally, both councils report directly through the new deputy chief of staff for policy rather than directly to the chief of staff and the president as they did in the Clinton administration. But it is clear that the councils seem likely to become increasingly institutionalized as a part of the White House as did the NSC some 53 years ago. Further, their ascendancy means that policy will continue to be managed at the White House level rather than being designated to an agency such as OMB or Treasury.

---

[21] Interview with Andy Rotherham, Progressive Policy Institute, January 16, 2002.

Key Agencies within the Executive Office of the President

Within the EOP there are several agencies serving the president that were established and are overseen by Congress. These include the Council on Environmental Quality (CEQ), the Council of Economic Advisers (CEA), the Office of National Drug Control Policy (ONDCP), and the Office of Science and Technology Policy (OSTP). Unlike their executive-appointed counterparts, these agencies run programs and implement regulations. Prior to the Clinton administration, they also coordinated policy for the president. As discussed earlier, during the Clinton administration, the role of policy coordination has been usurped by the policy councils as part of a general effort to reduce the conflict of interest resulting from agencies serving both Congress and the president. While they still play important roles in providing policy analysis for the president, they no longer drive the policy decision-making process (with the exception of the OMB and the Office of Trade Representative, both of which are cabinet agencies that are housed in the Executive Office of the President). Some of these entities have also declined in importance because of their heavy reliance on career staff who have no political allegiance to the president or their heavy emphasis on temporary academic staff with no policy or political experience.

The Council on Environmental Quality

Congress first established the Council on Environmental Quality (CEQ) within the Executive Office of the President as part of the National Environmental Policy Act (NEPA) of 1969. Additional responsibilities were provided by the Environmental Quality Improvement Act of 1970. The Council is headed by a chair, who is appointed by the president with the advice and consent of the Senate.

Specific functions of CEQ include the following:[22]

- Advise and assist the president in the development of environmental policies and proposed legislation as requested by the president
- Oversee federal agency implementation of the environmental impact assessment process and act as a referee for interagency disputes regarding the adequacy of such assessments
- Report annually to the president on the state of the environment through preparation of the annual Environmental Quality Report
- Interpret the NEPA and the CEQ regulations in response to requests from federal, state, and local agencies as well as from citizens
- Approve NEPA procedures and issue guidance to address systemic problems

---

[22] Council on Environmental Quality home page: http://www.whitehouse.gov/ceq/

The Council of Economic Advisers

Although the term *council* conjures up the image of a large committee, the CEA actually consists only of a chairman and two members. The chairman is legally responsible for establishing the positions taken by the council. The other two members direct research activities of the council in particular fields, represent the council at meetings with other agencies, and generally work with the chairman to formulate economic advice.[23]

In addition to the chairman and two other members, the CEA has a professional staff that is both small and unusual. It includes a group of about ten senior staff economists, generally professors on one- or two-year leaves from their universities. They, in turn, are assisted by an additional ten junior staff economists, typically advanced graduate students who also spend only a year or two at the CEA. In addition, four permanent economic statisticians assist in the interpretation and identification of economic data.

The academic nature of the staff and of most CEA members distinguishes it CEA from other government agencies, particularly the NEC, whose staff focuses more on policy making while the CEA staff focuses on economic analysis. Members and staff use their strong links in the academic community to obtain advice on technical issues. Many of their contributions result from the application of econometric analysis to the issues being discussed, and the ability to add new insights into economic policy debates.[24] Staffers often come to the CEA without the institutional knowledge of some of the issues with which they will deal and without any experience in the bureaucratic process of decision making. Experience suggests, however, that some of the senior staff economists have learned quite quickly how to be effective participants.

The Office of National Drug Control Policy

The principal purpose of the Office of National Drug Control Policy (ONDCP) is to establish policies and to identify and prioritize objectives for the nation's drug control program, the goals of which are to reduce illicit drug use, manufacturing, and trafficking; drug-related crime and violence; and drug-related health consequences. The director of the ONDCP is charged with producing the National Drug Control Strategy, which directs the nation's antidrug efforts and establishes a program, a budget, and guidelines for cooperation among federal, state, and local entities.[25]

By law, the director of the ONDCP also evaluates, coordinates, and oversees both the international and domestic antidrug efforts of executive branch agencies and ensures that such efforts sustain and complement state and local antidrug activities. The director advises the president regarding changes in the organization,

---

[23] The Council of Economic Advisers home page is http://www.whitehouse.gov/cea/

[24] See the CEA home page: http://www.whitehouse.gov/cea/

[25] See the Office of National Drug Control Policy home page: http://www.whitehousedrugpolicy.gov/

management, budgeting, and personnel of federal agencies that could affect the nation's antidrug efforts; he or she also reports on federal agency compliance with their obligations under the Strategy.[26] Because ONDCP has only a few programs under its direct control, its leverage relative to larger agencies with similar responsibilities is limited.

The Office of Science and Technology Policy

The mission of the Office of Science and Technology Policy (OSTP) is to provide scientific and technological analysis and judgment to the president with respect to major policies, plans, and programs of the federal government.

Under Public Law 94-282, OSTP is to

- Advise the president and others within the Executive Office of the President on the impacts of science and technology on domestic and international affairs
- Work with the private sector to ensure federal investments in science and technology contribute to economic prosperity, environmental quality, and national security
- Build strong partnerships among federal, state, and local governments, other countries, and the scientific community
- Evaluate the scale, quality, and effectiveness of the federal effort in science and technology

OSTP's Senate-confirmed director also serves as assistant to the president for science and technology. In this role, he or she cochairs the president's Committee of Advisors on Science and Technology (PCAST) and supports the president's National Science and Technology Council (NSTC). A Senate-confirmed associate director leads each of OSTP's divisions: Environment, National Security and International Affairs, Science, and Technology.[27] Like CEA, OSTP focuses more on analysis than policy development.

Conclusion

In an effort to centralize the policy-making process and strengthen the role of presidential appointees, the Clinton administration dramatically increased the role and power of the policy councils within the White House Office. To date, President George W. Bush has continued this trend. The Domestic Policy Council and National Economic Council now play a central role in developing the president's

[26] See the Office of National Drug Control Policy home page: http://www.whitehousedrugpolicy.gov/

[27] Office of Science and Technology Policy home page: http://www.whitehouse.gov/WH/EOP/OSTP/html/OSTP_Home.html.

policy-making agenda. They provide conduits for the flow of ideas, policy proposals, and recommendations from executive agencies and departments. They also act as honest brokers and mediators between competing policy makers. The combination of these tasks is the result of efforts to centralize the policy-making apparatus while leaving it sufficiently open to promote debate among agencies and departments with competing viewpoints and concerns. When this system is used appropriately, the policy council–centered organizational system enhances both the effectiveness and perceived legitimacy of the policy-making process. The role of other members of the White House staff in the policy-making process and their interaction with the policy councils is the topic of the next chapter.

Key Terms

Agency/Department: Departments and agencies are federal entities chartered by Congress or the president to develop policies, run programs, and/or issue regulations. Agencies tend to be narrower in function than departments and may exist within them or be independent.

Interagency Working Group: A working group that involves several agencies and is directed to develop a policy proposal or position on a policy area.

Principal and Principal-Level: A *principal* is a head of an agency, department, or office. *Principal-level* events or meetings generally involve mainly principals.

Deputy and Deputy-Level: A *deputy* refers to an individual who is directly subordinate to the head of an agency, department, or office. *Deputy-level* events or meetings generally involve only deputies.

Review Questions

1. What roles do the State of the Union address and the publication of the president's budget play in the policy-making process?

2. Describe the steps taken by the executive branch in preparing the president's budget plan.

3. Who chairs the National Economic Council (NEC)? How many members does the NEC have?

4. Describe the seven teams that comprised President Clinton's Domestic Policy Council (DPC).

5. How did President George W. Bush change the policy councils that existed or were created by the Clinton administration?

6. How do the White House policy councils and their counterparts in the Executive Office of the President differ?

CHAPTER 3

The White House Staff

PRESSURE, LOW PAY, LONG HOURS, AND THE CONSTANT THREAT
OF A SUBPOENA. WELCOME TO THE WHITE HOUSE.[1]

Working on the White House Staff

Stockbrokers on Wall Street claim they have the most challenging and high-pressured jobs in the world. Members of the White House staff are, however, likely to disagree. The following describes a typical morning for a policy maker in the White House.

Your supervisor emerges from a dawn meeting with the president and tells you that the **West Wing** wants a new proposal dealing with the cleanup of toxic sites (Superfund sites) in time for the president's Earth Day address in two weeks. Your proposal will be limited to $1 billion in precious taxpayer dollars, even though conservative estimates of the amount of money really needed to solve the problem are three times that amount. You identify six agencies that have a stake in the proposal. You have to get their support for the proposal as well as support (or **buy-in**) from as many interest groups as possible to avoid having some cabinet secretary rip you to shreds before the White House chief of staff. You establish an interagency working group and begin identifying points of consensus and disagreement among those involved.

Almost immediately, the White House communications director begins asking for an early version of the proposal to leak to the press. You do not want to give it out since you have not even called your first meeting of the working group, but the press office does not care—you are lucky if they even know how to spell

---

[1] Comment from a White House staffer in the Clinton administration.

chloroflurocarbons. Your main worry is that if you do not leak the policy proposal to a particular journalist, then that journalist will criticize the proposal and its proponents in the press and thus potentially dampen public support. In addition, the Office of Legislative Affairs is calling because they want you to brief 20 members of Congress who might be cosponsors. Of course this means that you will have to make 20 changes to the proposal to get their support. You describe a general policy approach which involves litigation against polluters to White House counsel and ask for a legal opinion. The attorneys question whether your proposed approach is constitutional and simultaneously hand you a subpoena for all your files concerning the housing policy project you worked on last month. So you call your lawyer at $300 per hour just to reassure yourself that you have done everything by the book. By the way, it's only lunch time. If you would like to work in this kind of environment, keep reading this chapter.

The White House staff has become an institutionalized component of policy making in the modern executive branch and it is critical to the president's success.[2] As executive branch policy makers including Richard Cheney and David Gergen have argued, the president's staff empowers him "to guide and direct government, to interact with the cabinet, to deal effectively with Congress, to manage his relationship with the press." They become his "intelligence gathering operation, his media management team, his congressional team, and the formulation of his policy."[3] To be effective the staff must recognize who the players are, what roles they play, and the tools, techniques, and processes they use to interact. This is vital because, while no individual, agency, or department has the capacity to make or implement policy, many have the capacity to inhibit its development or stall its implementation.[4]

Other Key Players in the White House

From Pennsylvania Avenue, off to the right of the White House, is a small, nondescript, three-story building known as the West Wing. Since it was first constructed under President Roosevelt, the West Wing of the White House has served as the office building of the White House staff. This building contains the Oval Office, the vice president's office, and the National Security Council's Situation Room, where the president's staff monitors the world. The ever-growing White House staff forced Roosevelt to add a third floor during World War II, and in the sixties large portions of the staff were moved across the street to the Eisenhower Executive Office Building.

---

[2] See Shirley Ann Warshaw, *The Domestic Presidency: Policymaking in the White House* (Boston: Allyn and Bacon, 1997).

[3] John H. Kessel, "The Presidency and the Political Environment," *Presidential Studies Quarterly* 31, no. 1 (March 2001): p. 25.

[4] In addition, it is important to note that although the tools and techniques we describe in this book have been used by multiple presidents, each president has his own working style. White House staff must adapt to the individual working habits of its own president as well as the needs of the external institutions and players with which the president has to interact. Ibid., 25–43.

George W. Bush White House Structure (2001–present)

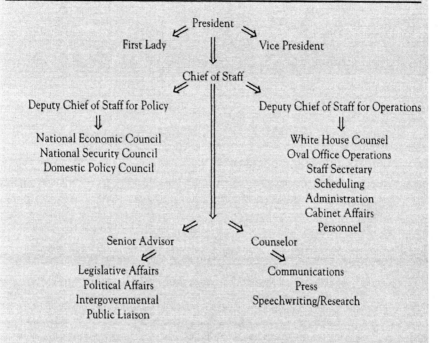

President

First Lady   Vice President

Chief of Staff

Deputy Chief of Staff for Policy   Deputy Chief of Staff for Operations

National Economic Council   White House Counsel
National Security Council   Oval Office Operations
Domestic Policy Council   Staff Secretary
                                                          Scheduling
                                                          Administration
                                                          Cabinet Affairs
                                                          Personnel

Senior Advisor   Counselor

Legislative Affairs   Communications
Political Affairs   Press
Intergovernmental   Speechwriting/Research
Public Liaison

William J. Clinton White House Structure (1993–2001)

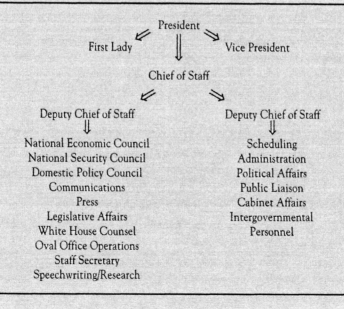

President

First Lady   Vice President

Chief of Staff

Deputy Chief of Staff   Deputy Chief of Staff

National Economic Council   Scheduling
National Security Council   Administration
Domestic Policy Council   Political Affairs
Communications   Public Liaison
Press   Cabinet Affairs
Legislative Affairs   Intergovernmental
White House Counsel   Personnel
Oval Office Operations
Staff Secretary
Speechwriting/Research

Today, the White House Office consists of some 18 different offices. In Chapter 2 we discussed the role of the White House policy councils—the National Economic Council (NEC), National Security Council (NSC), and the Domestic Policy Council (DPC). In this chapter we will focus on the responsibilities and functions of the 11 other major White House offices having responsibilities that relate to the policy development process. Of these, the chief of staff, the Office of Legislative Affairs and the Office of Intergovernmental Affairs have the most direct input into the policy-making process.

Chief of Staff

As the size of the White House Staff has grown, so has the power of the chief of staff (COS). Traditionally there have been three roles that the president's chief of staff has played in the White House.[5] The first of these is that of *confidant*—the president's closest adviser. In this capacity, the COS serves as a "behind-the-scenes" adviser whom the president entrusts with special assignments and uses as a sounding board for ideas and policy proposals as well as political and managerial issues. The second is that of *manager*. In this role, the chief of staff selects and manages key members of the White House staff. He or she also coordinates, and in some cases controls, personal access, information flows, and the decision-making processes on behalf of the president. In some cases, this power can be substantial. For example, the COS can act as a surrogate for the president and can often decide which decisions are worthy of presidential consideration and which are not. Third, the COS can serve as a *principal*, much like a cabinet secretary. This differs from the function of personal confidant for the president in that the COS plays this role both publically and within the confines of the White House. For example, the COS may negotiate with Congress and hold press conferences on behalf of the administration. Internally, the president sometimes designates the chief of staff as a member of his cabinet, which allows him to participate in formal policy decision-making meetings. In this capacity, the COS presents and protects the president's interests, while also operating as an honest broker among members of the executive branch and other stake holders.

In recent years the chief of staff has played an increasingly important role in the policy-making process. The COS provides his or her input through participation in policy council deliberations or when a decision memorandum is circulated to the president through the White House Staff secretary. For example, Andrew Card, COS for President Bush, has participated in NSC meetings on the war in Afghanistan. Leon Panetta, COS for President Clinton, was the lead negotiator on the budget with Congress in the early to mid-1990s.

As the role of the chief of staff has expanded, so has the size of his or her personal staff which has varied from eight to twelve individuals in recent administrations. Indeed, the size has grown large enough that some chiefs of staff have had their own chief of staff. Others have had their own personal foreign policy advisers and individu-

---

[5] For a review of the roles played by the chief of staff and additional insights based on interviews of several former chiefs of staff, see Charles E. Walcott, Shirley Anne Warshaw, and Stephen J. Wayne, "The Chief of Staff," *Presidential Studies Quarterly* 31, no. 3 (September 2001): 464–489.

als who are responsible for special projects that are of particular interest to him or her, such as an Olympics or a technology conference. Currently, President George W. Bush's chief of staff has two deputies as well as numerous support staff.

The Office of Legislative Affairs

The Office of Legislative Affairs (OLA) was established to manage all dealings between the president and Congress, specifically to coordinate the relationship be-tweeen White House policy offices and Congress. This function involves three re-sponsibilites. First, it serves as an intermediary that manages the policy interaction between the White House, members of Congress, and their staffs. Every member of Congress wants to be involved in what the president is doing, and just listening and responding to all their input is a full-time job. The OLA staffs are usually the first in the White House to take calls from members of Congress. It is up to the OLA whether to pass the contents of a call on to the appropriate White House staffer or simply to "hold onto" the information until it becomes timely.

Second, the OLA is responsible for maintaining good relations between Con-gress and the president. This includes everything from ensuring the "right" mem-bers are given access to the president's box at the Kennedy Center, to briefing the president on what to say when he meets with a senator or representative on a par-ticular piece of legislation.

Third, the OLA is intended to be the chief legislative strategist. This is a dif-ficult role to fulfill. The OLA often becomes so closely tied to the party leadership in Congress that its staff is unable to understand, or provide unbiased interpreta-tions of any conflicts between members of Congress in the president's party and the White House. A good OLA director will know how to build changing coalitions of members of Congress to pass or defeat legislation important to the president. In contrast, a weak or inexperienced OLA director will simply advise the president to follow his party leadership in Congress. Although this will deflect criticisms from the Hill, that party leadership does not always have the same interests or goals as the president. During the first two years of the Clinton administration, the OLA pursued a strategy intended to tie the president to the legislative agenda of the Democratic congressional leadership. As a result, many of President Clinton's chief legislative priorities, including welfare reform, the crime bill, healthcare reform, and campaign finance reform languished. Only after the president separated his goals from those of the Democrats in Congress did he begin to experience greater legisla-tive success. In the George W. Bush White House, the OLA has been placed under the direct control of the senior adviser to the president (currently Karl Rove), who also oversees the other three main political offices in the White House—the Office of Intergovernmental Affairs, the Office of Public Liaison, and the Office of Politi-cal Affairs. This new structure is designed to improve coordination of political strat-egy in the White House and to ensure that a single political message is delivered to the Congress, state, local, and tribal officials, and interest groups.

The relationship between the OLA and the policy councils is one of the most important in the White House. The policy councils maintain their role in the leg-islative process by running the interagency working groups on which the OLA sits.

Though the OLA does not have a seat on any of the policy councils, they have an open offer to attend any meeting the councils hold. If a decision memorandum (which we discuss in Chapter 5) is drafted on legislation, the views of the OLA are always included. Even on nonlegislative policy matters—such as an **Executive Order** issued by the president on federal hiring—the OLA's views will be sought out since Congress is responsible for overseeing executive branch actions, which encourages every member of Congress to express an opinion on the policies of the president.

There is often a great deal of tension between these offices. It is usual for the OLA staff to be more concerned about keeping members of Congress happy than are the policy councils' staff who, in turn, tend to be relatively more concerned about preserving the "true meaning" of the policy proposal at hand. Despite this tendency, the two organizations can work well together. Indeed, even competing organizations often make efforts to "strain toward agreement" in order to get a policy initiated.[6] When they do, the policy-making process works much more smoothly. For example, by the beginning of the second term of the Clinton administration both the OLA and the policy councils operated in strategic and not parochial terms. As a result, the administration experienced a good deal of legislative success at that time.

The Office of Intergovernmental Affairs

Parallel to the OLA's management of the relationship between the White House and Congress, the Office of Intergovernmental Affairs (OIA) is charged with maintaining relationships between the White House and the nation's governors; state, county, and local legislators; county and local officials including mayors; and Native American tribal governments. Like the OLA, the Office of Intergovernmental Affairs serves as a conduit and intermediary. The OIA is responsible for servicing and providing access to officials on various levels and communicating their concerns to the appropriate White House office. The OIA also works to convince state, local, and tribal governments to support the president's agenda. It works both with individual elected officials and umbrella organizations such as the National Governors' Associa- tion and the Conference of Mayors. In the George W. Bush White House, OIA has been somewhat downgraded in relation to other White House offices. The head of OIA is now a deputy assistant to the president rather than a full assistant in rank and reports directly to the senior adviser to the president.

The policy-making role of the OIA, and its interactions with the policy councils themselves, is centered around issues of particular concern to state, local, and tribal governments. For example, on issues of tobacco policy and welfare reform, the OIA played an important role in managing the interaction between individual governors, the National Governors' Association, and the policy councils. The OIA

---

[6] Roger Hilsman with Laura Gaughran and Patricia A. Weitsman, *The Politics of Policymaking in Defense and Foreign Affairs: Conceptual Models and Bureaucratic Politics*, 3d ed. (Englewood Cliffs, N.J.: Prentice Hall, 1993), 80–81; Warner Schilling, "The Politics of National Defense: Fiscal 1960," in *Strategy, Politics and Defense Budgets*, eds. Warner R. Schilling, Paul Y. Hammond, and Glenn H. Snyder (New York: Columbia University Press, 1962), 23.

is often not the only point of contact between the policy councils and nonfederal governments: the head of the Domestic Policy Council worked closely with the state attorneys general on the tobacco settlement. But the OIA and the policy councils often work closely together, particularly when there is a meeting of one of the umbrella organizations on policy matters. The National Governors' Association has two meetings each year in which policy resolutions are raised; usually the policy councils and the OIA combine efforts in responding to those resolutions.

The Office of Political Affairs

Originally designed to fulfill a parallel role to that of the OLA, the Office of Political Affairs (OPA) is responsible for keeping the president apprised of political issues that arise throughout the country. It serves as liaison to the various party entities such as the Republican National Committee (RNC), the Democratic Senatorial Campaign Committee (DSCC), and the Democratic National Committee (DNC). The office is broken down into regions, with a staffer covering each part of the country.

The OPA's task is to provide a political assessment of policy matters. As the role of outside political consultants has grown, however, the OPA's role has declined. Today, most consultants go around the OPA and deal directly with the president or the office of the chief of staff. The OPA's role is further undercut by a general belief among White House staff that they are politically adept and have little need for its input. As a consequence, the OPA currently has little or no direct involvement in the policy-making process. Most of the political input that actually goes into the policy decision-making process comes from other places within the White House, such as the chief of staff or the Office of Legislative Affairs. In part because of its decreasing relevance, the OPA, like the OIA, has been downgraded relative to other White House offices by the Bush administration. The office has been joined with the OIA and now is headed up by a deputy assistant to the president. It will be interesting to see if this reorganization will make the OPA more effective or if the growing importance of outside consultants will eventually make this office obsolete.

The Office of Cabinet Affairs

The Office of Cabinet Affairs (OCA) was originally created to serve as a deliberative body consisting of all the cabinet department heads. Because of its size and the disparate and often conflicting interests of all of the department heads, the Office of Cabinet Affairs has not operated effectively as a deliberate body. As a result, its role in policy making has diminished significantly. During the Clinton administration and continuing with the Bush administration, the responsibility for policy coordination has been largely taken over by the three White House policy councils, each of which includes smaller subsections of the cabinet. Interaction between the OCA and the policy councils is minimal. The OCA does not have a seat on any of the policy councils, and the councils themselves deal directly with the relevant federal agencies regarding policy matters. This has effectively negated the policy-making role of the OCA.

Today, the Office of Cabinet Affairs functions principally as a clearinghouse of information for the various cabinet agencies and as a coordinator of federal response efforts to natural disasters such as earthquakes, hurricanes, and floods. The roles of coordinating communications among cabinet agencies and "Disaster Affairs" have restored the relevance of the OCA. During disasters, the OCA enhances the government's legitimacy by providing a point of contact for disaster relief, it increases the efficiency of disaster relieve by centralizing disaster management, and it provides a means of communicating and amplifying the president's public communications.

Interaction with the Public

While the additional White House Offices—including the Office of Public Liaison, the Offices of Communications and the Press Office, and the Office of Cabinet Affairs—do not play a direct role in the policy formation process, they help to promote both the perception of legitimacy and efficiency of the system by providing points of contact and channels of communication between the White House and the public at large.

The Office of Public Liaison

The Office of Public Liaison (OPL) serves as the go-between for the ever-growing number of interest groups that play important roles in our democracy.[7] It was first created to help build support among the public for major presidential initiatives. In fulfillment of this role, the OPL pursues three primary missions: constituency building, policy advocacy, and policy facilitation. Constituency building is the primary mission of the OPL. The success of a presidential proposal is often determined by whether or not constituency groups can be brought into the fold. Policy advocacy is the second most important mission of the OPL. Specifically, the OPL is responsible for generating public understanding and support for presidential initiatives. Policy facilitation is its third mission. In reality, this means providing "access" and "services" to constituency groups with the policy councils and other White House offices.

The OPL also facilitates the policy-making process by gathering information not readily available from published sources from a variety of private sector organizations. The OPL provides a conduit for private sector organizations to express their concerns to the White House, but it does not act as an advocate for specific interest groups or concerns. While decision memoranda do reflect in some cases the concerns of interest groups, the policy councils rather than the OPL usually judge how relevant those concerns are. Nonetheless, by providing a means of communicating the concerns of private sector organizations, the OPL helps to promote the public perception of legitimacy of the policy-making process that, in turn, increases

---

[7] Heatherly and Pines, *Mandate for Leadership* (Washington, D.C.: American Heritage Institute, 1989).

the likelihood of support for policy outcomes. As a final, but important, duty, the OPL helps identify people for policy positions in government based on their expertise and ideological compatibility.

The Office of Communications, the Speechwriting Office, and the Press Office

People often ask what the difference is between the Office of Communications (OC) and the Press Office (PO). In principle, their roles are distinct; in practice they often overlap. The Office of Communications is charged with developing the long-term and daily communications strategy for the president.[8] Its role is to coordinate people, programs, and institutions in a way that best publicizes the goals and achievements of the president and the White House.[9] The Press Office is charged with implementing this strategy and gathering and disseminating White House information to the press on behalf of the president.[10] It serves as an information conduit and "fire wall" between the press and the White House, and is responsible for "servicing" press staff by granting formal and informal interview requests and helping them make their travel arrangements on presidential trips. It also helps present the views of the president, the White House Staff, and the press to one another, and it devotes a substantial amount of time to staging future events. The Press Office is divided into two parts: the West Wing Operations and the offices and staff in the Old Executive Office Building. The former are responsible for the White House press corps and support work for the press secretary, the latter work with specialized news groups and out-of-town press, as well as operations to facilitate radio and television coverage and plan advance work for the press corps.[11]

The administrative relationship between the PO and the OC have varied in recent administrations with the press secretary sometimes taking over the role of the communications director. For example, during much of the Carter administration, Press Secretary Jody Powell was directing communications operations.[12] Similarly, during the George H. W. Bush administration, Press Secretary Marlin Fitzwater took over the role. Sometimes, however, the hierarchy has been reversed. During the Clinton administration, for example, Press Secretary Dee Dee Myers reported to Communications Director George Stephanopoulos. Regardless, when the

---

[8] Martha Joynt Kumar, "The Office of Communications," *Presidential Studies Quarterly* 31, no. 4 (December 2001): 609–634. John Maltese, *Spin Control: The White House Office of Communications and the Management of Presidential News*, 2nd ed. (Chapel Hill, N.C.: University of North Carolina Press, 1994).

[9] Martha Joynt Kumar, "The office of Communications," *Presidential Studies Quarterly* 31, no. 4 (December 2001): 610–611.

[10] For a useful discussion of the role and functions of the Office of the Press Secretary, see Martha Joynt Kumar, "The Office of the Press Secretary," *Presidential Studies Quarterly* 31, no. 2 (June 2001), 296–322.

[11] Ibid., 306–307.

[12] Martha Joynt Kumar, "The Office of Communications," *Presidential Studies Quarterly* 31, no. 4 (December 2001): 610.

functions of these two organizations overlap, the resulting conflict can create confusion and result in a confused message to the public. In general, since the White House press secretary from the PO is the chief contact with the media, he or she often holds a great deal more leverage with the press than the head of the OC. On the other hand, the Speechwriting Office (SO) is under the authority of the OC. Since the president's speeches are the chief means of communicating, the OC has a significant impact on the material in which the press is interested. This restores some of the balance in the relationship. The Office of Communications is also responsible for designing and creating presidential events that convey White House positions and messages. The competition in roles between access to the media by the PO and Speechwriting and presentation of presidential ideas by the OC invariably creates a significant amount of tension between the two offices.

Although historically the press secretary has been responsible for communications planning within the White House—as was James Hagerty, who served as President Eisenhower's press secretary—the press secretary now focuses primarily on gathering and delivering information to reporters and plays a secondary role in communications planning.[13] The role of planning events involves the Scheduling Office, the Office of Chief of Staff, the Office of Communications, and the relevant policy councils.

The Press Office and Office of Communications interact frequently with the policy councils. The PO is responsible for ensuring that the president is fully briefed before he or she goes before the press, and it is the policy council's responsibility to draft the Q&A sheet that is given to the president. Of course, the PO also has an opinion regarding the president's responses to statements. The policy councils also are heavily involved with the OC in the drafting of speeches, especially when new policy proposals are being announced.

The close relationship between the PO, OC, and policy councils is vitally important for the preparation and marketing of policy proposals. However, it is rare for either the press secretary or the communications director to express views on policy matters in the decision-making process or memoranda. For the most part, they weigh in only when they feel very strongly that the press will destroy a policy proposal. Similarly, speechwriting plays no role in the policy development process. Once the policy is agreed upon, the policy councils work closely with speechwriters to guarantee that the ideas are framed and marketed effectively.

The White House Gatekeepers

Even though their official role in policy making is minimal, the offices of the White House counsel, Scheduling and Oval Office Operations, and the staff secretary play important, if indirect, roles as gatekeepers in the policy-making process.

---

[13] Martha Joynt Kumar, "The Office of the Press Secretary," *Presidential Studies Quarterly* 31, no. 2 (June 2001): 306.

The Office of Scheduling and Oval Office Operations

The Office of Scheduling and Oval Office Operations manage the president's calendar and his day-to-day interactions with staff, the press, and the public at large. When an organization or individual makes a request to meet the president, the request goes through the Office of Scheduling. Members of this office then coordinate its activities with all the other White House Offices and determine if a meeting with an individual or an event will be placed on the president's schedule. Although its function is primarily administrative, the White House scheduler has tremendous political influence since he or she controls the public's access to the president.

The Scheduling Office and Oval Office Operations are closely linked with the Office of the Chief of Staff. These offices provide the president's chief of staff with the ability to control the president's policy agenda and day-to-day activities. While the schedulers are concerned with ensuring that the president's day goes like clockwork and that the president has enough downtime, office time, and event time to fulfill his duties, they also can exert influence by proposing to eliminate policy events due to "time constraints." The level at which control of the schedule can influence policy depends on the management style and political strength of the White House chief of staff. In the Clinton administration, the Office of Scheduling was primarily concerned with ensuring that the president had enough rest time. As a result, it did not try to use its power to force policy items off the agenda. In previous administrations, more autocratic chiefs of staff used the Scheduling Office to control the policy agendas of agencies and the White House policy advisers.

Each week the president meets with his director of scheduling and the chief of staff to review the scheduling requests coming from the various White House offices and agencies within the executive branch. Any department wanting to schedule a policy event for the president must submit a "scheduling decision memorandum." This one-page memo summarizes the proposal, offers a recommendation, and includes a checkoff where the president can indicate his or her decision. (The format is similar to the decision memorandum discussed in Chapter 5.) The memo would include background on the proposed event, a summary of the policy proposal, and a list of potential participants in the program—people who can highlight the importance of the policy change and its impact.

In addition to the meetings with the president, the Scheduling Office and the Communications Office hold weekly meetings of all the relevant White House offices to coordinate policy and message for each week. Sometimes these meetings are broken up into short-term scheduling meetings (two weeks ahead), and long-term scheduling meetings (one to three months ahead). The Clinton administration tended to focus long-term scheduling from month to month with the schedule changing more regularly.[14] In contrast, the Bush administration has tried to enforce more scheduling discipline by planning meetings on a three-month basis—with the exception of issues involving the events of September 11.

---

[14] Interview with Karin Kullman, former White House scheduler.

Staff Secretary

The staff secretary controls the flow of paper going to the president from his staff and from agency heads. While the staff secretary almost never plays a role in the policy process, no paper or other materials get to the president without first going through the staff secretary. While this role is functionally administrative, it has important implications for policy making.[15] For example, establishing a routing list or routing procedures that specify who is included or excluded from particular memos or meetings is highly political and can affect the policy-making process. On sensitive issues like polling, the circulation may be limited, but on less sensitive issues, the policy proposals or recommendations from one policy council or agency are generally circulated to others who are the most likely critics.[16]

James Cicconi, staff secretary for President Bush in 1989 and 1990, summarized his role as one of an honest broker for stake holders in the policy-making process. Once he received a draft memo from an agency or policy council, the office of the staff secretary would circulate it for review, advice, and comments. Before sending it to the president, the staff secretary would circulate the comments to the authors of the memo and check to make sure that they responded to or accommodated the comment. In an interview with Martha Joynt Kumar in 1999, Cicconi argued that "If I wasn't satisfied with the answer, then I could overrule because I had the final responsibility for the paper that went to the president being full and complete and reflecting all the views of his advisers as honestly as possible.[17] In order to explain the complexity and diversity of views, staff secretaries often add summary memos to the material that goes to the president, crystalizing the primary disagreements and issues to be decided.[18]

Furthermore, once a memo to the president is completed, the staff secretary is the one who circulates it—or chooses not to circulate it—to the president and other key officials. This control of access is quite important to the policy councils. The staff secretary position is, thus, one of significant power and influence. The staff secretary is handpicked by the president's chief of staff, and former staff secretaries tend to move into positions of significance. Dick Darman, who later ran the Office of Management and Budget (OMB) was once staff secretary, as was President Clinton's last chief of staff, John Podesta.

Like the Office of Scheduling, the Staff Secretary Office is closely aligned with the White House chief of staff. Whereas the national security adviser has his or her own power base, the staff secretary relies on the influence of the chief of staff.

---

[15] Karen M. Hult and Kathryn Dunn Tenpas, "The Office of the Staff Secretary," *Presidential Studies Quarterly* 31, no. 2 (June 2001): 267.

[16] Ibid., 266–269.

[17] Interview with James Cicconi. White House Interview Program. Interview by Martha Joynt Kumar, Washington, D.C. November 12, 1999. Cited in Karen M. Hult and Kathryn Dunn Tenpas, "The Office of the Staff Secretary," *Presidential Studies Quarterly* 31, no. 2 (June 2001): 269.

[18] Karen M. Hult and Kathryn Dunn Tenpas, "The Office of the Staff Secretary," *Presidential Studies Quarterly* 31, no. 2 (June 2001): 268.

In the Reagan administration, this office was used to filter all memos going to the president. There was no guaranteed access to the president through the staff secretary. In the Clinton administration, the Office of Staff Secretary focused on ensuring support for the decision-making process by making certain all interested parties received relevant memoranda.

White House Counsel

The White House counsel offers legal advice on official matters for the president and the White House staff. Although the office has grown over the years, especially as the number of congressional investigations of the White House has increased, its basic functions have remained the same since they were shaped by counsel Fred Fielding during the Nixon administration.[19] These functions include: advising the president and the White House staff on the exercise of presidential powers, defending the president's constitutional prerogatives, and overseeing presidential nominations and appointments to the executive and judiciary branches. In addition, the counsel's office decides what is appropriate and what is not, both legally and ethically, for the president and his staff. It also provides training for all White House staff about ethics rules and records management and monitors their adherence when ethical issues arise. The counsel's office acts as a point of contact between the Executive Office of the President and the Justice Department and works with the Justice Department in determining the constitutional or other legal implications of policy proposals. Finally, the office works with White House personnel in "vetting" the qualifications of possible political appointees throughout the executive branch of government.

The counsel's office sits at the intersection of law, politics, and policy, and it is charged with advising the president and the White House staff on what is legally sound, yet politically astute.[20] When it is not mired in addressing scandals or confirmation matters, the White House counsel is significantly involved in the policy-making process. The counsel's office does not draft legislation submitted by the White House to Congress. That is done by an agency, the Office of Management and Budget, or someone in the policy councils. But, the counsel's office sometimes drafts Executive Orders or presidential memoranda that carry the same force of law as legislation. For example, the president can issue an Executive Order decreasing the size of the federal workforce without the approval of Congress, as President Clinton did early in his administration. Similarly, President George H. W. Bush made extensive use of Executive Orders when he responded to Iraq's invasion of Kuwait in 1991 (see Chapter 11). In addition, the counsel's office often fulfills a variety of functions related to the legislative process. These include: reviewing legislative proposals and bills presented for presidential signature or veto.[21] Furthermore,

---

[19] Mary Anne Borrelli, Karen Hult, and Nancy Kassop, "The White House Counsel's Office," *Presidential Studies Quarterly* 31, no. 4 (December 2001), 563–573.

[20] Ibid., 562.

[21] Ibid., 568.

the counsel's views are considered throughout the policy process, especially on policy matters before the courts—such as lawsuits against gun manufacturers, which could impact gun control legislation.

In its gatekeeper role, the counsel will use its authority as the president's legal adviser to influence policy proposals. If the counsel declares that a policy proposal developed by one of the policy councils is unconstitutional, the policy will have to be revamped or discarded. Policy councils rarely challenge the legal interpretations of the White House counsel, unless they can get a different legal opinion from the Justice Department. However, the Justice Department tends to adopt narrower interpretations of what is constitutional than the White House counsel. In an effort to reduce some of the legal leverage of the counsel's office, the policy councils in recent years have hired lawyers to provide legal ammunition. However, the counsel's office and its authority continue to grow as presidents rely on the office for a variety of legal services.

Conclusion

In this chapter we discussed the role of several White House offices in the policy-making process. These offices have distinct and important roles in the process. In particular, they serve as conduits through which the concerns of various constituencies at the national, state, and local levels are transmitted to the president. The more these constituents believe that their views and concerns have been considered by the chief policy maker, the more likely they are to accept the process and the policy outcome. Consequently, while the role of the White House Office in the policy-making process is less direct than that of the policy councils, it is no less important. In the next chapter, we analyze how policy is implemented. We will describe the role of agencies and interagency policy working groups, and how to determine who needs to be consulted in the policy implementation process and who does not.

Key Terms

Buy-in: Support for a proposal. Gaining buy-in from all interested parties is equivalent to achieving a consensus that the proposal should move forward.

Executive Orders: Presidential directives with the force of law. They do not require the approval of Congress to take effect.

West Wing: Since it was first constructed under President Theodore Roosevelt, the West Wing of the White House has served as the office building of the White House staff. This building contains the Oval Office, the vice president's office, and the National Security Council's Situation Room, where the president's staff monitors the world.

Review Questions

1. What are the three primary roles of the Office of Legislative Affairs (OLA)?

2. What role does the Office of Intergovernmental Affairs (OIA) play in the policy-making process?

3. How can the Office of Public Liaison (OPL) facilitate the policy-making process?

4. What role does the White House counsel play in policy making?

CHAPTER 4

Agencies and Policy Implementation

Executive Agencies and Departments and Executive Branch Policy Making

Even though the policy-making process since the presidency of Franklin Roosevelt has become increasingly centralized in the White House, federal agencies continue to play an important and dynamic role in the process. Because of the sheer number of government programs and decisions that need to be made, a large portion of the policy-making process remains outside the White House in executive branch agencies.[1] The term *agency* refers to organizations with "Agency" in their titles (the Environmental Protection Agency or Central Intelligence Agency for example), as well as departments like the Department of State or Department of Defense, and bureaus like the Federal Bureau of Investigation. As chief executive, the president is responsible for executing and implementing government policies; however, this role is often delegated to executive branch agencies. These agencies have the programmatic knowledge and substantive expertise needed to carry out this task. In addition, they control the programs, bud-

---

[1] Although controlling the federal bureaucracy is difficult, the president has a variety of means he can use to alter bureaucratic behavior. These include working through the OMB to modify organizational budgets and monitor bureaucratic activities, pursuing countervailing legislation, or pursuing limited administrative reorganizations. Recent studies suggest that the most potent means of presidential influence over the bureaucracy rests with the president's ability to make and rescind political appointments. Based on the Civil Service Reform Act of 1978, the president can choose senior executives based on compatibility with his agenda, he can reorganize bureaucracies so that power is centralized in the hands of political allies, and he can use reductions in force or transfers to adjust lower bureaucratic levels. See B. Dan Wood and Richard W. Waterman, "The Dynamics of Political Control of the Bureaucracy," *American Political Science Review* 85, no. 5 (1991): 804–805, Terry N. Moe, "Control and Feedback in Economic Regulations: The Case of the NLRB," *American Political Science Review* 79 (1985): 1094–1116, Terry N. Moe, "The Politicized Presidency," in John Chudd and Paul Peterson, eds. *The New Directions in American Politics* (Washington, D.C.: Brookings, 1985).

gets, and regulatory and rule-making processes that make policy implementation a reality.[2]

In this chapter, we will identify the roles and responsibilities of agencies in policy making and policy implementation. It is important to recognize that the implementation process begins—rather than ends—when the president makes a decision and signs a bill into law or issues an Executive Order. Agencies draft regulations, fill in the details on legislation submitted by the president to Congress, and are often designated to carry out presidential decisions presented in Executive Orders. The four primary means of implementing policy decisions are:

1. Submitting Legislation
2. Executive Orders and other Executive Actions
3. Regulations and rule making[3]

We will analyze these implementation mechanisms and specify the conditions under which each is likely to be used.

The Role of Agencies

There are 14 cabinet agencies and scores of independent agencies, commissions, and other government organizations in the executive branch of government. Some of these are **cabinet-level agencies,** meaning Congress has determined that these agencies should serve as preeminent advisors to the president and that the programs and responsibilities they carry forward are of vital national interest. The president can include the heads of particular agencies in his cabinet, but only Congress can grant the whole agency cabinet status. For example, President Clinton made the administrator of the Environmental Protection Agency a member of his cabinet but Congress failed to enact legislation that would provide the agency with cabinet-rank status. The box on page 56 provides a list of all the cabinet-level agencies.

Most agencies are organized into **program offices** and **nonprogram offices**. Program offices run the specific programs that Congress has established by statute—such as Head Start, Pell Grants, and food stamps. Nonprogram offices include an agency's budget office, the office of the general counsel, the office of the chief of staff, and an agency's policy and research office. Policy development in most federal agencies is coordinated by the office of the chief of staff and the policy development office. The budget process is directed by the budget office while rule implementation (regulations) is controlled by an agency's general counsel office.

---

[2] For an overview of the problems and issues that the president faces when attempting to implement policy, see George Edwards and Stephen Wayne, *Presidential Leadership: Politics and Policy Making*, 5th ed. (New York: St. Martin's/Worth Publishing, 1999), 283–322.

[3] A fourth way the president can promote action on a particular policy is through the use of the bully pulpit. For an analysis of Ronald Reagan's use of the bully pulpit, see William Ker Muir, Jr. *The Bully Pulpit, the Presidential Leadership of Ronald Reagan* (San Francisco, Calif.: Center for Self Governance of the Institute for Contemporary Studies, 1992).

Cabinet-Level Agencies

Department of Agriculture	Department of the Interior
Department of Commerce	Department of Justice
Department of Defense	Department of Labor
Department of Education	Department of State
Department of Energy	Department of Transportation
Department of Health and Human Services	Department of the Treasury
Department of Housing and Urban Development	Department of Veterans Affairs

Like the White House Office, cabinet agencies follow a specific set of internal processes and guidelines when developing policy. If a cabinet secretary wants an agency to prepare an options memorandum in a specific policy area, he or she will assign someone in the chief of staff's office or policy development operation the task of setting up an **intra-agency working group**. The working group will usually include someone from the general counsel's office, the agency's budget office, and its relevant program office(s). In a fashion that mirrors the White House policy process, the interagency group will continue to meet until a memorandum is readied. Before the memo is submitted, however, a formal **concurrence/nonconcurrence sheet** is circulated to the agency senior staff. Each member of the senior staff *must* express his or her viewpoint before the memorandum is submitted to the secretary.[4]

The difference between cabinet agencies and agencies whose director is a member of a particular president's cabinet can seem confusing and arcane. For example, at President Clinton's State of the Union addresses, Congress treated the administrator of EPA as a cabinet member by seating her with the other cabinet officers. This implied congressional acquiescence to EPA being a cabinet agency. EPA has a larger budget than several other cabinet agencies, and Congress conducts regular oversight of the EPA just as it does with cabinet departments. Yet EPA is not a cabinet agency. For practical purposes, the differences between some cabinet departments and large noncabinet agencies like EPA are often nonexistent. However, there is a distinct political difference in terms of the degree of clout. For example, for reasons of continuity in government and clear lines of succession in the event of a catastrophe, one cabinet officer always fails to attend the State of the Union address. The missing officer is always a congressionally designated cabinet agency.[5] Thus, even though President Clinton treated the head of the EPA as a cabinet officer, and even though his own Office of Cabinet Affairs (OCA) believed that the president has the authority to make an agency a cabinet department without

---

[4] Interview with Jacquie Lawing, former chief of staff to the secretary of Housing and Urban Development, May 7, 2001.

[5] Interview with Thurgood Marshall Jr., former secretary of the cabinet, April 3, 2001.

congressional approval, the OCA did not allow the head of the EPA to be the missing cabinet official. This recognition of political clout carries over into policy meetings where there is often a subtle difference in the way cabinet agencies versus noncabinet agencies are treated by White House staff.

Noncabinet-level agencies tend to have either a narrow program or issue area focus. Two examples of agencies with a singular area focus are the Federal Emergency Management Agency (FEMA) and the General Services Administration (GSA). FEMA is the agency responsible for coordinating the federal government's response to emergencies including natural disasters. GSA manages all the administrative services for the federal government; they negotiate the leases for agencies that want to rent business space, and they purchase all the office furniture and supplies for all federal government agencies. Another good example of a single-issue or single-program agency is the Peace Corps. Founded by President Kennedy, the Peace Corps currently has a budget of only about $260 million. Yet it is well known because it was one of President Kennedy's signature programs. The Corps logically could have been placed in the State Department. But there was concern that many developing countries would have balked at hosting Peace Corps volunteers if they thought they were really State Department diplomats or spies rather than engineers, teachers, and agricultural advisers. So a new agency was formed.

The box below lists all the major noncabinet-level agencies that report directly to the president. Some of the heads of these agencies serve on the president's cabinet, and others do not.

Important Noncabinet-Level Executive Agencies

Central Intelligence Agency	National Aeronautics and Space Administration (NASA)
Corporation for Community and National Service	Office of Personnel Management
Environmental Protection Agency	Peace Corps
Federal Bureau of Investigation	Small Business Administration
Federal Emergency Management Administration	Social Security Administration
General Services Administration	

Some single-issue or single-program agencies have grown beyond their original mandates and could become cabinet agencies if Congress acquiesced. The EPA, as we mentioned before, is an example of an agency that has over time become larger than several other cabinet departments, yet for a variety of political reasons has not been made a cabinet-level agency. Actually, these agencies play a much greater role in the policy process than originally intended. The EPA is now involved in almost every interagency process regarding environmental policy—even when the discussion involves programs not run by the agency. In contrast to cabinet agencies—such as Treasury, which can participate in almost any discussion regardless of any

Independent Agencies, Departments, Bureaus, and Other Entities

Commission on Civil Rights

Commodity Futures Trading Commission

Consumer Product Safety Commission

Defense Nuclear Facilities Safety Board

Export-Import Bank of the United States

Federal Communications Commission

Federal Deposit Insurance Corporation

Federal Election Commission

Federal Housing Finance Board

Federal Maritime Commission

Federal Mediation and Conciliation Service

Federal Reserve System

Federal Retirement Thrift Investment Board

Federal Trade Commission

Merit Systems Protection Board

National Archives and Records Administration

National Credit Union Administration

National Labor Relations Board

National Railroad Passenger Corporation

National Transportation Safety Board

Nuclear Regulatory Commission

Office of Government Ethics

Pension Benefit Guaranty Corporation

Railroad Retirement Board

Securities and Exchange Commission

Selective Service System

United States International Trade Commission

United States Postal Service

direct responsibility for the programs being discussed—most single-issue or program agencies participate in policy processes only when the programs being discussed are ones run by their particular agencies. This is the practical difference between cabinet departments and an agency like the Small Business Administration.

Independent agencies, departments, bureaus, and other entities exist within the executive branch but their day-to-day operations are not overseen by the president and the White House staff. These independent entities were created to ensure that they carried out their responsibilities without regular political interference from the executive and congressional branches. These entities tend to be either regulatory bodies or government corporations that are chartered to provide a specific service to business or consumers (i.e., United States Postal Service). Independent regulatory agencies are also typically defined by term appointment rather than appointments at the pleasure of the presidency, and by law their members typically represent both parties.[6] The best known, and arguably most powerful, independent agency is the Federal Reserve Board, which serves as the nation's central bank. Others include the Federal Communications Commission (FCC), which regulates the telecommunications industry, and the Federal Elections Commission (FEC), which oversees our country's election laws. The president's primary authority over these agencies is through nominating the heads and board members of these depart-

---

[6] Interview, Thurgood Marshall Jr., former secretary of the cabinet, April 3, 2001.

ments, and, in some cases, designating the chairperson of these agencies. Although the president can formally request these agencies to take certain actions, he or she cannot order or direct them to do so. And, unlike non-independent agencies, independent agencies can simply ignore the president's requests. For example, in 1997 President Clinton asked the Federal Communications Commission to require broadcasters to provide free television to candidates for federal office as part of his overall campaign finance reform agenda. Then FCC Chairman Bill Kennard expressed some initial interest in the proposal, but the Commission soon found that appropriators on Capitol Hill did not warm to the idea, and the FCC failed to act on the president's official request.

Implementing Policy Decisions

Once a policy decision has been made, the implementation process begins. Decision memoranda generally contain both policy recommendations and policy implementation recommendations (see Chapter 5). For example, in 1993 President Clinton was given a decision memorandum that recommended he reform the Community Reinvestment Act (CRA). Under CRA, commercial banks and savings and loans are required to reinvest in the communities in which they are chartered and take deposits. The purpose of the law is to ensure that all communities have access to basic banking services. Yet throughout the 1980s CRA was criticized for being overly bureaucratic and concerned more about paperwork than performance. President Clinton's advisers suggested that CRA be streamlined and that the regulations be made performance-based—tied to actual lending and investment benchmarks—instead of based on highly subjective criteria such as the number of meetings with community groups. In their decision memo to the president, his advisers suggested he send a presidential directive to the four banking regulators asking them to revise CRA regulations. Thus, the advisers provided not only a proposed policy change but a tool to implement those recommended changes. In the case of CRA reform, the tool of choice was a presidential directive. On other occasions it could be legislation, regulatory change, or simply the use of the presidential bully pulpit. The choice of the tool is driven sometimes by the policies chosen and sometimes by the political climate. For example, presidents often rely on Executive Orders when they lack political support in Congress. In the remaining sections of this chapter we will discuss the policy implementation process and the role of the White House offices and the agencies in it.

Executive Orders and Other Executive Actions

The president is the chief executive of the executive branch of the federal government. As chief executive, he has ultimate supervision over the various administrative agencies. In addition, he or she has wide, if vague, authority to further the public interest. In the secession crisis of 1861, for example, President Lincoln suspended, by proclamation, the writ of habeas corpus. Under the Constitution, the president is also the commander in chief and the head of state responsible for the directing of foreign relations.[7] He also has considerable decision-making authority in matters of foreign trade. The primary means by which the president exercises authority in these areas is through the issuance of proclamations and Executive Orders (EO).

Proclamations and Executive Orders have much the same legal effect, but they are usually used for different purposes: proclamations for ceremonial statements, executive orders for policy determinations under statutory authority. Proclamations are usually used for ceremonial statements of general interest (such as declaring National Flag Day), but in the past occasionally these were used for substantive statements of general policy (such as Lincoln's Emancipation Proclamation) or for announcements of certain presidential decisions, especially in the fields of foreign relations and trade.

The first Executive Order was issued in 1789, but none was numbered or issued uniformly until 1907 when the State Department began a numbering system and designated an 1862 order as Executive Order #1. Orders issued between 1789 and 1862 are referred to as "unnumbered executive orders."[8] Executive Orders are essentially presidential directives with the force of law and do not require the approval of Congress to take effect. The Constitution is silent on the subject of Executive Orders, but the courts have upheld them in principle—based on the implied powers inherent in the grant of "executive power" to the president in Article II, section 1 and in the constitutional language in Article II, section 3, that says presidents are "to take care that the laws be faithfully executed." In addition to this general constitutional authority, some Executive Orders are issued under direct statutory authority delegated specifically to the president by Congress in limited policy areas.[9] Executive memoranda or presidential directives are similar to Executive Orders but they are less formal and some jurists believe they have less legal authority.[10] More recently, several executive orders have received substantial public attention. These include President Roosevelt's Executive Order 9066, which provided the basis for imprisonment of Japanese Americans in World War II, President George H. W. Bush's orders concerning Haitian refugees, and President Clinton's Executive Orders regarding the environment and the rights of minorities.[11]

---

[7] The Constitution does not specify the president's power to act unilaterally. Scholars have argued that modern presidents have used this ambiguity to expand their institutional powers to act unilaterally and create law on their own. Terry M. Moe and William G. Howell, "Unilateral Action and Presidential Power: A Theory," *Presidential Studies Quarterly* 29, no. 4 (1999): 850–872.

[8] University of Florida Levin College of Law Web page, April 9, 2001.

[9] C-Span Web page, April 10, 2001.

[10] See Stephen J. Wayne, G. Calvin MacKenzie, David M. O'Brien, and Richard L. Cole, *The Politics of American Government*, 3d ed. (New York: St. Martin's/Worth Publishing, 1999), 502, and Phillip J. Cooper, "The Law: Presidential Memoranda and Executive Orders: Of Patchwork Quilts, Trump Cards, and Shell Games," *Presidential Studies Quarterly* 31, no. 1 (March 2001): 126–141.

[11] Phillip J. Cooper, "The Law: Presidential Memoranda and Executive Orders: Of Patchwork Quilts, Trump Cards, and Shell Games," *Presidential Studies Quarterly* 31, no. 1 (March 2001): 127.

Executive Orders

1. The president agrees to issue an Executive Order.

2. The relevant policy council identifies a lead entity to draft the Executive Order. Potential lead entities include a policy council or an agency, the White House counsel, or the OMB.

3. A draft Executive Order is completed and sent back to the relevant policy council for editing and review.

4. A final draft is submitted to the White House staff secretary.

5. The White House staff secretary circulates to all White House and Executive Office of the President agencies and, if appropriate, to the relevant departments for concurrence or nonconcurrence recommendation.

6. The final Executive Order is sent to the president with an information memorandum.

7. The president signs the Executive Order.

Congress often gives considerable leeway to the executive branch in carrying out its legislation. Details are often left out of statutory language—either because of a desire to leave the federal agencies involved some flexibility in implementing a bill, or simply because Congress feels unable or unwilling to spell out every detail for a bill's execution.[12] If members of Congress feel that an Executive Order contradicts the original legislative intent of the law or has no underlying statutory authority, a lawsuit can be filed to change or rescind the Order. Congress can also pass a bill repealing or modifying a specific Executive Order. That bill would, however, be subject to a presidential veto.[13]

Like the legislative drafting process, the process for preparing Executive Orders and other executive directives is controlled for the most part by the policy councils, as long as the Orders are related to policy. On the other hand, when it comes to implementing policy, Executive Orders share all the same advantages as regulations and share the disadvantage of being restricted by statutory and constitutional limitations. However, the process for issuing an Executive Order (see the accompanying box) is not as long as it is for issuing a regulation and there is no public comment period.

Submitting Legislation

When a president signs into law legislation he or she submitted to Congress, it is often considered a milestone event from a policy, political, and communications perspective. Bill signings are big events, and legislative achievements are given high

---

[12] C-Span Web page, April 10, 2001.

[13] Ibid.

consideration by political commentators and historians. Using legislation to implement policy has several advantages over Executive Orders and Executive Directives. First, legislation is generally broader in scope than Executive Orders or regulations. While Executive Orders and regulations are limited by statutes, legislation can be as far-reaching as its authors desire and is constrained only by the degree of political consensus in Congress and the White House and constraints imposed by the Constitution. Second, legislation that is enacted into law carries an aura of legitimacy derived from the legislative process. Specifically, any legislation that becomes law has the support of majorities in the House and Senate and at least the acquiescence of the president. Executive actions and regulations, since they are implemented by the executive branch solely, do not carry the same political weight because they lack the legitimacy that comes from wider participation in the policy-making process.

Despite the benefits of using legislation to implement policy, there are several drawbacks that make it inappropriate under certain circumstances. First, no legislation passes without compromise. While a president can have control over executive actions, legislation must go through the congressional process. In some cases, what comes out at the end of the process may look very different from what the president proposed. Second, the legislative process is usually long and arduous. Sometimes bills take years to pass, and other times Congress just ignores them. In contrast, policy can be implemented very quickly using Executive Orders. For example, within 12 hours of being informed that Iraq had invaded Kuwait, President George H. W. Bush had signed Executive Orders freezing Iraqi and Kuwaiti assets in the United States (see Chapter 11). Third, to get legislation enacted, the president must spend political capital. Many presidents have wasted a great deal of political influence on legislation that never got out of Congress. Despite these drawbacks, presidents continue to submit legislation to Congress because it offers them the best chance to achieve real, substantial changes in policies, programs, and systems.

The box on page 63 outlines the process by which legislation is drafted and then submitted to the Congress. Like the policy-making process discussed in earlier chapters, an interagency process to develop the bill is led by the policy councils. A lead agency is designated to draft the language of the bill, and a series of meetings is held to review, edit, and redraft the legislation until a consensus is reached. Once the interagency group has completed its work, the bill is moved through the OMB LRM process for review by any interested party of government. If a disagreement cannot be resolved, a decision memorandum is drafted and the president is presented with the recommendations of the group. However, several different groups of advisers meet—in the hopes of resolving any differences—before the president is required to engage. If a consensus is reached, the president receives an information memorandum that the bill is ready and a timetable for when it will be sent up.

Regulations and the Rule-making Process

Issuing regulations is one of the key means by which policies are implemented. Agencies can issue and revise regulations using existing statutory authority. They generally do so either when Congress has enacted legislation, when the president

Preparing Legislation

1. The president directs the appropriate White House policy council to implement his decision to draft legislation.

2. A White House policy council establishes a working group to write a draft of the legislation.

3. The chair of the White House working group chooses a lead agency to provide first draft of legislation.

4. The lead agency divides up drafting responsibilities between its general counsel's office, the relevant program office, and the relevant policy office.

5. An interagency working group meets to review first draft of legislation. The policy council coordinates the revisions and recommendations received from other agencies in working group. The policy council resolves any disagreements.

6. The lead agency reincorporates the revisions.

7. The redrafted bill is submitted to the OMB Legislative Referral Management process.

8. The OMB circulates the draft bill to the relevant agencies.

9. The OMB incorporates the revisions and recommendations it receives from the agencies. Unresolved issues go to policy councils. If major disagreement exists, the issue is bumped up to principals-level meeting (agency heads). If disagreement still exists, the policy council drafts a decision memorandum for the president.

10. The final legislation is prepared by lead agency. The lead agency identifies members of Congress to submit legislation on behalf of the president.

11. The legislation is submitted. The congressional review process begins.

has asked for a new rule, or the agency itself determines that a regulation should be reviewed and/or revised.

The advantages of using the regulatory process as a means of implementing policy for the executive branch are that the process is under the control of the rule-making agency and the impact can be immediate once the rule is completed. The limitations are that the effect of regulations is limited by the statutes on which they are based; the regulatory process can be long and arduous and is subject to public comment which can often create political problems for the executive branch; and new regulations often create new requirements and paperwork burdens, which are generally politically unpopular.

Federal agencies are authorized to issue regulations by their enabling statutes, by statutes establishing new programs, and by statutes amending and extending the duties and responsibilities of those agencies. Most regulations are issued informally, under the notice-and-comment procedure established by the Administrative Procedure Act (APA). Less frequently, certain agencies are required to add elements of adjudicatory proceedings such as cross-examination and rebuttal witnesses to the notice-and-comment requirements. These agencies include the Federal Trade

The Rule-making Process

1. An agency begins the rule-making process.
2. The appropriate agency program office and general counsel's office write a draft of the regulation.
3. The first draft of the regulation circulates within the agency.
4. Revisions and recommendations are sent back to the appropriate agency program office and general counsel's office.
5. The draft regulation is circulated through the agency again along with a concur/not concur sheet. All senior agency staff personnel must reply before the process continues.
6. A final "drop dead" meeting takes place in which all final comments are made and reviewed.
7. The secretary's or agency head's office clears final rule.
8. The Office of Information and Regulatory Review (OIRA) coordinates the review of the regulation by the OMB and White House, though only economically significant regulations require OMB review.
9. OIRA establishes a regulatory working group that includes the White House policy councils and the Office of the Vice President to review the regulation.
10. OIRA assembles the revisions and sends them back to the agency that originated the regulation. If there is no disagreement, OIRA will provide the agency with a regulation number which allows the regulation to be published in *Federal Register*.[14] If there are disagreements over the revised regulation, the vice president's working group convenes and resolves differences. In unique circumstances a decision memorandum can be presented to the president.
11. The regulation is sent to relevant congressional committees (authorizing committees) for a short waiting period.
12. The regulation is published in *Federal Register* for public comment. On occasion public hearings are held on proposed rules. Comment periods are at least 60 days.
13. The regulations are revised to incorporate public comments.
14. Steps 5 through 11 are repeated.
15. The final regulation is printed in *Federal Register*. If parts of regulation are set aside for further consideration, an interim final rule is published instead. Rules take effect no earlier than 30 days after publication.

Commission, the Consumer Product Safety Commission, and the Occupational Safety and Health Administration. Very rarely, some agencies must conduct their rule-making exercises in a formal adjudicatory proceeding.[15]

---

[14] Interview with Jacquie Lawing, former chief of staff of the Department of Housing and Urban Development, March 5, 2001.

[15] Rogelio Garcia, "Federal Regulatory Reform: An Overview," *The Semiannual Regulatory Agenda*, IB95035. Congressional Research Service: Government and Finance Division (October 24, 2000).

More than a hundred federal agencies and units within agencies issue regulations. Depending on their relationship to the president, the agencies may be divided into two categories: those subject to the president's direction and control (executive departments and agencies), and those relatively independent of such direction and control (independent agencies). The Consumer Product Safety Commission, the Federal Energy Regulatory Commission, the Federal Reserve System, the Federal Trade Commission, and the Securities and Exchange Commission are all examples of independent agencies.[16]

Approximately 90 percent of all regulations issued by agencies are subject to Executive Order 12866, which gives the president considerable oversight authority. Most of these agencies are involved with issuing the more controversial social regulations. They include the Environmental Protection Agency, the Occupational Safety and Health Administration, and the Mine Safety and Health Administration (both in the Department of Labor), the Food and Drug Administration (Department of Health and Human Services), the Department of Energy, the Department of the Interior, the Department of Agriculture, and the Department of Transportation (especially the National Highway Safety Administration).

Once the rule-making process starts, however, the White House cannot comment to the drafting agency on the proposed regulation until it has been sent to the Office of Information and Regulatory Review (OIRA) for review.[17] However, while OIRA controls the editing process for regulations, the White House offices—and the policy councils in particular—have tremendous influence over the process and the final outcome once the regulation is circulated by OIRA.[18] The knowledge that the policy councils are senior policy advisers to the president and can submit any dispute to him gives the councils a great deal of leverage in any negotiation over disagreements.[19] If there are disagreements about the regulation between the drafting agency and a White House policy council, OIRA generally brings the parties together to negotiate a compromise rather than imposing its will on them.

Presidents Nixon, Ford, and Carter directed agencies to consider costs and various regulatory alternatives to reduce those costs when developing regulations. But it was EO 12291 that dramatically changed the procedure under which agencies develop and issue regulations. EO 12291 directed agencies to employ cost-benefit analysis when developing regulations and established centralized review of rulemaking. It also directed agencies, to the extent permitted by law, to issue only those

---

[16] Ibid.

[17] However, OIRA only reviews rules that are significant. A significant regulation is defined as one that may have an annual effect on the economy of $100 million or more, or adversely affect in a material way the economy, a sector of the economy, productivity, competition, jobs, the environment or public health or safety, or state, local, or tribal governments or communities (regulations in this category are considered economically significant, requiring detailed cost-benefit analyses and OMB review); interfere with an action taken or planned by another agency; or may materially alter the budgetary impact of entitlements, grants, user fees, or loan programs or the rights and obligations of recipients; or raise novel legal or policy issues arising out of legal mandates, the president's priorities, or the principles for regulatory planning and review specified in the order.

[18] Interview with Cynthia Rice, former special assistant to the president for domestic policy, May 1, 2001.

[19] Ibid.

The Regulatory Review Process[20]

Week Ending Friday, October 1, 1993 Executive Order 12866—Regulatory Planning and Review September 30, 1993

The American people deserve a regulatory system that works for them, not against them: a regulatory system that protects and improves their health, safety, environment, and well-being and improves the performance of the economy without imposing unacceptable or unreasonable costs on society; regulatory policies that recognize that the private sector and private markets are the best engine for economic growth; regulatory approaches that respect the role of State, local, and tribal governments; and regulations that are effective, consistent, sensible, and understandable. We do not have such a regulatory system today. With this Executive order, the Federal Government begins a program to reform and make more efficient the regulatory process. The objectives of this Executive order are to enhance planning and coordination with respect to both new and existing regulations; to reaffirm the primacy of Federal agencies in the regulatory decision-making process; to restore the integrity and legitimacy of regulatory review and oversight; and to make the process more accessible and open to the public. In pursuing these objectives, the regulatory process shall be conducted so as to meet applicable statutory requirements and with due regard to the discretion that has been entrusted to the Federal agencies. Accordingly, by the authority vested in me as President by the Constitution and the laws of the United States of America, it is hereby ordered as follows:

. . .

Sec. 2. Organization. An efficient regulatory planning and review process is vital to ensure that the Federal Government's regulatory system best serves the American people. (a) The Agencies. Because Federal agencies are the repositories of significant substantive expertise and experience, they are responsible for developing regulations and assuring that the regulations are consistent with applicable law, the President's priorities, and the principles set forth in this Executive order. (b) The Office of Management and Budget. Coordinated review of agency rule-making is necessary to ensure that regulations are consistent with applicable law, the President's priorities, and the principles set forth in this Executive order, and that decisions made by one agency do not conflict with the policies or actions taken or planned by another agency. The Office of Management and Budget (OMB) shall carry out that review function. Within OMB, the Office of Information and Regulatory Affairs (OIRA) is the repository of expertise concerning regulatory issues, including methodologies and procedures that affect more than one agency, this Executive order, and the President's regulatory policies. To the extent permitted by law, OMB shall provide guidance to agencies and assist the President, the Vice President, and other regulatory policy advisors to the President in regulatory planning and shall be the entity that reviews individual regulations, as provided by this Executive order. (c) The Vice President. The Vice President is the principal advisor to the President on, and shall coordinate the development and presentation of recommendations concerning regulatory policy, planning, and review, as set forth in this Executive order. In fulfilling their

---

[20] Excerpts from Executive Order 12866, Office of the *Federal Register* Web page, 4/5/2001.

responsibilities under this Executive order, the President and the Vice President shall be assisted by the regulatory policy advisors within the Executive Office of the President and by such agency officials and personnel as the President and the Vice President may, from time to time, consult.

. . .

Sec. 7. Resolution of Conflicts. To the extent permitted by law, disagreements or conflicts between or among agency heads or between OMB and any agency that cannot be resolved by the Administrator of OIRA shall be resolved by the President, or by the Vice President acting at the request of the President, with the relevant agency head (and, as appropriate, other interested government officials). Vice Presidential and Presidential consideration of such disagreements may be initiated only by the Director, by the head of the issuing agency, or by the head of an agency that has a significant interest in the regulatory action at issue. Such review will not be undertaken at the request of other persons, entities, or their agents. Resolution of such conflicts shall be informed by recommendations developed by the Vice President, after consultation with the Advisors (and other executive branch officials or personnel whose responsibilities to the President include the subject matter at issue). The development of these recommendations shall be concluded within 60 days after review has been requested. During the Vice Presidential and Presidential review period, communications with any person not employed by the Federal Government relating to the substance of the regulatory action under review and directed to the Advisors or their staffs or to the staff of the Vice President shall be in writing and shall be forwarded by the recipient to the affected agency(ies) for inclusion in the public docket(s). When the communication is not in writing, such Advisors or staff members shall inform the outside party that the matter is under review and that any comments should be submitted in writing. At the end of this review process, the President, or the Vice President acting at the request of the President, shall notify the affected agency and the Administrator of OIRA of the President's decision with respect to the matter.

Sec. 9. Agency Authority. Nothing in this order shall be construed as displacing the agencies' authority or responsibilities, as authorized by law.

Sec. 10. Judicial Review. Nothing in this Executive order shall affect any otherwise available judicial review of agency action. This Executive order is intended only to improve the internal management of the Federal Government and does not create any right or benefit, substantive or procedural, enforceable at law or equity by a party against the United States, its agencies or instrumentalities, its officers or employees, or any other person.

Sec. 11. Revocations. Executive Orders Nos. 12291 and 12498; all amendments to those Executive orders; all guidelines issued under those orders; and any exemptions from those orders heretofore granted for any category of rule are revoked.

William J. Clinton, The White House, September 30, 1993

[Filed with the Office of the *Federal Register*, 12:12 p.m., October 1, 1993] *Note:* This Executive order was published in the *Federal Register* on October 4.

regulations for which benefits outweigh costs and to prepare cost-benefit analyses when developing major regulations. To assure compliance, agencies were required to submit their proposed and final regulations to OMB for review and clearance. When President Clinton assumed office in 1993, he continued the reform process by issuing Executive Order 12866 and revoking E.O. 12291. The new order maintained, with minor revisions, the cost-benefit analysis requirements as well as the requirement that regulations be reviewed and cleared by the OMB. Independent regulatory boards and commissions again were exempted from the order.

The **Congressional Review Act**, Subtitle E (110 Stat. 868), requires agencies to submit new regulations to the Congress and the General Accounting Office (GAO) before they can take effect. GAO is to prepare a report on each major rule, which it sends to Congress, to ensure that the agency has complied with procedural requirements regarding cost-benefit analysis, regulatory flexibility analysis, and specified sections of the Unfunded Mandates Reform Act. Congress has 60 session days in which to block the regulation by passing a joint resolution of disapproval, which must be signed by the president. The regulation goes into effect if the president vetoes the joint resolution and the veto is not overridden.[21]

The box on pages 66–67 provides excerpts from Executive Order 12866 which set forth the procedures for regulatory review in the executive branch of government.

Conclusion

Even though the policy-making process has been increasingly centralized in the White House, federal agencies, departments, and bureaus continue to play an important and dynamic role in the policy-making process. Their programmatic expertise and their control of budgetary resources and their role in the regulatory and rule-making processes make them essential players in the making and implementation of policy in the executive branch.

Key Terms

Cabinet Status or Cabinet-Level Status: *Cabinet status or cabinet-level status is* granted to agencies or individuals that Congress has determined should serve as preeminent advisers to the president and that the programs and responsibilities they carry forward are of vital national interest. The president can include the heads of particular agencies in his cabinet, but only Congress can grant the whole agency cabinet status. A cabinet-level agency is one which has been designated by Congress as "cabinet-level."

Concurrence/nonconcurrence Sheet: A *concurrence/nonconcurrence sheet* is circulated to agency senior staff before a memorandum from an interagency work-

---

[21] Rogelio Garcia, *Federal Regulatory Reform: An Overview* (Washington, D.C.: Congressional Research Service, Government and Finance Division, October 24, 2000).

ing group is submitted to a cabinet secretary. Each member of the senior staff must express their viewpoint on the memorandum before it is submitted.

Congressional Review Act: The Congressional Review Act, Subtitle E (110 Stat. 868), requires agencies to submit new regulations to the Congress and the General Accounting Office (GAO) before they can take effect.

Independent Agencies, Departments, Bureaus, and Other Entities: Each exists within the executive branch, but these are not overseen by the president and the White House staff. These agencies tend to be either regulatory agencies or government corporations that are chartered to provide a specific service to business or consumers (i.e., United States Postal Service).

Intra-agency Working Group: A working group within one agency charged with addressing a specific issue.

Proclamations: Generally ceremonial statements made by the executive that are of general interest (such as declaring National Flag Day). Occasionally, however, they are used for substantive statements of general policy (such as Lincoln's Emancipation Proclamation) or for announcements of certain presidential decisions, especially in the fields of foreign relations and trade.

Program Offices and Nonprogram Offices: *Program offices* in an executive branch agency run the specific programs that Congress has established by statute. Examples include Head Start, Pell Grants, and food stamps. *Non-program offices* include an agency's budget office, the Office of the General Counsel, the Office of the Chief of Staff, and an agency's policy and research office.

Review Questions

1. How many executive branch agencies are cabinet-level agencies? What difference does that designation make?

2. What is a "single-issue" or "single-program" agency?

3. What is an independent regulatory agency?

4. When was the first Executive Order issued? How can Executive Orders be challenged?

5. What are the advantages and disadvantages of issuing Executive Orders?

6. Describe the 11 steps taken by the federal government in preparing legislation to be submitted to Congress.

7. What are some of the advantages to utilizing the rule-making process as a means of implementing policy?

CHAPTER 5

Policy-making Memoranda

The Tools of Policy Making

The process of making policy within the executive branch involves the collective action of a wide range of individuals, policy councils, agencies, and departments with common as well as competing policy ideas and preferences. To participate in the policy-making process, each of these groups must be able to communicate their ideas, evaluate competing policy proposals, resolve differences, and make recommendations in a clear and recognized manner. Within the executive branch, standard tools of the trade—including decision-making memoranda, polling, and legislative clearance mechanisms—enable policy makers to convey their ideas concisely and clearly. These tools provide a common and standardized mode of communication that facilitates the interchange of ideas in the policy-making process and, thereby, maximizes its effectiveness as well as its legitimacy in the eyes of policy stake holders.

The president has the unique capability of setting the policy agenda and communicating his policy priorities at major events like the State of the Union address or when he submits an annual budget to Congress. The State of the Union address, given in January, is critical because it establishes the 10 to 20 policy initiatives to which the administration will give top priority in the year ahead. The budget, in turn, specifies the funding for hundreds of policies, projects, and programs that will be maintained or implemented in that year. Yet even events like these, where the president can use his bully pulpit to shape the policy-making agenda, require a great deal of communication and exchange of ideas among competing groups within the executive branch.[1] This, in turn, requires the use of various tools of the trade.

Preparations for the budget and the State of the Union address begin each year in August or September. Work on new policy initiatives and budget proposals for the

---

[1] Other key annual events include the Economic Report to the President by the Council of Economic Advisors in mid-February which specifies the economic status of the country, the Mid-Session Review by the OMB in June or July, which evaluates the government's surplus or deficit about half way through the fiscal year, and congressional and presidential elections (when held, these take place in November).

next year accelerates after Congress passes the budget for the current year, usually in October or November. Late in the fall, all executive agencies and departments submit their proposed budgets to the Office of Management and Budget (OMB), the OMB then gives them a "**pass back**" (which specifies the amount of funding it is willing to grant), the agencies and departments appeal, and—with the guidance of the relevant policy councils—the OMB and the respective agencies or departments negotiate a compromise. If no compromise is reached, the president intervenes and, by the end of December, budgetary decisions are finalized. The process of developing policy initiatives follows a similar pattern. The budgetary and financial impacts of each initiative are evaluated by the OMB, while the policy evaluation is managed by the relevant policy councils. Thus, although the processes of articulating the State of the Union and the budget enable the president to define the policy-making agenda in the federal government, creating those proposals involves a long process of exchange between a wide range of participants within the executive branch, each of whom must be able to communicate with one another effectively.

In addition to annual announcements like the State of the Union address, policy making within and outside of the executive branch is often driven by sudden and changing events. These can involve a wide range of phenomena including military and political crises, sudden economic changes at home or abroad, or natural disasters. Decision makers in the executive branch must often respond to these crises quickly, despite having little time to consider the problems at hand and often either too little or too much information at their disposal. In the face of severe time and information constraints, assistants to these decision makers must determine which of these crises requires the policy maker's attention. They must provide the decision maker with policy options and recommend a course of action in response to the crisis, and they must decide how the policy is to be implemented.[2] Following standard policy-making procedures and using the appropriate tools to initiate, analyze, and implement policy is critical because they provide continuity and structure that would otherwise be absent in a world of crisis management.

Adherence to a standardized process enables all policy makers to anticipate, understand, and use the tools of the policy-making process to voice their concerns and present their proposals to the chief decision maker. The ability to do so increases the efficiency of the process and provides a sense of legitimacy that enhances the commitment of all players to the policy outcome. Furthermore, by facilitating the input of multiple policy makers, use of standard policy-making tools, techniques and processes increases the likelihood that policy making under crisis conditions will be consistent with the overall policy goals of an administration, and it helps ensure that appropriate, persuasive, balanced, and well-justified policy decisions are made. In contrast, an ad hoc structure process or inappropriate use of

---

[2] In addition, as the Bush administration's experience during the Gulf War suggests (see Chapter 11), it is important to provide relevant policy makers with information about and input into the policy-making process even before the initial crisis period is over.

policy-making tools will create the perception that the policy chosen does not represent a consensus within the administration.

The next four chapters evaluate the most widely used and important tools for developing and conveying ideas and recommendations in the executive branch policy-making process.[3] This chapter emphasizes the most important tool in the process—the memorandum. It describes how to write decision and other types of memoranda for senior government officials. Using the formats developed by the Office of the White House Staff Secretary, we guide readers through the memo-writing process and how to distinguish the form and purpose of decision memoranda, briefing memoranda, and information memoranda. It is important to note that the formats and processes discussed in this book have been utilized, approximately, since the end of World War II and are still in effect today in President George W. Bush's administration. Subsequent chapters analyze polling, legislative clearance and coordination mechanisms, and the appropriate mechanisms for marketing policy.

The Role of Memoranda

In early 1993 a large number of advisers sat with the president in the Roosevelt Room in the heart of the West Wing of the White House. The purpose of the meeting was to discuss a decision memorandum regarding whether to submit legislation to Congress that would create *Empowerment Zones*, geographic zones in distressed areas that would receive special tax incentives and federal aid. The meeting with the president was tense because no consensus had been reached beforehand on whether to send Congress the Empowerment Zone legislation in its current form; a decision memo had been drafted for the president with several options but no consensual recommendation. The meeting was an early test of the new decision-making system put into place by the Clinton White House, in which unresolved policy issues of presidential importance would be put forth in a memo to the president to present all the options and views of the interested agencies.

Memoranda, specifically the **decision-making memorandum,** the **information memorandum,** and the **weekly report** are among the most important tools in the policy-making process. Decision memoranda are the mechanisms by which ideas are presented, options discussed, and resolutions on policy matters are reached. Without the ability to convey ideas concisely and clearly, a policy maker is effectively marginalized. This is bad for the individual policy maker and often has negative repercussions for the policy-making process.

---

[3] The role of memoranda has varied slightly across administrations depending on the president's decision-making style. Some, like Presidents Nixon and Carter, preferred to make decisions based on detailed memoranda that specified the pros and cons of policy options, while others, like Presidents Eisenhower, Kennedy, Johnson, Ford, Bush (Sr.), and Clinton, used them to focus and organize policy discussions and debates. George C. Edwards III and Stephen J. Wayne, *Presidential Leadership: Politics and Policy Making*, 5th ed. (New York: St. Martin's/Worth Publishing, 1999), 224–226.

Following a consistent format for each type of memorandum standardizes the policy-making process and maximizes its effectiveness. Although the reading tastes of different presidents or heads of agencies differ, and they may prefer a slightly different format or set of procedures than those described in this chapter, the basic structure and purpose of the memoranda remain constant, as do the most common mistakes made by inexperienced staffers. For example, the most common error made by policy makers when writing decision memoranda is the tendency to alter the format of the memorandum to provide additional information. The basic rule is that no memorandum should go beyond three pages in length, but there is often a desire on the part of staff to provide more information by attaching addenda to the back of a memorandum. Memorandum writers often argue that additional information must be made available to the president or agency head before they make their decision. Such an exercise is futile. Decision makers face severe time and informational constraints. Indeed, one of the most important roles of the memorandum is to compensate for those constraints by presenting *only* critically important information and doing so in a way that evaluates and suggests certain justifiable and coherent courses of action. If you know that your chief executive does not have time to read more than three pages of information, then why provide him or her with ten pages of addenda? It is a disservice to the decision-maker and to the issue discussed in the memorandum.

Since the purpose of the memorandum is to enable the president to make a good decision under extreme information and time constraints, it must succinctly filter through the mass of data about a particular event, identify information that is critical for the decision maker to know, and make a series of recommendations about appropriate courses of action. Good memorandum writers must exhibit clear thinking based on a solid understanding of how the event in question evolved and how it is related to other ongoing domestic and international phenomena of importance to the executive. Long memoranda tend to indicate a lack of clear thinking, while concise memos are much more effective in conveying ideas and proposals. If the president or his senior advisers desire more information, they will mark "Discuss Further" on the memorandum and ask the relevant agencies or departments to provide it.

Decision-making Memorandum

The required format for decision-making memoranda for the president of the United States as specified by the White House Staff Secretary's office is presented in the accompanying box. The decision-making memorandum plays a critical role in three primary phases of the policy-making process: the problem-identification and agenda-setting phase, the policy-formulation phase, and the policy-implementation phase. Of these three, the first and most important roles of the decision-making memorandum is to set the agenda by identifying which events have sufficient importance to the executive and to the United States of America to necessitate the policy maker's attention, and bring that action-forcing event to his or her attention. The driving force behind a decision memorandum is, thus, the action-forcing event.

Format for a Decision-making Memorandum

MEMORANDUM FOR THE PRESIDENT

FROM:

SUBJECT:

I. **Action-Forcing Event:**

Specify the nature of the event requiring or suggesting action and the degree of flexibility associated with it.

II. **Background/Analysis:**

Outline the current status and relevant history of the action-forcing event. Provide a succinct assessment of essential information about the key issues, principal actors, and primary constituents affected by the action-forcing event so that an informed, well justified, and persuasive decision can be made.

III. **Policy Options:**

Summarize options stating the advantages and disadvantages of each proposal.

IV. **Recommendation:**

Indicate a single recommendation or list options. Identify and provide responses to the most important benefits and criticisms of the chosen option.

V. **Decision:**

_____ Approve   _____ Approve As Amended   _____ Reject   _____ Discuss Further

The Action-forcing Event

An action-forcing event is a potential or existing situation that necessitates the need for presidential action and/or review. Action-forcing events include military conflict, an upcoming vote on important legislation, or the issuing of an Executive Order by the president. All three of the following are actual action-forcing events.

- Intelligence reports that North Korea has mobilized six divisions in response to South Korea's purchase of a nuclear reactor from Russia
- Twenty-five Senators, including the Majority and Minority Leader, plan to introduce a comprehensive welfare reform bill when Congress returns from recess
- During the last presidential campaign, you promised to cut 100,000 employees from the federal government workforce; attached is an Executive Order prepared by the Domestic Policy Council and OMB's Legal Counsel which would direct all federal agencies to make these cuts by the beginning of the next fiscal year

An action-forcing event is something significant enough that senior advisers do not believe that they can act under the authority of the president or an agency head without his or her specific consent. Of course the threshold for acting without specific presidential consent changes from administration to administration. In some White Houses, the president has relied heavily on the **cabinet government**—including his cabinet secretaries and appointees such as the chief of staff, national security adviser, or other senior-level advisers—for advice and information.[4] In administrations with this decentralized policy-making style, a lead adviser or agency often is empowered to make major decisions without specific consent on every situation and takes the lead role in promoting or implementing policy. The combination of the authority vested in their positions as commissioned officers to the president plus their relationship to the chief executive gives the adviser or agency considerable latitude to act alone. The Reagan administration often relied on his cabinet government to coordinate policy making. In other administrations, with more centralized or *presidential* styles of decision making, decisions of all types may be placed before the president. The Nixon, Carter, and Clinton administrations often used a more centralized presidential style of policy making.

If the president relies heavily on a cabinet government to coordinate policy making, the decision-making memorandum must obviously be directed to the appropriate advisers and governmental agencies. Yet, even if the president prefers that all major decision-making memoranda are written primarily to himself, a memo must still identify the views of the major agencies affected by both the event and the recommended response to it. If the input of relevant agencies is not anticipated and considered during the policy-making process, the neglected agencies will find alternative ways in which to move their views forward—such as circumventing the traditional policy-making apparatus. These could include direct contact with the president or other senior officers in the White House, such as the vice president, First Lady, or chief of staff, communication with members of Congress, or the disclosure of information to the press.

The potential for policy **leaks** is considerable. Indeed, *approved leaks* (information that is intentionally provided to the media in an informal manner in order to mobilize public support) and *unapproved leaks* (information that is provided to people outside of the formal decision-making apparatus without the knowledge or consent of the executive) take place on virtually every important issue. The authority of a presidency can be greatly damaged by the release of unapproved leaks (as opposed to strategic leaks designed to promote the president's agenda). Uncontrolled leaks weaken the president by making the internal control mechanisms seem irrelevant and thus promoting chaos within an administration. In addition, policy ideas that are delivered directly to the president from an agency head or outside source are not filtered by the established policy process and are, consequently, not likely to include other options or dissenting views which can provide the president with a broader perspective before he makes a decision. Since members of the policy-making community are most likely to go outside of the standard policy-making process when they feel that their views or concerns are not being presented to the president, one way that the White House staff can minimize leaks and other nonstandard

---

[4] Roger Porter, *Presidential Decision Making: The Economic Policy Board* (Cambridge, England: Cambridge University Press, 1980), 23–29.

practices is to make sure that the information and memoranda presented to the president represent the input of the relevant players. This does not mean that everyone in the policy-making process must agree on the policies being promoted, but there must be a consensus that the information presented to the president conveys the opposing views of all of the primary parties in the policy-making process.

Background Information and Analysis

The background information and analysis section of the decision-making memorandum often determines the length of the document. While the action-forcing event should be no more than a sentence or two, the background/analysis section can be anywhere from a paragraph to a page. This section must:

- Provide a quick overview of the issue, including any specific, recent events that create the need for presidential action
- Give the relevant historical or contextual background
- Provide essential information about the key issues, principal players, and the primary constituents affected by the crisis and the various policy options so that an informed, well-justified, and persuasive decision can be made.

While the amount of detail included in this section can be modified based on the familiarity of the president or agency head with the issue at hand, it is essential that this section meets two primary objectives. First, it must provide enough convincing evidence to build a consensus among various constituencies within the policy-making process. Second, it must be persuasive enough to convince these constituencies that a particular policy option, or set of policy options, is called for and represents the most effective means of pursuing fundamental goals and objectives that the president and the executive branch feel are of vital interest to the United States. The ability of the decision-making memorandum to filter and interpret information makes it an extremely powerful policy tool.

Policy Options

In the options portion of the decision memorandum, the author lays out various proposals to address the action-forcing event in some detail. If there is only one recommended option, then this section is not necessary and the recommendation section alone will suffice. However, if there are several options, it is important that the author of the memorandum present the proposals in this section as an honest broker and reserve his or her views until the recommendation section. To do so before the options are presented would prejudice the decision maker.

Each option should also include a section outlining the advantages and disadvantages of the proposition. The views of all the parties need to be taken into account. This helps to ensure that the decision memorandum serves as the sole deliverer of information on a given issue, and that the participants in the decision process will not feel the need to undermine the resolution mechanism. Pros and cons related to both policy and political concerns need to be included. Stake holders—such as interest groups, key members of Congress, local leaders, etc.—and their views should be identified.

The need to be fair and open to all options must be weighed against the desire to provide the decision maker with concise, clear, relevant, and good choices. It is important that the decision memorandum not become a free-for-all forum for ideas that will confuse the decision maker and cloud the issues surrounding the action-forcing event. Therefore, it is vital that the author(s) of the memo work to build a consensus around those options that are consistent with the goals that the president and the executive branch feel are of vital interest to the United States. One way to limit the number of options while ensuring open discussion is for the author(s) to encourage agencies that disagree with the majority to unify behind one alternative option that would include some but not necessarily all of their views. Agencies that recognize the power of numbers will cooperate as long as they feel they will get something out of the process. However, there are instances where the participants in the decision process will feel—for ideological or political reasons— that they want to submit their own option to the decision maker. In these cases, the author(s) of the decision memorandum, after having exhausted all attempts at building a consensus, must either include that option or face the reality that the process will be seen as illegitimate and may break down.

Recommendation

In the recommendation section, the authors have the opportunity—assuming they have built a consensus among key constituents around the option that they support—to make their recommendation. However, it is common for the lead writers of the decision memorandum to side with a policy option preferred by a minority of the constituents. If that is the case, the majority option should be given first billing, rather than the proposal the authors support. In addition, the authors need to be clear as to who is recommending what option. Each participant in the process should be listed as supporting what option.

The recommendation section should not be long. What is being conveyed to the decision maker is the recommended option and a statement of who supports that position. An exception to this rule exists when there is only one option and the recommendation section becomes the place where the consensus proposal is discussed and the pros and cons of the proposal being considered are laid out before the decision maker.

Decision

There are three actions that a decision maker can take in response to a memorandum. If the president or designated decision maker agrees with the recommendation as is or as amended, several actions are set into motion. If the memorandum calls for an executive action (which can include issuing of an Executive Order or a

Sample Decision-making Memorandum to the President

MEMORANDUM FOR THE PRESIDENT

FROM: Domestic Policy Council

SUBJECT: **Executive Order Reducing the Federal Bureaucracy by at Least 100,000 Positions**

I. Action-Forcing Event:

You are tentatively scheduled to announce reductions in the federal bureaucracy on Wednesday, February 10, 1993.

II. Background/Analysis:

This Executive Order seeks to satisfy your campaign pledge to cut the federal bureaucracy by at least 100,000 positions through attrition, as a way to eliminate unnecessary layers of management and improve productivity.

One of every six dollars we spend on domestic programs goes to wages and benefits for Federal workers—not counting administrative costs. Eliminating 100,000 positions in the bureaucracy would save $3 to $4 billion a year by FY 1996.

This measure will reduce the Government's civilian workforce of 2.2 million people by four percent over the next three years. It orders the Office of Management and Budget to issue detailed instructions directing the executive departments and agencies with over 100 employees to achieve 25 percent of the cuts in FY 1993, 62.5 percent by the end of FY 1994 and 100 percent by the end of FY 1995. At least ten percent of the reductions would come from management (Senior Executive Service, GS-14, and GS-15). Independent agencies are requested to make similar reductions voluntarily.

III. Recommendation:

This action will help fulfill one of your most visible campaign promises. We recommend that you approve the proposed Executive Order.

IV. Decision:

_____ Approve   _____ Approve As Amended   _____ Reject   _____ Discuss Further

Source: Domestic Policy Council, the White House.

---

phone call to a head of state) or for new legislation (which requires congressional approval), the executive branch policy councils will direct the appropriate federal agency to begin drafting the recommended policy. These drafts will be developed jointly by the agency policy and legal counsel offices. Once completed, the legislation or Executive Order is submitted by the policy councils, in coordination with the Office of Management and Budget, to other relevant agencies for comment. The executive branch policy councils then are responsible for ensuring the action is completed, as are the relevant policy offices in each agency.

A second possible action stems from the president or designated decision maker wanting additional information. In this case, he or she will check the "Discuss Further" option, implying dissatisfaction with the options presented. This may indicate a desire for additional options. Alternatively, the president might support one of the options but decide that events dictate that the decision should be postponed. If more information is required, the policy councils, or the relevant offices in agencies, will prepare additional materials, in coordination with the agencies or other persons from inside or outside of the executive branch that the decision maker requests information from, and resubmit a new memorandum. If the executive chooses to delay a decision, those same offices are responsible for raising the issue at a subsequent, more appropriate time.

Third, the president or designated decision maker may decide to reject the recommendations because the action-forcing event did not or no longer rises to a level where he or she believes a decision must be made. This option is rarely exercised because while events may overtake the issues raised in the action-forcing event, a good policy maker should never submit a memo in which the action-forcing event is not action-forcing.

A sample decision-making memorandum from the Domestic Policy Council to the president is presented on page 78. Note that in this particular memo, policy options were not offered since there was a consensus recommendation among the president's advisers.

The Information Memorandum

The information memorandum is another important tool for policy makers. The key difference between the information memorandum and the decision-making memorandum is that the information memo should *not* raise issues for decision. Instead, the information memorandum serves two primary functions. First, it provides

---

Format for an Information Memorandum

INFORMATION
MEMORANDUM FOR THE PRESIDENT
FROM:
SUBJECT:

I. Summary
Three sentences or less that state the subject at hand and summarize the changes or provide an update on relevant information related to it.

II. Discussion
Highlight any problems or unresolved issues regarding the subject at hand.

---

information that will be helpful on an issue or potential action item requiring a de-cision at a later date. For example, information memoranda of two to three pages can update the executive on commissions that are reviewing issues of large scope, such as Social Security reform, and strengthen his or her knowledge base prior to the delivery of a set of recommendations at the end of the commission's study. Sec-ond, it keeps the executive informed of the progress or regression of an issue on which he or she has already made a decision. A case in point concerns the follow-up to the Executive Order described in the Sample Decision-making Memorandum to the President (page 78). The White House staff would send information memo-randa to the president when certain benchmarks were reached, including the final target number. The format of the information memorandum is exhibited in the box on page 79.

Summary Section

The Summary section should quickly state the change or update in information. Using the Executive Order to reduce the size of government as an example, the summary would read as follows:

> On June 17th, the Office of Personnel Management is prepared to report that we have met the goal stated in Executive Order (#) to reduce the size of the fed-eral government through attrition by 100,000.[5]

Discussion Section

The discussion section should highlight any problems. Using the above reduction of the federal government as an example, the president's advisers may use the dis-cussion section to underscore the fact that 60 percent of the reduction came from the Department of Defense and that this might open the administration up to criti-cism. However, not all discussion issues are by nature negative. The White House staff may, for example, also use the discussion section to report that the reductions in personnel will save more budget funds than previously estimated in the follow-ing years.

The Weekly Report

An additional mechanism to provide the decision maker with timely information is the weekly report. The staff of each cabinet-level agency and White House office submits weekly reports to the president, vice president, White House chief of staff, and agency heads. The style of these reports depends in part on the objective of the writer.

---

[5] Domestic Policy Council, the White House.

Potential Issues Raised on a Weekly Report

WEEKLY REPORT

MEMORANDUM FOR VICE PRESIDENT GORE

FROM: Carol Browner, Environmental Protection Agency

SUBJECT: Weekly Report

I. Key Agency News

On 4/13 and 4/14 the Administrator of the Environmental Protection Agency testified before the House Appropriations Subcommittee on the Veterans, HUD, and Independent Agencies on the Administration's environmental budget.

II. Press Releases

On 12/3, the Secretary will announce the Electricity Restructuring Bill, a new energy plan that uses resources more efficiently, cuts electric bills for the consumers and businesses, and protects public health and the environment. The event will be open to press and questions will be taken at the end of the announcement.

III. Weekly Schedule

A list of the key event for each day of the coming week is attached.

Source: Office of the Vice President, the White House.

Some agencies use weekly reports as a way to summarize the events of the prior week. A report may be broken down into several sections. One section might describe speech and meeting activities with outside groups, such as interest groups, lobbyists, and elected officials. This section could also include important legislative activity. Another section of the report will focus on press activity. A fourth section describes the future schedule of important individuals in the administration or agency. Above is an example of what might be included in a typical weekly report from the EPA to the vice president.

Others may utilize a weekly report to pursue an ongoing dialogue with the decision maker on issues that are high on the decision maker's agenda. For example, the report can be used to respond to questions from the decision maker, provide timely information on an issue of importance, or seek guidance on an issue. Agencies may also use the weekly report as a way to subliminally suggest issues that they believe the decision maker should engage in. Below are two real examples from the weekly reports of the White House Domestic Policy Council.

Health Care—Medicare Annual Cap on Rehabilitative Services: You recently asked about the $1500 annual cap on Medicare payments for outpatient physical therapy and other rehabilitative services. This cap was included in the Balanced Budget Act at Congressman Thomas' insistence; we had opposed it for fear that

> it would have had an adverse impact on chronically ill beneficiaries. Providers and advocates are now arguing that the cap has had just such an impact, pointing to a recent study showing that almost 13 percent of Medicare beneficiaries incur significant out-of-pocket expenditures as a result of the cap. Senator Grassley has proposed legislation that would allow Medicare beneficiaries to exceed the cap if they have an illness that clearly requires additional services. This proposal, however, may prove very costly; we are scoring it now as well as reviewing alternatives.[6]

This paragraph underscores the report's use as a way to respond to a question from the decision maker directly, and as a way to seek guidance indirectly. The last sentence is intentionally leading. It suggests that there may be some alternatives and subtly asks if the decision maker wants to pursue them. And, in fact, President Clinton's written response was to encourage the development of alternatives.

> Tobacco—Oregon Verdict: A jury in Oregon last week ordered Philip Morris to pay $81 million in damages (including $79.5 million in punitives) to the family of a man who died of lung cancer after smoking for 40 years. The verdict was the largest ever against a tobacco company, exceeding the $51.5 million verdict awarded by a California jury against Philip Morris earlier this year. Shares of tobacco companies fell sharply this week as a result of the verdict.[7]

This paragraph provides a classic example of the information power of the weekly report. It is simply a factual description of an important event from the week on a high-profile issue, yet because the information is timely and noted to be important, it raises the salience of the tobacco issue sufficiently to place it on the president's agenda.

Conclusion

The memorandum is one of the most important and influential tools in the decision-making process. It initiates the decision-making process by identifying an action-forcing event and bringing that event to the relevant decision maker's attention, it compensates for severe information and time constraints in the decision-making process by identifying the specific background information and analysis needed to make a decision, and it suggests an informed, balanced, well-justified, and strongly supported policy option. To do this, the memorandum must be well written, but it is important to remember that all decision memoranda, information memoranda, and weekly reports will be judged by the results they produce. What happens after a memorandum is written is even more important than the writing of the document itself. In particular, it is the action that a decision maker takes once he or she has read the memorandum that completes the decision-making process.

---

[6] Domestic Policy Council, the White House.

[7] Domestic Policy Council, the White House

In the next chapter, we will show how memorandum writers can use public opinion to refine and promote particular policy options. Successful pollsters use polling data not only to identify popular ideas but to learn how to market proposals that decision makers want to pursue. Good polling data also help policy makers refine ideas that they have already developed to ensure continued support throughout the policy-making process. The next chapter will demonstrate how to prepare and interpret opinion polls to ensure that they provide accurate and reliable information.

Key Terms

Cabinet Government: A policy-making style in which the president relies heavily on his cabinet secretaries and appointees such as the chief of staff, national security adviser, or other senior level advisers for advice and information. The lead adviser or agency is often empowered to make major decisions without specific presidential consent and takes the lead role in promoting or implementing policy.

Decision-making Memorandum: One of the primary means of communicating and exchanging ideas in the policy-making process. It plays a critical role in agenda setting, policy formation, and policy implementation. The most important of these roles is setting the agenda by identifying which events have sufficient importance to the executive and to the United States of America to necessitate the policy maker's attention and bring that action-forcing event to his or her attention.

Information Memorandum: A memo providing information that will be helpful on an issue/potential action item requiring a decision at a later date. Unlike the decision-making memorandum, the information memorandum should *not* raise issues for decision.

Leaks: *Approved* leaks refer to information that is intentionally provided to the media in an informal manner in order to mobilize public support. *Unapproved* leaks refer to information that is provided to people outside of the formal decision-making apparatus without the knowledge or consent of the executive. Uncontrolled leaks can weaken the president by making the internal control mechanisms seem irrelevant and thus promoting chaos within an administration.

Pass Back: Late in the fall, all executive agencies and departments submit their proposed budgets to the Office of Management and Budget. The OMB then gives them a *pass back*, which specifies the amount of funding it is willing to grant. The agencies and departments may appeal, and, with the guidance of the relevant policy councils, the OMB and the respective agencies or departments negotiate a compromise.

Weekly Report: A mechanism that provides decision makers with important information on a regularly scheduled basis.

Review Questions

1. What is the primary purpose of a decision-making memorandum? What role do decision memos play in the policy-making process?

2. What is the difference between a decision-making memorandum and an information memorandum?

3. What is the most common error made by policy makers when writing decision memoranda?

4. What are the three actions a decision maker can take in response to a decision-making memorandum?

5. What constitutes an action-forcing event?

6. How do federal agencies utilize weekly reports?

CHAPTER 6

Polling and the Policy-making Process

Polling and Policy Making: Myths and Realities

Since President Herbert Hoover first systematically quantified newspaper editorials and undertook sophisticated surveys of public opinion to gauge support for his policies, presidents have used polling to inform themselves and others, shape policy, write speeches, and design political strategies.[1] Polling has been institutionalized in the White House since the late 1960s,[2] yet several recent presidents downplayed their use of polls because of fears about potential negative public perceptions regarding their use. For example, fearing that they would be criticized for relying on polls the way that the Johnson administration had been, the Nixon and Ford administrations made efforts not to make public references to polling.[3] In contrast, the Clinton administration was relatively open about its use of polling

---

[1] Robert M. Eisenger and Jeremy Brown, "Polling as a Means Toward Presidential Autonomy: Emily Hurja, Hadley Cantril, and the Roosevelt Administration," *International Journal of Public Opinion Research* 10 (1998): 238–256; Robert M. Eisinger, "Gauging Public Opinion in the Hoover White House: Understanding the Roots of Presidential Polling," *Presidential Studies Quarterly* 30, no. 4 (December 2000): 643–661; Diane J. Heith, "Presidential Polling and the Potential for Leadership," in *Presidential Power: Forging the Presidency for the 21st Century*, ed. Lawrence Jacobs, Martha Kumar, and Robert Shapiro, (New York: Columbia University Press, 2000) 380–407; Lawrence R. Jacobs, *The Health of Nations: Public Opinion and the Making of American and British Health Policy* (Ithaca, N.Y.: Cornell University Press, 1993); Lawrence R. Jacobs and Robert Y. Shapiro, "The Rise of Presidential Polling: The Nixon White House in Historical Perspective," *Public Opinion Quarterly* 59 (1995): 163–195, and Lawrence R. Jacobs and Robert Y. Shapiro, *Politicians Don't Pander: Political Leadership, Public Opinion and American Politics* (Chicago: University of Chicago Press, 2000).

[2] See Diane J. Heith, "*The Polls:* Polling for a Defense: The White House Public Opinion Apparatus and the Clinton Impeachment," *Presidential Studies Quarterly* 30, no. 4 (December 2000): 783–790.

[3] Ibid., 784.

for marketing policy prescriptions.[4] The George W. Bush administration, on the other hand, has sought to portray the president as unconcerned about polls.

Political pundits, editorial pages, and politicians looking for a campaign issue have publically debated the use of polling by policy makers in the executive branch. Some critics of polling argue that truly great leaders should ignore polls, that polls are untrustworthy, and that polling is somehow undemocratic. These assertions are unfortunate because they mischaracterize polling and undermine the public's confidence and general understanding of the critical role it plays in the policy-making process. Contrary to the exhortations of its critics, we argue that polling enhances the democratic nature of policy making by providing a conduit through which information about constituents' concerns are channeled to policy makers.[5] This can enhance the legitimacy of the policy-making process by enabling policy makers to be more responsive and accountable to their constituents.

Particularly when presidents cannot count on members of their party in congress to support their policies, demonstrating public support for a particular policy agenda can help them build successful legislative coalitions.[6] At a minimum, public support for presidential initiatives bolsters the bargaining power of his supporters within the executive branch by reducing the likelihood that the president's critics in Congress and elsewhere will mobilize in opposition to the policy. This also generally enhances the president's ability to work with Congress and with those within the executive branch who hold competing ideas on a variety of related issues. Alternatively, low ratings in the polls can undermine executive and congressional support for a particular policy initiative by increasing the incentives of critics to attack the policy and eroding the president's ability to negotiate and resolve policy disagreements with Congress. It is, therefore, critical to recognize the power of polling.

Throughout this book we argue that the policy-making process in the executive branch works most efficiently when policy makers believe that the process itself is a legitimate and effective means of expressing their views to the president. By providing a channel for the public to express their viewpoints on policy initiatives at various stages in development, polling can further enhance the legitimacy of the policy-making process by informing policy makers about how a potential policy

---

[4] Colin Campbell and Bert Rockman, eds. *The Clinton Presidency: First Appraisals* (Chatham, N.J.: Chatham House, 1996); Dick Morris, *Behind the Oval Office: Getting Reelected Against All Odds* (Los Angeles: Renaissance, 1999); George Stephanopoulos, *All Too Human* (Boston: Little Brown, 1999).

[5] This premise is valid as long as the executive branch modifies its policies to some extent in response to the polling results. Scholars including Robert Y. Shapiro and Lawrence R. Jacobs argue that despite the increase in polling, the White House may not have become more responsive to public opinion. See Lawrence R. Jacobs and Robert Y. Shapiro, *Politicians Don't Pander: Political Manipulation and the Loss of Democratic Responsiveness* (Chicago: University of Chicago Press, 2000). For a review of the scholarly literature on the relationship between presidents, polling, and public opinion, see Robert Y. Shapiro and Lawrence R. Jacobs, "*Source Material*: Presidents and Polling: Politicians, Pandering, and the Study of Democratic Responsiveness," *Presidential Studies Quarterly* 31, no. 1 (March 2001): 150–167.

[6] Researchers have found, for example, that popular presidents received more congressional support regardless of party affiliation. See George C. Edwards III, *At the Margins* (New Haven, Conn.: Yale University Press, 1989), 124; Fred I. Greenstein, ed. *Leadership in the Modern Presidency* (Cambridge, Mass.: Harvard University Press, 1988), and Samuel Kernell, *Going Public: New Strategies of Presidential Leadership* (Washington, D.C.: Congressional Quarterly Press, 1986).

initiative might be received or how well a current policy is working. Polling also provides the public with a de facto means of bolstering the bargaining power of those who support popular proposals and undermining the bargaining power of those who do not.

This chapter introduces the basics of polling in the executive branch. It specifies who does the polling in the White House, when it is useful to conduct polls, and how polls have been used to promote the policy-making process. As an introduction, it is useful to consider some of the popular myths about polling and politics.

> *Myth:* Polling is damaging to the democratic process. Elections provide the appropriate means for the public as a whole to voice its concerns. Polling undermines the importance of elections by enabling the small group of people interviewed to circumvent the electoral process and exercise a substantial amount of influence.
>
> *Reality:* The reality is that polling can help strengthen the democratic process by providing an additional channel through which a diverse set of constituents express their views and concerns to executive and congressional decision makers. If polling is done correctly, it often provides a better indicator of what the American people as a whole feel about a particular set of issues than do elections or even referenda on those same issues.

> *Myth:* Politicians use polling to decide their position on issues.
>
> *Reality:* Scholars have argued that because presidents have only limited institutional and political resources and cannot respond to every issue, they will tend to pay attention to events and respond to issues that the public deems most important.[7] However, policy ideas are generally developed first, then polling is done to see how broadly the ideas will be supported and how to best market them. As Clinton Domestic Policy Adviser Bruce Reed points out:

>> We sometimes get accused of having an agenda of poll-driven ideas . . . I think it was actually the other way around. We would come up with a host of ideas and we'd use whatever channels we could to convince people around here to do them. It wouldn't hurt if something was popular, but that wasn't where we got the idea in the first place. . . . I think the President had always been interested in the use of public opinion to figure out what are public feelings, not to make the policy decisions.[8]

> *Myth:* Pollsters manipulate data.
>
> *Reality:* Unquestionably, pollsters can alter the manner in which questions are asked, how polls are conducted, and how polling results are presented.

---

[7] George C. Edwards III and B. Dan Wood, "Who Influences Whom? The President, Congress, and the Media," *American Political Science Review* 93 (June 1996): 327–344.

[8] Bradley H. Patterson Jr., "The White House Staff: Inside the West Wing and Beyond," (Washington, D.C.: Brookings Institution Press, 2000).

Indeed, there are many intentional and unintentional ways to create bias in polling. In practice, however, intentional manipulation of polls by professional pollsters is more limited than one might imagine. Pollsters who tilt questions or the interpretation of the responses to achieve results that they or their clients want to see will soon be viewed as unreliable, ineffective and unemployed. Questionable polling practices undermine the integrity and usefulness of polls. Biasing results denies policy makers the information that makes polling such a powerful tool—indeed, rather than enhancing the policy-making process and empowering decision makers, biased polling can misdirect decision makers and undermine the policy-making process by encouraging them to promote unpopular or unsupported policies. As a result, regardless of their particular viewpoints or the answer they "want" the results to support, politicians quickly lose patience with pollsters whose data or analyses they believe are inaccurate or misleading.

Myth: Polling has become a substitute for leadership.

Reality: Certainly some politicians shift their policy positions when polls indicate that those positions are no longer supported. Responding to polling data does not, however, necessarily reflect a lack of leadership. Nearly all politicians use polling data to evaluate their policy decisions and most, appropriately, weigh public opinion in their analysis of the policy's success. More than an evaluation tool, however, polling can be used to promote and empower leadership. The best politicians use polling to help them sell ideas they believe are in the best interest of the country. Polling is most effective when used as a way to market positions already taken both to the public at large and to critics in the policy-making process itself. In his book, *Behind the Oval Office,* Dick Morris points out that President Clinton used polling to support positions he believed were right for the country, but unpopular:

> Clinton had decided to oppose a constitutional amendment to allow school prayer, but polls showed that the public supported the amendment. Deadlock? No. Our polling identified the specific religion, spiritual, and moral activities the public wanted in schools, activities that had been subsumed under the rubric of "school prayer." But we found that prayer itself was not that high on the list: people really wanted schools to teach values, ethics, and morals. Armed with this information, Clinton explained that the First Amendment did not limit the teaching of any of these subjects and that there was no justification for tinkering with it. The demand of school prayer abated.[9]

Myth: Charisma drives popular opinion. The public will support the agenda of a popular president and is generally uninterested in the specific substance of the issues he is promoting.

---

[9] Dick Morris, *Behind the Oval Office: Getting Reelected Against All Odds* (Los Angeles: Renaissance Books, 1999), 338.

Reality: Although the public tends to be receptive to presidents in general, studies suggest when presidents are popular and when the prestige and integrity of the executive branch are high, presidents can lead public opinion on specific issues. When these factors are low, generating public support is much more difficult and efforts to promote public support can be counterproductive.[10] To counter low approval ratings, presidents often try to pursue strategies—such as making major policy speeches, traveling abroad, or pursuing domestic trips—to increase their popularity, competence, and prestige.[11] On the other hand, public expectations of the ability of the president and the executive branch to address societal demands or implement campaign promises often exceeds their ability to do so.[12] Consequently, presidential popularity tends to decline over time and efforts to bolster it have only short-term effects.

Polling Basics

Polling is an important and useful tool of policy making. At a minimum, it democratizes the policy-making process by providing policy makers with a source of information about the views of the public at large. While giving the public a de facto means of bolstering support for popular initiatives and undermining support for unpopular initiatives, it enables policy makers to test new ideas and determine how best to market them, and it can enhance political leadership on popular issues by giving the executive branch additional justification for promoting widely supported proposals. The beauty of polling is that by sampling a small number of randomly chosen citizens, a well-orchestrated survey can provide a good approximation of the general public's likely response to a potential policy initiative or its likely choice in an upcoming election. Polls can be captivating, and the statistics, graphs, tables, and charts created from them can appear authoritative and compelling—yet they can also be deceptive. In order to use polls effectively, it is important to know their strengths and limitations. The bottom line is that polls and the statistics they generate can never speak for themselves, and two equally intelligent and honest people can legitimately interpret the same polling questions, and the survey results they generate, differently. The phrasing of a polling question, the demographics of the people being asked the questions, and the techniques used in analyzing and presenting the results can all affect how the results are interpreted and, consequently, how they are used.

---

[10] Jeffrey E. Cohen, "Presidential Rhetoric and the Public Agenda," *American Journal of Political Science* 39, no. 1 (February 1995): 87–88. See also George C. Edwards III, *The Public Presidency: The Pursuit of Popular Support* (New York: St. Martin's Press, 1983) and Samuel Kernell, *Going Public: New Strategies of Presidential Leadership*, 2d ed. (Washington, D.C.: CQ Press, 1993).

[11] Recent research suggests that these strategies have a mixed and short-term effect on the popularity of the president and support for specific policies. See Paul Brace and Barbara Hinckley, *Follow the Leader* (New York: Basic Books, 1992).

[12] The classic book on this topic is R. E. Neustadt, *Presidential Power and the Modern Presidents* (New York: Free Press, 1990).

Ten Steps to Making a Good Poll

1. **Ask the right questions.** Be sure that the questions asked are valid, so that they ask about precisely what you want to know, and that they are reliable and nonleading so that different people at different times will interpret the question the same way. How the questions are worded is key. The wording of questions can affect the response. For example, if a poll asks if you agree with a plan to reduce aid for textbooks for school children, few would concur. But if a poll asks if you agree or disagree with a plan to shift money from textbooks to computers, the response might be different.

2. **Order the questions correctly.** How questions are ordered can impact the results of a poll. If you ask, for example, if someone support tax cuts then ask a question about a spending proposal, you might impact the results of the poll.

3. **Time the polling well.** The most reliable polls are taken over several days. Polls conducted during the week generally produce more representative samples than those conducted over weekends, when many people are not at home. Furthermore a single-night poll, say one that occurs on Thursday, is less representative of the voting population because it misses everyone who works on Thursday night.

4. **Check the evening news.** Check to see what events are occurring during the polling. Voters' responses often are based on the last thing they hear reported about an issue. Polls taken after major news events can be distorted. For example, a poll on gun control taken right after a gun shooting at a school might be distorted.

5. **Ask the right people.** If and only if people from the population are selected randomly, so that everyone in the population has an equal or known probability of being interviewed, can the responses of everyone in the population be inferred from the results of a poll of a small sample of that population. If not, the results will be biased in favor of those who

Does this suggest that all that surveys yield are "Lies, Damn Lies, and Statistics?"[13] No. But it does suggest that polls and the statistics they produce are powerful tools that can easily be misused. To use polls with greatest effectiveness and to avoid being seduced or misdirected by them, you need to identify what specific information you want to know, then follow a few simple guidelines indicated in the box above.[14]

---

[13] See Darrell Huff, *How to Lie with Statistics* (New York: Norton, 1982).

[14] A variety of useful sources provide information on polling and statistical analyses. These include "About Polling," www.publicagenda.org/aboutpubopinion/aboutpubop1.htm; Earl Babbie, *The Practice of Social Research* (Belmont, Calif.: Wadsworth Publishing, 1995); Damodar Gujarati, *Basic Econometrics* (New York: McGraw-Hill, Inc. 1995); David Freedman, Robert Pisani, Roger Purves, *Statistics* (New York: W. W. Norton, 1998); Jeffrey Katzer, Kenneth Cook, and Wayne Crouch, *Evaluating Information: A Guide for Users of Social Science Research* (Reading, Mass.: Addison Wesley, 1998); and King, Keohane, and Verba, *Designing Social Inquiry* (Princeton, N.J.: Princeton University Press, 1994).

were included in the sample. The samples in some "quickie" polls that are conducted overnight and surveys in which people vote on the Internet are neither random nor necessarily representative of the voting population.

6. **Ask enough people.** Generally, the greater the sample size, the more likely the results accurately reflect the views of the public at large. Good national samples are generally comprised of at least 1000 individuals.

7. **Identify the respondents.** Who is included in the sample? Is the poll surveying all adults? registered voters or likely voters? the opinion of urban dwellers or suburbanites? Politicians are often most interested in the opinions of likely voters because only about half of all adults and two-thirds of registered voters actually cast ballots in presidential races. Regardless of the subset of the population one is interested in, everyone in that group must have an equal chance or known probability of being chosen to take the poll. If not the results will be biased.

8. **Interpret and present the results effectively.** The results should be presented in an easily assessable manner that highlights their implications for the policy issues at hand.

9. **Use the appropriate techniques to analyze the results.** Standards of statistical analysis should be followed at all times to minimize biases in the data and misinterpretation of the results.

10. **Estimate an acceptable confidence interval.** All polls have sampling errors. Estimating a confidence interval around the data provides a good assessment of the accuracy of the data. Polling statistics indicating that 59 percent of the American public support for tougher gun control with a margin of error of +/–3 percent, means that if the survey were repeated 100 times, the polster is confident that 95 of the repeated polls would have confidence intervals that included values between 56 percent and 62 percent.

The Questions

To begin with, pollsters must ask the right questions. The way that questions are phrased and the context in which they are asked can have a profound impact on how people interpret and respond to them. For example, one of the most important policy issues in the 2000 presidential election involved the role of government. Claims and counterclaims were exchanged regarding the dangers of big government versus the benefits of smaller government and putting power in the hands of "the people." Polls regarding the public's impression of Vice President Gore and Governor Bush's policies on the role of the government varied considerably depending on how the question was asked. ABC NEWS results showed, for example, that Governor Bush had a big edge in "holding down the size of government"—but that likely voters by a 2-1 margin said "providing needed services" is more important than

[15] http://www.abcnews.go.com/sections/politics/DailyNews/trackingpoll_001025.html

cutting governemnt.[15] Asking the right questions means asking questions that are valid—that is, do the questions address the specific issue you are interested in? The results of the ABC NEWS poll suggest that while the public supports Bush's anti-"Big Government" initiative, it does not support a reduction in services. This type of nuance would not be clear if the survey only asked people whether they supported Bush's plan to reduce Big Government. A **valid question** is one that unambiguously refers to the specific issue that the pollster wants to evaluate. It is important to recognize that any single policy may have multiple social, political, or economic dimensions to it. As a consequence, no single question will be able to provide a valid indication of public opinion on all of those dimensions. Instead, one must ask a number of questions focused on the various dimensions of a policy to get a clear picture of the public perception of the policy as a whole.

The right question must also be reliable. A **reliable question** is one that is asked in a way likely to ellicit similar interpretations by people with different backgrounds, at different times, and in different contexts. Will Big government be interpreted differently by teenagers who do not rely heavily on government services and elderly people on Medicare? A reliable question is one that is likely to be interpreted the same way regardless of who is responding to the survey and when. Unfortunately, this may be more difficult than it first appears because voters' responses are also often affected by events outside of the survey itself—such as their most recent experiences or the last thing they heard about a particular issue. For example, polls taken after major news events can be distorted. As a consequence, it would be a mistake to interpret a poll on public support for gun control taken the day after a gun shooting at a school as a reliable indicator of general public support for gun control.

In order to increase their reliability, polls are often taken over several days. Polls conducted during the week generally produce more representative samples than those conducted over weekends, when many people are not at home. A single-night poll, say one that occurs on Thursday, is less representative of the voting population because it misses everyone who works on Thursday night.

In addition to the timing of questions, the wording of questions can affect a respondent's answer. If, for example, a poll asks if you agree or disagree with a plan to reduce aid for textbooks for school children, few would concur. But if a poll asks if you agree or disagree with a plan to shift money from textbooks to computers, the response might be different.

How questions are ordered can also impact the results of a poll. For example, people are more likely to respond positively to a question regarding increased government spending on public services if the question preceding it on the survey asked who should get the most credit for eight years of growth and rising national incomes than if the question preceding it on the survey asked them to evaluate new tax policy. Effective pollsters can avoid leading—or they can lead—respondents to particular answers by altering the wording or the order of the questions asked. If this is a concern, multiple polls are conducted using slightly different questions or with the questions in a different order to test for this type of bias.

The Respondents

Once focused, nonleading questions have been chosen, it is important to ask the "right" people to answer them.[16] The power of polling and statistics comes from the ability of the pollsters to infer what the American people think about a particular set of issues from surveying a small sample of them. Due to the beauty of statistical inference, a sample of as few as a thousand people can provide a reasonably accurate picture of a population of several tens of millions. The key to this capability, however, rests on the ability of the pollster to select the survey respondents randomly. To be randomly selected, everyone in the population must have an equal or known nonzero probability of being chosen as a potential respondent. When this occurs, variations in responses within the sample interviewed will tend to parallel those in the population at large. This remarkable phenomenon (known as the **central limits theorem** in statistics) only works if the sample of people chosen to be interviewed is truly selected randomly. If a poll of "the American people" is conducted randomly, then people from urban neighborhoods in North Philadelphia must have as good a chance of being selected as those from Ames, Iowa or Corpus Christi, Texas. If people in all of these areas do not have an equal chance of being chosen, but it is possible to determine the probability that they would be missed, then the survey results can be weighted accordingly so that their views are given the weight that they would have had if they were all counted. If everyone in the population does not have an equal or known probability of being selected for a poll, then the sample is not considered to be a **random sample** and will be biased; its results will reflect the preferences of those in the sample but will not reflect those of the overall population of the United States.

One common polling technique is to have a computer randomly dial telephone numbers of potential respondents. This works fairly well in randomly selecting people with telephones, but it will tend to reflect the views of people with more than one phone more heavily than those who have only one or those who do not have access to a phone of their own. To correct for this problem, the results of telephone surveys should be weighted so that the responses from households with multiple phones are discounted proportionately based on the increased probability that they would be selected for the survey.[17]

In addition to polling the entire country, decision makers are often interested in distinct subsets of the American population. For example, because currently registered voters are more likely to vote in upcoming elections than unregistered voters, policy makers may be particularly interested in finding out what registered voters think about a particular policy initiative. If all registered voters had an equal chance of being polled, then the sample of respondents could be considered random, and inferences about all registered voters could be made from

---

[16] For a good review of the practice of using surveys and the problems of sampling, see David Freedman, Robert Pisani, Roger Purves, *Statistics*, 3d ed. (New York: W. W. Norton, 1998), 333–437.

[17] Ibid. 346–348.

the results of the sample. Such a survey would, however, provide no information about what nonregistered voters think about the issues at hand. Focused surveys like this can be taken for groups designated by race, gender, religion, income level, union membership, party affiliation, or any other common characteristic that can be used to identify the group in which one is interested. For purposes of cost or efficiency, pollsters use different kinds of random sampling techniques—including simple random samples, stratified random samples, clustered random samples, and even multistage sampling that combines two or more of the other strategies. Each represents a variety of random or probability samples.[18]

Generally, the greater the sample size, the more likely the results from the poll will accurately reflect the views of the public at large. All polls have a sampling error that indicates how likely a poll reflects actual public opinion. Increasing sample size can help reduce the error. The bigger the sample, the smaller the error, but once you get past a certain point—say, a sample size of 800 or 1000—the improvement is very small. The results of a survey of 300 people will likely be correct within 6 percentage points, while a survey of 1000 will be correct within 3 percentage points. But that is where the dramatic differences end; when a sample is increased to 2000 respondents, the error drops only slightly, to 2 percentage points.[19]

In addition to reporting the statistical significance of particular survey results, polling results are often presented with a **confidence interval** to give an indication of their accuracy. For example, polling statistics may report that 59 percent of the American public support tougher gun control with a 95 percent confidence interval of +/– 3 percent. This indicates that although the researcher's best approximation is that 59 percent of the American public support tougher gun control, the actual number is unlikely to be exactly 59 percent. To compensate, the research provides a *confidence interval* around the result. A 95 percent confidence interval of +/– 3 percent indicates that if the survey was repeated 100 times the polster is confident that 95 of the repeated polls would have confidence intervals that included values between 56 and 62 percent.[20]

The second commonly used type of polling is known as the **dial group** or **focus group.** This is a group of individuals with specific similar characteristics who are asked to view or listen to a speech, commercial, or policy statement while holding an opinion "dial" that allows the participants to state the degree of approval or disapproval to certain phrases, words, or proposals. The information is then analyzed to identify the degree of approval or disapproval of the material that is being tested. A graph is created to show the approval or disapproval levels for each

[18] Jeffrey Katzer, Kenneth Cook, and Wayne Crouch, *Evaluating Information: A Guide for Users of Social Science Research,* 3d ed. (New York: McGraw-Hill, 1991), 180 and, more generally, 175–187.

[19] For a review of polling and statistical sampling, see "About Polling," www.publicagenda.org/aboutpubopinion/aboutpubop1.htm; David Freedman, Robert Pisani, and Roger Purves, *Statistics,* 3d ed. (New York: W. W. Norton, 1998), 333–437.

[20] Jeffrey Katzer, Kenneth Cook, and Wayne Crouch, *Evaluating Information: A Guide for Users of Social Science Research,* 3d ed. (New York: McGraw-Hill, 1991), 182–183.

proposal.[21] Like a targeted sample, polls taken from a focus group will be biased toward the feelings of a particular group. The participants in focus groups are generally small in number and not selected randomly. As a result, generalizations based on the polling results will be biased in favor of the opinions of the specific focus group and may not reflect those of the larger subset of the population they are intended to represent.

A third commonly used technique is the **mall intercept method.** In this approach, space is set up at a mall, shopping center, or storefront. Passersby are asked to review clips of speeches, commercials, or rebuttals to ads or attack statements. The viewing is followed by a questionnaire in which opinions are solicited and evaluated by the consultants.[22] While useful, this technique is the least accurate of the three discussed. Its respondents may appear to be random to the extent they are not chosen by the interviewer, but this is not truly a random sample since only people shopping at the mall who walk past the interviewer have a chance of being selected. As a consequence, the results from such a poll will be biased and will tend to reflect the views of a narrow set of people who likely have the average income of the people in the shopping center, and who like to shop at that time of day and at the location where the interview took place. Such a sample is not scientific because it suffers from multiple biases that make it difficult to draw general conclusions from its findings.

The Results

Once the sample has been chosen and the polls taken, it is important that the analyst uses the appropriate techniques for analyzing and interpreting the data. Our goal here is not to introduce and evaluate different statistical techniques, measures of association or the concept of statistical significance, but it is vitally important that all consumers of polling data recognize that statistics provide probabilistic answers. Regardless of how definitive the results look, they are *approximations*. Equally important, even if the results are very precise, and show a strong, positive, and statistically significant relationship between two variables—say party affiliation and one's race or religion—the statistical result does not prove that the two variables are causally related. It merely shows that—for whatever reasons (and there may be several)—changes in the two variables coincide with one another. Cause and effect, like beauty, are in the eye of the beholder.

Finally, once the data have been analyzed, they must be presented in order to be useful. Presentation matters. Simple techniques such as changing the scale on the side of a graph can make small changes in trends look dramatic, or large changes in trends look insignificant. Big bullet points and colorful graphs grab people's attention and can easily direct them toward (or away from) the issues at hand. Masters of presentation, like 1992 presidential candidate Ross Perot, can effectively use graphs and tables to give the sense of authority and decisiveness in response to

---

[21] Ibid., 215.

[22] Bradley H. Patterson Jr., *The White House Staff: Inside the West Wing and Beyond,* (Washington, D.C.: Brookings Institution Press, 2000), 215.

1996 Campaign Poll

Issues for President's Speech, Train Trip, Gore Speech

In this poll, we ranked every issue we are thinking of using by their likelihood of making people vote for Clinton and then tested them for their feasibility in accomplishing their goals. The numbers indicate percentage of respondents that chose more likely—the percentage of those that chose less likely.

These 44 proposals all test above 60 percent and all but two test with feasibility over 50 percent.

	Likelihood of Support for Clinton	Feasibility
Welfare-to-work	80-17	51-43 (cumulative)
Welfare/work in neighborhoods	79-20	51-43 (cumulative)
College tax credit	78-28	75-20
Cop killer bullet ban	78-18	70-24
Track sex crimes	76-20	68-24
No guns for felons	74-23	57-40
Clean drinking water	74-21	68-26 (cumulative)
Enviro crimes/lien	73-22	64-30 (cumulative)
Adult college tax credit	73-24	77-18
Trigger locks	72-23	68-27
100,000 cops	72-23	71-24
3 hours educational TV	72-22	76-21
Enviro right to know	72-24	70-25 (cumulative)
Ban racial preference in adoption	72-19	76-16
75 percent cleanup toxic waste	71-25	54-45
Welfare employee tax credit	71-25	51-43 (cumulative)
Education savings bonds	71-22	68-26
IRS deadbeat dads	71-27	74-21

complex and nuanced problems. Once the table or graph is presented, the audience will focus on it—rather than where it came from, whether it was the best or most appropriate means for presenting the results, or whether it really gets to the heart of the problem or left out something important.[23]

Who Polls for the White House

Contrary to popular belief, there is no official pollster within the White House. In fact, it is the national political parties—the Democratic National Committee

---

[23] A useful reference for people interested in conducting polls is found in "About Polling," available on the Web at www.publicagenda.org/aboutpubopinion/aboutpubop1.htm

	Likelihood of Support for Clinton	Feasibility
School health clinics meet primary medical needs of kids	70-28	
State standardized test for promotion	70-26	68-27
No tax deductions for deadbeat dads	69-28	72-22
Brady bill dom violence misdems	68-27	57-36
State standardized test graduation	68-28	71-22
Fed govt. standardized test/promotion	68-29	74-21
Welfare/placement bonus	68-27	51-43 (cumulative)
No guns under 21	68-24	53-43
Iran/Libya sanctions	68-25	49-45
50,000 literacy teachers	67-31	73-23
Welfare-staffed child care	67-30	51-43
HMO notification/alt treatment	67-26	
TV family hour	65-26	68-25
6 yr bal budget plan	65-29	61-33
Violence on kids' TV	64-28	71-25
Ban cig ads at kids	64-31	59-36
Mandatory adoption if abuse	64-26	66-26
Targeted tax cuts	64-26	62-30
Health ins for unemployed	63-33	
No firing of HMO doctor	63-26	
Penalize drug countries	62-31	44-48
Teen gangs RICO	61-33	50-43
No cap gains on home sale	61-33	50-43
Adopt after 1 year foster care	60-27	68-24
Ban meth (drug)	58-33	52-34

Source: Dick Morris, *Behind the Oval Office* (Los Angeles: Renaissance Books, 1999), 627–628.

(DNC) and the Republican National Committee (RNC)—who hire the pollsters who work for the president. These pollsters are paid by dollars raised from DNC or RNC supporters, not taxpayer funds. Since the president is the head of his or her respective national party, he or she chooses which pollster works for the DNC or the RNC. In effect, the pollster works for the president, but not the White House.

The pollster is a political consultant and not a government official. Therefore, his or her interaction with White House staff is limited and controlled by ethics laws. For example, political meetings can only be held in a few designated areas of within the White House complex: the family residence atop the White House; the Ceremonial Office of the Vice President in the Eisenhower Executive Office Building; and the Ward Room located in the basement of the West Wing.

Polling questions are not actually drafted by White House staff. They are crafted by employees of the polling firm. However, White House staffers talk with pollsters when they are preparing the questions to make certain that the questions are factually correct. In the Clinton White House, pollsters would conduct surveys in the field once a week to twice a month. During campaign seasons (typically one year before an election), the polling occurs each week. These field polls include a range of questions, voter preference surveys, and presidential job performance ratings, among others. The polls also include questions regarding new policy proposals, existing legislative disagreements between the president and Congress, and policies already enacted and implemented.

In addition to using polling to determine how best to market ideas that the president wants to support, the executive branch uses polling to identify the relationship between the presidential favorability ratings and particular policies or political issues. The box on pages 96–97 provides such a chart compiled by White House consultant Dick Morris. Many of the issues and related policies like welfare-to-work were first raised by Clinton's 1992 presidential campaign committee, and then were modified and fine tuned by the policy development staff in the White House. They were then tested against the president's popularity ratings.

The Role of the Office of Political Affairs

Within the White House, the office that chiefly interacts with pollsters and the political consultants is the White House Office of Political Affairs (OPA). In contrast to the pollsters and political consultants, the OPA is like all members of the White House staff. People working in the OPA are federal employees and are subject to ethics, conflict of interest, and financial disclosure rules.[24] As a result, the OPA often serves as the reporter, rather than the provider, of political information. For example, OPA's weekly report to the president includes a breakdown of all national, publicly released polling. These data are widely shared throughout the White House. On the other hand, the private polling is handed out on a need-to-know basis only. Most of the information on polling is shared between the consultants, the head of OPA, the president, and selected staff, at the weekly residence meetings.

As shown in the sample Polling Update and Briefing, polling is conducted once a proposal is in play, either under consideration in Congress or during the regulatory process. As this poll underscores, no one can predict completely accurately public opinion, and one must remember that a poll is only a snapshot of a particular moment in time. At the time this survey was taken, there was strong support for President Clinton's 1993 stimulus package. The author of the poll in fact implies that support for the stimulus package was at a similar level to support for cutting government. This is a somewhat contradictory finding. The data also indicated that there was 58 percent support for the stimulus package even when the person being interviewed was apprised that it would cost $160 billion in new domestic spending.

---

[24] Bradley H. Patterson Jr., "The White House Staff: Inside the West Wing and Beyond," (Washington, D.C.: Brookings Institution Press, 2000), 205.

Polling Update and Briefing

Date: March 9, 1993

Re: Polling Update
        The Clinton Economic Program

The President's economic program continues to enjoy broad support across nearly all the national surveys: 60 percent approve the program—twice the number who oppose it (ABC, CNN, Democratic National Committee). Support has been sustained from the night of the "Joint Session" address and now pervades the country—even in more conservative states in the South and central parts of the country. The support is rooted in the program's balance—particularly the investment to achieve growth.

Voters want further spending cuts. That has been widely reported, as the public discussion has centered on that task. But the debate is obscuring the very strong public desire to do something affirmative on the economy, beginning with the economic stimulus.

- Just 29 percent of the electorate believes the economy is recovering.
- 56 percent of the electorate says the program does not go far enough in stimulating the economy.
- Three-quarters say maintain or expand the stimulus part of the economic program.
- 58 percent support the spending side of the program, even when it is described as 160 billion dollars of new spending on domestic programs.

Support for the program is strong in states that have not traditionally turned to national Democrats for direction on the economy. State polls conducted last week in Nebraska, Georgia, Louisiana, and North Dakota (Democratic National Committee polls) show remarkably strong support for the Clinton economic program.

	Clinton Economic Program	
	Approve	Disapprove
Nebraska	56%	32%
Georgia	57%	32%
Louisiana	54%	35%
North Dakota	57%	30%

Source: Stan Greenberg, March 9, 1993.

Based on this type of information, President Clinton pushed for a stimulus plan that he was eventually forced to drop in response to strong congressional opposition and a lack of popular support. This shows how polling data can be misleading and how events can change between the time a poll is taken and when a policy initiative works its way through the policy-making process.

Polling is also conducted to determine the public's perception of the president, his political initiatives, and the policies his administration has implemented. Ironically, there is often a sharp divide between the president's actions and the public's perceptions of what he has or has not accomplished. During the Clinton administration, polls often showed that the public was not aware of, or failed to give credit to, the executive branch for actions in a variety of policy arenas. For example, President Clinton was particularly upset by polls indicating that the three things people most remember about the first months of the administration were the summit with Yeltsin, healthcare, and gays in the military. The public did recognize the administration's role in promoting a strong economy, reducing the deficit, lowering taxes for the middle class, or reducing interest rates.[25] For example, according to a CBS/New York Times Poll conducted 8–11 September 1994, only 24 percent of respondents thought that his economic plan and budget would help the economy, and a Newsweek Poll one month later indicated that 65 percent of the public thought that taxes on the middle class had increased rather than decreased during the first two years of the Clinton presidency.[26] Lack of a clearly focused policy agenda, poor publicity, the failures of healthcare reform, and a general public perception that the president was unable to work with the Congress may explain the disconnect between the president's actions and the public's reaction. Regardless, the lack of public recognition of the executive's actions gave the administration a strong incentive to reinvigorate its policy-making efforts in 1994. This lead to major successes in welfare and other areas (see Chapter 10).

When to Poll Policy Ideas

At the beginning of this chapter we discussed the myth that politicians use polling to determine their positions on issues. In fact, polling is most effectively used to help market policy proposals that have already been developed. In 1997, at the request of the president and the vice president, the DPC and the NEC began developing ideas to address the issue of urban sprawl. The working group produced a range of ideas. One proposal that was developed was the Better America Bond program. Under this proposal the Treasury Department would authorize state and local communities to issue bonds from which the proceeds would be used to purchase open spaces and parkland, and to clean up so-called "brownfields" (contaminated former industrial sites).

After developing the proposal, the idea was tested by the president's pollster, Mark Penn. Penn tested the basic idea, to provide communities with funds to purchase open spaces to save for future generations, in one of his weekly surveys. His

---

[25] Elizabeth Drew, On the Edge (New York: Simon & Schuster, 1994), 125.

[26] George C. Edwards, "Frustration and Folly: Bill Clinton and the Public Presidency," in The Clinton Presidency: First Appraisals, ed. Colin Campbell and Bert Rockman (Chatham, N.J.: Chatham House Publishers, 1996), 240.

firm also tested potential names for the program. The polling data found at least 70 percent support for the basic idea. Better America Bonds was the name chosen over "Green Bonds" and "Better Community Bonds." In this case, the polling data provided additional support for sending the Better America Bond legislation to Congress. Polling was also used to help decide how to "spin" or market the proposal.

Of course, polling does not end when the policy proposal is sent to Congress or an Executive Order is issued. If a proposal is in play—for example, the idea is being debated by a congressional committee—then the proposal will continue to be polled to see if public opinion is altered by the congressional debate.

Conclusion

Critics of polling often point out that President Clinton relied more heavily on polling than previous presidents. He conducted three or four polls and three or four focus groups per month and, while George Bush spent $216,000 for public opinion polls in 1989 and 1990, President Clinton spent $1,986,410 in 1993 alone. At best, critics argued, this indicated a lack of leadership, and at worst, it undermined the democratic process. Such criticisms are misplaced. Rather than indicating a lack of leadership, supportive polling results can enhance leadership by bolstering the president and his policies, while unsupportive results, in turn, empower critics within the executive branch and Congress.

Even if the president's policies achieve their objectives, if the public does not recognize or associate the benefits they receive from the policy initiative, the president will not receive credit for the policy, and the policy process will not be improved. Lack of public awareness that middle income taxes had decreased and that President Clinton's economic plan had dramatic and positive implications for the nation's economy are important, because they highlight the divide between policy makers' perceptions of their actions within the Beltway and national perceptions of those actions from outside of Washington. Polling provides an essential conduit and channel for those opinions to be heard and, thereby, enables the executive to respond to public demands and recognize a need to educate the public on its activities. This enhances both the democratic process and the ability of the executive branch to be responsive to public concerns.

In summary, polling can be used to test the public's receptiveness to particular policy proposals. Once the proposals have been implemented, polling can also be used to test the public's awareness of the links between various policy initiatives and its economic, political, and social well-being and, by doing so, help policy makers determine how best to market the policies and inform the public of these benefits. In addition, polling helps keep executive branch and congressional policy makers informed about public opinions and perceptions and thereby helps make the policy-making process more responsive to the concerns of their multiple constituents. By providing these functions, polling can add legitimacy to the policy-making process in the executive branch, making it more efficient, more effective, and more likely to be supported by decision makers in Congress and the public at large.

Key Terms

Central Limits Theorem: A theorem that provides the mathematical justification for making inferences about a population based on a sample.

Confidence Interval: This gives the range of the unknown variable within a population estimated from a sample and the confidence level that the range covers the true value.

Dial Group or Focus Group: A group of individuals with specific similar characteristics who are asked to view or listen to a speech, commercial, or policy statement while holding an opinion "dial" which allows the participants to state the degree of approval or disapproval to certain phrases, words, or proposals. The information is then analyzed to identify the degree of approval or disapproval with the material that is being tested.

Mall Intercept Model: A method of polling in which passersby are asked to review clips of speeches, commercials, or rebuttals to ads or attack statements. The viewing is followed by a questionnaire in which opinions are solicited and evaluated by the consultants.

Random Sample: One in which all respondents have an equal chance of being chosen or a known probability that they will be missed.

Reliable Question: One that will be interpreted the same way by different respondents or by the same respondent at different times.

Valid Question: One that clearly reflects the underlying issue in which the researcher is interested.

Review Questions

1. Name four guidelines that pollsters should follow when polling policy proposals.

2. What is a dial or focus group? How does this commonly used polling technique differ from the mall intercept and random sample methods? What are the strengths and limitations of these techniques?

3. What are the ten steps to conducting a useful poll?

4. Who drafts polling questions for the White House?

5. At what points in the policy-making process is it most useful to take polls? Why?

CHAPTER 7

Legislative Clearance and Coordination: SAPs, LRMs, and Other Policy Acronyms

Legislative Clearance and Coordination

You are a new employee in a federal agency and are trying to find your way through a bureaucracy of almost two million. How do you make an impact early? Get yourself on the Office of Management and Budget's Legislative Referral Distribution List, and soon every official statement and testimony, as well as other documents, will come across your desk. Getting your name on the OMB distribution list is like getting on the "A" party list. Now you can get past the bouncer at the door, but what you do at the party is a whole other story.

In this chapter, we will discuss how administration policy is cleared through the executive branch. In particular, we will highlight the influential role that the OMB plays by overseeing policy and legislative proposals to be adopted as **administration policy.** The Bureau of the Budget was renamed the Office of Management and Budget in 1970 by President Nixon, who dramatically expanded its policy management and advisory functions, as well as its role as a monitor of executive branch activity and advocate of the president's position.[1] The OMB provides accountability to the executive branch by routinely monitoring day-to-day activities of the entire government. It has the authority to determine whether pending legislation or regulations are consistent with the president's objectives and intentions, and it has the power to issue administration positions on policy matters. In this chapter, we will explain and evaluate how the formal oversight process run by the OMB, the Legislative Referral Memorandum (LRM) process, and the OMB's

---

[1] The Bureau of the Budget was established in 1921 to help the president prepare his annual budget for submission to Congress. For a discussion of its evolution and the expansion of its roles over time, see George C. Edwards III and Stephen J. Wayne, *Presidential Leadership: Politics and Policymaking*, 5th ed. (New York: Worth/St. Martin's Press, 1999), 405–411.

preparation of Statements of Administration Policy (SAPs) affect the policy-making process.

Like decision memoranda, LRMs and SAPs enable interested parties to engage in the policy-making process in a more fair, coordinated, and centralized manner than would otherwise be the case. Specifically, they provide a means for the OMB to communicate executive policy positions and solicit input from all agencies and departments on every policy proposal being considered by the executive. The appropriate use of these tools thus provides a conduit for the exchange of ideas with the chief decision maker. As a result, it enhances the perceived legitimacy of the system. This, in turn, tends to increase the commitment among policy makers to support the resulting policy. It also makes the policy outcomes better, to the extent that they tend to reflect a wider range of inputs than it would if these channels did not exist.

Legislative Responsibility in the Executive Branch

The president's legislative responsibilities are founded in his or her constitutional duties and powers to:

- Require in writing the opinion of the principal officer in each of the executive departments
- Take care that the laws are faithfully executed
- Give the Congress information on the State of the Union
- Recommend to the Congress such measures as he or she judges necessary
- Approve or disapprove bills passed by the Congress
- Convene either or both Houses of the Congress

In order to fulfill these duties, the president presides as the chief executive officer in charge of a vast policy-making and coordinating body called the Executive Office of the President (EOP). The EOP consists of roughly 1800 employees who work in congressionally mandated executive agencies with specific programmatic responsibilities or are members of the president's White House staff. Congressionally mandated agencies include organizations like the Office of Management and Budget (OMB), the U.S. Trade Representative, the Council of Economic Advisers, and the Council on Environmental Quality. The president's White House staff, in turn, includes both people who maintain the White House residence (taking care of the First Family meals, cleaning, laundry, etc.), and the people who serve on executive policy councils such as the Domestic Policy Council, the National Economic Council, and the National Security Council, which are charged with managing policy decisions for the president. (See the box on page 105.)

Given the large cadre of employees within the Executive Office of the President (EOP), the task of coordinating policy and communicating regarding legislation between the EOP and the executive branch of government—cabinet departments

The White House Office and the Executive Office of the President

The White House Office	Executive Office of the President
Office of the Chief of Staff	White House Office
Office of the Vice President	Council of Economic Advisers
Advance	Council on Environmental Quality
Cabinet Affairs	Office of Management and Budget
Communications/Speechwriting	Office of National Drug Control Policy
White House Counsel	Office of Science and Technology Policy
Domestic Policy Council	United States Trade Representative
Office of the First Lady	President's Foreign Intelligence Advisory Board
Intergovernmental Affairs	
Legislative Affairs	
Administration	
National Economic Council	
National Security Council	
Political Affairs	
Press Secretary	
Public Liaison	
Scheduling	
Staff Secretary	

and smaller agencies—can be very complicated. Coordination of the policy-making processes within the EOP takes place at two levels. At the highest level, major policy decisions are controlled by the White House policy councils (see Chapter 2), which develop and implement major policy decisions using the decision-making memoranda we discussed in Chapter 5. The resulting decisions are then run through a formal clearance process conducted by the Office of Management and Budget called the Legislative Referral Memorandum (LRM) process.

Most legislative issues relating to congressional bills and other policy matters such as Executive Orders and presidential decrees, however, do not necessitate presidential involvement. These issues, such as clearing congressional testimony or providing the views of the administration on a particular legislative bill, are handled primarily by the Office of Management and Budget itself through the LRM clearance process and do not necessarily involve the White House policy councils. When the White House policy councils are not involved, the OMB plays a critical role in resolving policy conflicts and guaranteeing that resulting legislation or actions are consistent with the policies and objectives of the president.

This power is one that is closely guarded by OMB and is often a point of contention between the various agencies in the executive branch which often believe OMB does not always act as an honest broker but forces decisions based solely on budgetary concerns (how much will it cost), and not on the broader policy goals of the administration. OMB counters that budgetary concerns should have a high priority regarding any policy decision and that discussions over the cost of proposals lead to more precise and well-thought-out policy proposals. As we discussed in Chapter 2, the debate over OMB's role has led to the ever-growing role of the White House policy councils. However despite the growing role of the policy councils, the sheer number of decisions that must be reviewed necessitates that OMB, with its larger bureaucracy, run the day-to-day clearance process.

The Clearance Process

The Office of Management and Budget's LRM clearance process is intended to do the following:

- Permit the coordinated development, review, and approval of legislative proposals needed to carry out the president's agenda
- Help the agencies develop draft bills that are consistent with and that carry out the president's policy objectives
- Clearly identify for Congress those bills that are part of the president's program and the relationship of other bills to that program
- Assure that Congress receives coordinated and informative agency views on legislation under consideration
- Assure that bills and position statements submitted to Congress by one agency properly take into account the interests and concerns of all affected agencies
- Provide a means whereby divergent agency views can be reconciled

OMB Circular number A-19 sets the basic guidelines and procedures for carrying out its clearance process. The LRM clearance function covers agency legislative proposals, agency reports and testimony on pending legislation, Statements of Administration Policy (SAPs), and enrolled bills. These procedures have been substantially the same for more than 50 years. An example of a Legislative Referral Memorandum (LRM) is included on page 107.

Legislative Proposals

All legislative proposals that agencies in the EOP wish to transmit to the Congress must be sent to the OMB for clearance. OMB circulates the bills to affected agencies and appropriate EOP staff. The EOP agencies or staff may favor it or have no objection. They may also propose substantive or technical amendments, or perhaps a complete substitute. Divergent views can be reconciled by telephone, letters, emails or meetings.

After review, analysis, resolution of issues, and obtaining policy guidance from the relevant EOP agencies, the OMB may offer the proposing agency positive feedback by advising it that (1) there is "no objection" from the standpoint of the

Sample Legislative Referral Memorandum

LRM ID REJ42

Executive Office of the President
Office of Management and Budget
Washington, D.C. 20503-0001

Thursday, April 23, 1997

LEGISLATIVE REFERRAL MEMORANDUM

TO: Legislative Liaison Officer (See distribution of agencies and names below)

FROM: Assistant Director for Legislative Reference

SUBJECT: Testimony of the Undersecretary of Treasury for Enforcement Before the
            Senate Judiciary Committee

DEADLINE: Noon, April 27, 1999

> In accordance with OMB Circular A-19, OMB requests the view of your agency on
> the above subject before advising on its relationship to the program of the President.
> Please advise us if this item will affect direct spending or receipts for purposes of the
> "Pay-As-You-Go" provisions of Title XIII of the Omnibus Budget Reconciliation Act
> of 1990.

Distribution List

Agencies:

> Department of Justice
> Department of Treasury, Alcohol & Tobacco and Firearms (ATF)
> Office of National Drug Control Policy

Executive Office of the President

> Assistant to the President for Domestic Policy
> Assistant to the President for Legislative Affairs

---

administration's program to the submission of the proposed draft bill to the Congress, or (2) the proposed bill is "in accord with the president's program," if it implements a presidential proposal. This "advice" is conveyed then by the submitting agency to the Congress in its transmittal letter. Major legislation is sometimes transmitted personally by the president. On the other hand, if the OMB decides that the proposed bill conflicts with an important administration objective, or is not in accord with the president's program, it can stop the bill from being be transmitted to the Congress. In such cases, disagreements between the OMB and executive agencies must be resolved before the bill can be transmitted.

Clearance of Agency Testimony and Reports on Pending Legislation

If a congressional committee asks an agency in the executive branch to report or testify on pending legislation, or if an EOP agency wishes to volunteer a report on an issue being considered by a congressional committee, similar clearance procedures are followed. Congressional testimony is a useful means for an executive agency to convey the administration's views on legislation or other congressional matters without directly involving the president. Indeed, the White House often prefers that an agency takes the lead on noncritical or controversial issues or legislation. The strategy of allowing **agency-owned issues** enables the president to stay above the fray and it protects him or her from potentially contentious debates on issues or legislative proposals that are not of major importance to the country as a whole. In such instances, the LRM process allows the White House staff to oversee and coordinate these agency-owned issues without direct presidential involvement and without expending a scarce resource known as "presidential prestige."

Statement of Administration Policy (SAP)

The OMB also prepares a Statement of Administrative Policy (SAP) for major bills scheduled for House or Senate floor action as well as those to be considered by major congressional committees such as the House Rules Committee. SAPs are also prepared for so-called "noncontroversial" bills considered in the House under suspension of the rules—bills that are voted on without the opportunity to offer amendments.

The SAP process coordinates, systematizes, and rationalizes the administration and formulation of the president's policy. SAPs are important because they provide a direct and authoritative way for the administration to let the Congress and, via the press, the American people know the views of the president on a particular bill or legislative issue. The SAP may be used to indicate support for legislation by the administration and the president. It may also be used to clarify the president's position in support of the whole bill or specific components of the legislation. Alternatively, the SAP may be used to indicate the administration's and the president's disapproval of all or part of a particular bill. When disapproval is strong enough, the SAP may contain a veto threat from the president. There are three levels of veto threats used in SAPs. In order of strength these are: (1) "The president will veto"; (2) "Senior advisors will recommend to the president that he should veto this legislation"; (3) "The secretary of treasury (or whichever is the relevant agency) will recommend to the president that he should veto this legislation."

An example of a SAP is included on page 109. The OMB prepares SAPs in coordination with the agency or agencies principally concerned and other relevant EOP units. Once the SAP has passed through the clearance process, it is sent to Congress by OMB's Legislative Affairs.

Enrolled Bills

At the end of the legislative process, after Congress has voted and passed a particular bill, it is enrolled—that is, sent to the president for his approval or disapproval.

Sample Statement of Administration Policy

August 5, 1999

(House Rules)

H.R. 417 - BIPARTISAN CAMPAIGN FINANCE REFORM ACT OF 1999

(Shays (R) CT and 138 cosponsors)

The Administration strongly supports House passage of H.R. 417, the bipartisan campaign finance reform legislation offered by Reps. Christopher Shays and Marty Meehan. The Shays-Meehan legislation meets the test of real, comprehensive, bipartisan reform. It would ban unregulated "soft money" raised by both parties, address backdoor campaign spending by outside organizations, and strengthen public disclosure. This bipartisan measure is the best chance in years to reduce the role of special interests, give voters a louder voice, and treat fairly incumbents and challengers of both parties.

The Administration urges that the rule for floor debate ensures that the House has an opportunity to vote on the Shays-Meehan text.

*****

This Statement of Administration Policy was developed by the Legislative Reference Division in consultation with White House Counsel, White House Legislative Affairs, and the Domestic Policy Council.

Treasury, Justice, OMB/General Counsel, did not respond to our request for views on this SAP.

Administration Position to Date

The President has previously endorsed the Shays-Meehan bill.

Summary of H.R. 417

H.R. 417 would:

1. Ban "Soft Money" contributions to national political parties, and to State-level parties when it would influence a Federal election; increase contribution limits for State committees of political parties from $5,000 per year to $10,000 per year, and aggregate contribution limits for individuals from $25,000 to $30,000 per year.

Pay-As-You-Go Scoring

OMB's pay-as-you-go scoring estimates of H.R. 417 is under development.

LEGISLATIVE REFERENCE DIVISION

AUGUST 5, 1999 (11:16 AM)

The Constitution provides that the president shall take action within ten days of receipt of the bill, not including Sundays.

To assist the president in determining a course of action on a bill, a review process—which is similar to the LRM process for bills submitted to Congress by the president—is set into motion. OMB requests each interested agency to submit its analysis and recommendation to the OMB within 48 hours. These **views letters** are signed by the head of the agency or a presidential appointee. Before transmitting a views letter to Congress, OMB prepares a memorandum to the president on the enrolled bill with a summary of significant issues and various agency and OMB recommendations. If an agency recommends disapproval or a signing statement, it is responsible for preparing a draft of an appropriate statement for the president's consideration. While OMB recommendations to approve enrolled bills are almost always accepted, scholars have found that its recommendations to veto enrolled bills are followed only a little more than half the time, although the president is more likely to veto an enrolled bill when executive agencies join the OMB in urging him to do so.[2]

Conclusion

In this chapter, we discussed how administration policy is cleared through the executive branch. We highlighted the influential role that the Office of Management and Budget (OMB) plays by overseeing and clearing policy and legislative proposals. Through the Legislative Referral Memorandum (LRM) process and the preparation of Statements of Administration Policy (SAPs), the OMB provides accountability to governmental actions, guarantees that positions taken by the EOP are consistent with the president's policies and agenda, and provides Congress and the American public with a direct and authoritative statement about the president's position on important policies and legislation. These tools enable everyone to engage in the policy-making process in a manner more fair, coordinated, and centralized than would otherwise be the case. As a result, when used effectively, they can enhance the perceived legitimacy of the system. This, in turn, tends to increase the commitment among policy makers to support the resulting policy. To the extent that the resulting policy outcome reflects a wider range of inputs, it is also likely to be better balanced and satisfy more concerns than would otherwise be the case.

In the next chapter we will build on this theme by explaining the role of the press and communications office in presenting and marketing policies. In particular, we will discuss how to draft press statements, Question and Answer sheets, and backgrounders that the press office can use to sell a policy agenda to Congress and the general public.

Key Terms

Administration Policy: Policy becomes official *administration policy* when the Office of Management and Budget prepares a Statement of Administrative Policy (SAP). SAPs provide a direct and authoritative way for the administration to let the Congress and, via the press, the American people know the views of the president on a particular bill or legislative issue.

---

[2] Richard L. Cole, James F. C. Hyde, and Stephen J. Wayne, "Advising the President on Enrolled Legislation: Patterns of Executive Influence," *Political Science Quarterly* (Summer 1979): 303–316.

Agency-owned Issues: As part of the Legislative Referral Memorandum process, executive agencies may oversee and coordinate issues without direct presidential involvement. The strategy of identifying *agency-owned* issues allows the president to stay out of potentially contentious debates on issues or legislative proposals that are not of major importance to the country as a whole.

Views Letters: To assist the president in deciding his course of action on a bill, the OMB may request that each interested agency submit within 48 hours *views letters* that specify its analysis and recommendation of a particular policy proposal. OMB prepares a memorandum to the president on the enrolled bill which transmits these views and summarizes the bill, significant issues, and various agency and OMB recommendations.

Review Questions

1. When does a policy become "Administration Policy?"

2. What are the executive branch's legislative responsibilities?

3. What is the purpose of the Legislative Referral Memorandum (LRM) clearance process?

4. Describe the three levels of veto threats in a Statement of Administration Policy (SAP).

5. What is the role of the Office of Management and Budget in the legislative clearance process?

6. Under what circumstances does the White House encourage or approve of "agency-owned" issues?

CHAPTER 8

Communicating and Marketing Policy

The Importance of Communicating and Marketing Policy

Throughout the policy-making process, and particularly once the policy proposal is near completion, it is critical to communicate and market the policy initiative to policy makers outside of the executive branch and to the public at large.[1] President Theodore Roosevelt was one the first presidents to make extensive use of the press to promote his policies in the public arena. President Franklin Roosevelt, in turn, became famous for using the radio to present his fireside chats, and he and his wife Eleanor Roosevelt were very successful in using the media to garner public support. Communicating and marketing policy to the public is a powerful tool because it adds the force of public opinion to a president's capabilities when selling his policies to others in the executive branch and when negotiating with Congress.[2]

Ironically, the advent of the Internet and 24-hour coverage of political events by the media has increased rather than decreased the importance of clear and effective communication and marketing of government policies to the public. The massive increase in the availability of instantaneous information has increased the public's awareness of political issues, but it has also dramatically increased the likelihood that the public will be bombarded by a cacophony of disparate bits of information that can easily be misunderstood. In the face of an information overload, people unconsciously

---

[1] For a discussion of the impact of going public on securing support for policy initiatives, see Samuel Kernell, *Going Public*, 3rd ed. (Washington, D.C.: The Congressional Quarterly, 1997), and Richard J. Powell, "Going Public Revisited: Presidential Speechmaking and the Bargaining Setting in Congress," *Congress and the Presidency* 26 (Fall 1999): 171–191.

[2] Some scholars argue that presidents tend to make appeals for public support and call on Congress to take action regarding economic policy initiatives more often than they do regarding foreign policy initiatives. David Lewis, "The Two Rhetorical Presidencies: An Analysis of Televised Presidential Speeches, 1947–1991," *American Politics Quarterly* 25, no. 3 (July 1997): 380–395.

tend to fit the new information into their preconceived notions of what they expect to see (so-called "**cognitive bias**") or what they want to see (so-called "**motivated bias**").[3] In such circumstances, sound bites can be very appealing, though they are also easily misinterpreted. Furthermore, if people fail to see the relevance of a particular policy to their own needs, they may lose interest and ignore new information about it all together.

It is also important to recognize that mobilizing public support can create a double-edged sword by raising public expectations about the president's ability to implement the policy and distribute the benefits that policy promises to deliver. If these expectations become unrealistic, failure to implement a policy that the public has been convinced is necessary and beneficial can be detrimental to the president's political prestige and undermine the ability of the executive branch to gain support for future policy initiatives.[4] To gain public and congressional support, policy makers must provide clear and persuasive information about the policy under consideration and acknowledge its merits and deficiencies. If that support does not materialize, the policy is not likely to be implemented.

In this chapter we analyze several of the most important tools policy makers use to communicate and market policy proposals. These include fact sheets and press sheets, question and answer documents, and speeches. We will focus on how these materials are written and when and why these tools are used. We will also specify how policy makers interact with the Speechwriting Office, the Office of Communications, and the Press Office that exist in the White House and in each federal agency that is responsible for interacting with the press and directing and implementing a communications strategy.

The Speechwriting Office is charged with preparing all remarks, radio addresses, and public speeches for the president or agency heads. It alone produces approximately 2500 pages of public statements each year. The Communications Office is responsible for developing a media strategy that emphasizes the policy and legislative strategies of each executive agency involved in the policy process. The Press Office, in turn, is responsible for day-to-day contact with the media, including the management of press logistics and scheduling, and the provision of immediate answers to real-time questions or concerns. Policy makers in the White House and federal agencies interact with all three offices on a daily and sometimes hourly basis. The relationship between policy makers and these offices is occasionally adversarial, often complex, and always important.

Some argue that good policies speak for themselves. Others believe that effective marketing can sell any policy, good or bad. We argue that the truth lies somewhere in between. A good policy that cannot be articulated in an accessible manner is not likely to gain wide support. Furthermore, a policy decision that cannot

---

[3] For a discussion of the impact of cognitive and motivated biases on perceptions and decision making, see Robert Jervis, Richard Ned Lebow, and Janice Gross Stein, *Psychology and Deterrence* (Baltimore: Johns Hopkins University Press, 1985), 18–33.

[4] Samuel Kernell, *Going Public*, 2d ed. (Washington, D.C.: Congressional Quarterly, 1993).

be accurately and clearly transmitted to the appropriate agencies may not be implemented in a manner that reflects the intentions of the president. This is why it is important for policy makers to consider how best to communicate and market their ideas throughout the entire policy-making process.

Speechwriting

Before the advent of the Internet and 24-hour cable news, the speech was the primary tool by which leaders conveyed a policy to the public. The more modern venues are very good sources of raw information about policy initiatives, but speeches remain unique and important tools to communicate with the public because they provide a forum for policy makers to present, explain, and market a policy to a focused audience. For example, speeches are often used to frame debates at the start of a policy campaign. They enable policy makers to set the agenda for the discussion against which their opponents will have to argue. The first public speech on a particular issue is like a shot across the bow of other ships in the policy arena. If a policy speech is not successful, it can set back an effort to pass legislation or open up a proposed regulation or Executive Order to being lambasted by those opposing the proposals.

The relationship between speechwriting and policy making is complicated yet complementary. Speechwriters are the translators of the intricacies of policies to the public, yet speechwriters do not participate formally in the policy-making process and they often disdain the involvement of policy staff in the writing of speeches. The policy-making staff provides a summary of the policy to the speechwriters before a speech is written, yet policy speeches generally contain only a few lines of detailed information about the policy itself. Based on the policy summary, the speechwriters will produce a draft about three days before the actual speech (one exception to this time frame is the State of the Union address, where speechwriters begin working on a first draft weeks ahead of the address). After the draft is completed, it is circulated to policy staff for their factual review. Policy staff are asked to correct any "technical" errors and return the draft to the speechwriters.

The **fact checking** of a speech is critical and often more complicated than it first appears. Sometimes a factual discrepancy may be incredibly subtle. What appears to be factually accurate to a speechwriter may be a major error to a policy maker. For example, during the 2000 election Al Gore was criticized for supposedly exaggerating the administration's record on community policing when he claimed the Clinton-Gore administration had put 100,000 more police officers on our streets. Although the administration had made enough grants to communities to enable them to place 100,000 more cops on the beat but the communities had not yet spent all the funds and hired all the police. What may have seemed an innocuous discrepancy to the speechwriter was a major faux pas from a policy perspective, and it created some uncomfortable problems for candidate Gore in the 2000 election. That mistake underscores the importance of the quality and level of communication between speechwriters and policy staff. The more involved policy staff are in the editing and rewriting of a particular speech, the less likely the number of factual errors. At the same time, it is important for policy staff to understand that the more they try to clarify a speech with details and information, the duller and less effective the speech will be in marketing a policy proposal.

Speechwriters are often called on to draft opinion/advocacy pieces to help build support for policy initiatives. While policy makers provide speechwriters with a specific proposal to defend as well as detailed information about the pros and cons of the policy they will be writing about, the advocacy component of the speechwriting process is similar to the opinion and editorial (op-ed) writing process used in major newspapers. John Timpane, the op-ed editor of the *Philadelphia Inquirer*, provides potential op-ed writers with an excellent set of guidelines for writing advocacy statements that may be used by op-ed and speechwriters alike.[5] Timpane argues that the first thing a good commentary or advocacy piece should do is express an opinion. He receives scores of pieces in which the authors write "about" something that interests him or her, but they fail to advocate a particular position on the issue at hand. As a result, their writing may be informative, but it is not persuasive and, consequently, will not be accepted as an op-ed.

A good opinion piece should state an opinion within the first two or three sentences. The most common way to assert a position in an op-ed piece is to argue that something is or is not so, something is or is not worthy of attention, something should or should not be done, or something will or will not happen unless action is taken. In the policy world, the comparable assertions could be the following. "It's true/not true that welfare programs create a culture of dependency." "If we pass the new tax-cut bill, our gross national product will plummet." In addition, according to Timpane, a good op-ed should be linked to the current concerns of its readership. In the policy realm, this suggests that policy proposals should be designed to clearly address the concerns of constituents. Finally, op-eds and policy proposals alike will be stronger if they include concrete evidence to support their propositions and undermine potential counterproposals.

Likewise there is a set of rules to follow when preparing a speech announcing a new policy or set of policies. In order for a speech to effectively convey and sell a policy, the speech should[6]

- Explain the policy in simple terms. In fact, one can argue that any policy that cannot be described clearly and coherently may not be effective since the people it is designed to help will not understand how to take advantage of the proposal. If you need a whole speech to explain all the nuances of a particular proposal, then you probably are going to have a great deal of difficulty in garnering support for an idea. This does not

---

[5] Interview with John Timpane, April 2001.

[6] Thanks to Jim Kestler, a former speechwriter for Senator Charles Schumer, for his suggestions on this section.

mean that the proposal itself cannot be detailed and sophisticated, but the basic goal of the policy and how it will be achieved must be clear and easily explained.

- Define a specific problem of public concern that the policy is going to address and make a persuasive argument that the policy is needed and is the appropriate solution to the problem at hand. A speech is a linear form of communication. If the problem is under-specified or vague, then the purpose of the speech will remain unclear, and support for the policy will be weak.
- Use evidence to show that the problem exists and that the proposed solutions will address it.
- Persuade the audience to agree with the problem and the solution—the policy proposal—that you have developed.

Communications

The Communications Office is charged with long-term message planning and coordination. It is responsible for developing the broad themes that provide a recognizable framework for the president's (or chief decision maker's) ideas and policies. The Communications Office focuses on how public events are staged and how they will look and sound to the audience. It works closely with the scheduling offices and often serves as the intermediary between scheduling offices and the policy offices and staff. Coordination between the policy offices and the Communications Office is critical. Coordinating activities can, however, be difficult because the two groups have potentially competing objectives.

In particular, in contrast to the policy staff, the communications staff is far less concerned with the policy itself, and what the policy is intended to do, than with how the proposal fits into the theme of the moment. To avoid conflict and maximize synergies, the policy staff will often try to coordinate the public announcement of its proposals with the Communication Office's message calendar and use this timing of an event as a deadline for preparing any proposals under development. Thus, if the Communications Office is planning on emphasizing the president's education agenda around the time that students are going back to school, the policy councils will use that date as a deadline for completing policy proposals related to education.

Once an event is scheduled, the policy offices are charged with helping the Communications Office produce the public materials that will be disseminated at the event. Specially, in advance of a scheduled event, the Communications Office and policy councils will develop a **fact sheet** and **press paper** (these are sometimes the same, or are differentiated by the inclusion of a message component in the press paper). If appropriate, they may also prepare a report on the proposal and a state-by-state impact, background information on the site and why it was chosen, background information on the people or activities highlighted in the event as examples of beneficiaries of the policy, and whatever charts or graphs are needed to support the points being made at the event. The involvement of the policy offices in the White House and other executive agencies is required to guarantee that the policies are portrayed accurately.

Unlike speeches, fact sheets and press papers are first developed by the policy staff. The Communications Office staff only begins to edit the material after a draft is completed by the policy councils. Thus, press sheets tend to be more detailed and specific than speeches. As a consequence, reporters and others who are interested in more detailed information about a particular issue or policy tend to rely on fact sheets rather than speeches as the primary source of information. Press or fact sheets have become increasingly important with the advent of the Internet because they provide a credible on-line source of information about the administration's policy.

One of the primary objectives of writing a strong fact sheet or press paper is to control the information that is made available to the public. A well-written fact sheet can also relieve the pressure on the Press Office and Communications Office to comment on the details of policies with which they are not familiar. A strong fact sheet or press paper should contain enough facts so the majority of reporters can write their stories without having to interview policy staff in an agency or at the White House. This is important because most policy staffers do not have clearance to talk with the press. This restriction is generally imposed both as a way of controlling leaks and, more important, as a means of reducing the chance that policy staff could provide policy details that could either cause the reporter to lose interest in writing the story or direct the reporter's attention toward details that distract the reporter from the primary story.

A second objective of a fact sheet or press paper is to drive home the message that the communications staff wants the public to receive from the event. See the example on pages 118–119 of a typical press/fact sheet prepared by the policy and press offices. It provides considerable detail of the gun buyback plan announced by the Clinton administration including cost, numbers of guns to be purchased, and how many committees are already participating in the program. It also highlights the administration's overall theme of using so-called "common sense" gun measures, which focus on keeping guns away from criminals as a way of reducing gun violence. This theme is underscored in the headings describing different aspects of the program in the announcement.

Press Office

The Press Office became institutionalized in its current form during the Eisenhower administration, and President Eisenhower's press secretary, James C. Hagerty, is often cited as the standard by which press secretaries since have been judged.[7] Now every agency has a press office modeled on the White House operation. Since that time, the Press Office's primary responsibilities have been to interact with the

---

[7] For an evaluation of press secretaries since the Eisenhower administration, see Michael Towle, "On Behalf of the President: Four Factors Affecting the Success of the Presidential Press Secretary," *Presidential Studies Quarterly* 27, no. 2 (Spring 1997): 297–319.

President Clinton Announces Gun Buyback Partnership with the District of Columbia, April 28, 2000

Today, President Clinton, joined by District of Columbia Mayor Williams, Metropolitan Police Chief Ramsey, and Housing Secretary Cuomo, will announce a new gun buyback partnership between the District of Columbia and the Department of Housing and Urban Development. Under the initiative—the largest ever in D.C. and one of the largest ever in the country—a total of $350,000 will be made available to purchase an estimated 7000 guns through a local gun buyback program jointly administered by the Washington Public Housing Authority and the Metropolitan Police Department. In addition, the Bureau of Alcohol, Tobacco and Firearms will trace all guns recovered in the buyback. A total of 85 communities across the country are now participating in the first round of HUD's BuyBack America program to launch similar local gun buyback programs and to take tens of thousands of unwanted guns out of circulation. Today's initiative is part of a comprehensive effort by the Clinton Administration to provide more tools for communities to reduce gun violence, and to advance common sense gun safety legislation to keep guns out of the wrong hands.

Taking Thousands of Guns out of Circulation in Washington

In the wake of the recent shooting at the National Zoo, President Clinton today will announce a major partnership between the federal government and the District of Columbia to fund the largest gun buyback in the city's history. Under today's partnership, HUD's BuyBack America program will provide $100,000 and the Metropolitan Police Department will provide $250,000 to fund the buyback, which will be held June 23rd and 24th. The District of Columbia Public Housing Authority will partner with the Metropolitan Police Department to conduct the buyback, which will fund the purchase of an estimated 7000 guns and take them off the street and out of circulation permanently. Last August, the Metropolitan Police Department conducted two successful buybacks. The first, funded in part by HUD, yielded 600 guns; the second, 2300 guns. According to an ATF report on the buybacks, the vast majority of firearms recovered (2200) were handguns, and far exceeded the District's average annual recovery rate of 2105 crime guns. Among the firearms frequently recovered were the types of guns often used in crimes and illegally trafficked by unlicensed dealers.

Providing Resources to Fund Buybacks Across the Country

A recent study released by HUD shows that people living in public housing are more than twice as likely to suffer from gun-related victimization as the general population. And while

media on a daily basis, to respond to public inquiries of the day regarding governmental activities, to advise the president on communications matters, and to implement the communications strategy. Implementing the communications strategy includes "spinning" the message of the day, managing the release of information and executive messages to the public, and preparing briefings by policy experts in the administration.

It is important to note that while the term **spin** has become a value-laden term often used by the media to refer to efforts by politicians to evade questions or mislead others into thinking that policy actions benefit them, it is not a derogatory term. In policy circles, spin refers to marketing efforts used to promote support for a

gun crime is down by 35 percent since 1992, nearly 12 children are still killed every day by gunfire. To help reduce the toll of gun violence, President Clinton last September unveiled a $15 million HUD gun buyback initiative—the largest gun buyback program in history. Under the first round of the BuyBack America Initiative, HUD is providing funding to a total of 85 communities to enable Public Housing Authorities (PHAs) to partner with local law enforcement agencies to conduct local gun buyback programs. By reducing the number of firearms in circulation, buyback programs can help prevent accidental shootings, gun suicides, gun crime and unauthorized gun use. The HUD buyback program encourages a cap of $50 for each working gun, and encourages PHAs to provide the awards in the form of gift certificates for goods or services rather than cash. Every HUD-sponsored buyback must be run by a local police department—with no amnesty given for any crimes committed with returned firearms. And to ensure permanent removal from circulation, all guns are destroyed unless they are relevant to an ongoing law enforcement investigation, or they have been stolen from their lawful owner.

Working with D.C. Law Enforcement to Combat Gun Crime

Today's initiative is another example of efforts by the federal government and the District of Columbia to work together to combat gun crime. Under innovative programs such as Operation Cease fire, which has received nearly $1 million in federal funding since 1995, local police are partnering with the U.S. Attorney and the ATF to increase gun enforcement and gun crime prevention programs. Also, through the Administration's Youth Crime Gun Interdiction Initiative, local police are working with the ATF to trace all crime guns recovered in the District to crack down on illegal gun traffickers that supply guns to juveniles and criminals.

Keeping up Pressure to Enact Common Sense Gun Legislation

In addition to announcing these new tools to combat gun violence, the President will again emphasize the importance of common sense gun measures that can reduce gun violence by keeping guns out of the wrong hands. Noting that the Congress missed an opportunity to pass gun safety legislation by the April 20th anniversary of the Columbine shootings, the President will urge Congress to complete work on juvenile crime legislation and pass a final bill that closes the gun show loophole, requires child safety locks for handguns, bars the importation of large capacity ammunition clips, and bans violent juveniles from owning guns for life.

Source: White House Web page.

particular policy. Policy spin is factual evidence presented in a way that support a proposal or position. It is not meant to mislead but rather to inform the public in a way that puts a proposal in the best light.

There are three primary subdivisions of the Press Office: the specialty press, the regional press, and the radio office. The specialty press subdivision focuses on demographic sectors of the media. For example, it will target trade and industry journals, as well as media that target specific groups in society, like women or minorities. The regional press subdivision focuses on four press regions: the Northeast, Midwest, South, and West. Finally, the Radio Office focuses on radio talk shows and DJs, and it coordinates other broadcast media.

Gun Buyback Event, Q&A, April 28, 2000

Q: Critics say that gun buybacks don't actually take guns out of the hands of criminals. Is there any evidence to suggest that gun buybacks actually reduce gun crime?

A: Every time we take a gun out of circulation through a buyback program, we help reduce the incidence of gun violence—not only gun crime, but also gun-related accidents, suicides, and other unintentional uses of guns. For instance, people living in a home with a gun have a suicide risk that is five times greater than those who live in a home without a gun. We also know that of the nearly 12 young people who are killed every day by gunfire, more than a third are by gun suicides and accidents. And many of the firearms obtained through buybacks are the types of guns frequently used in crimes. Unfortunately, there haven't been any truly comprehensive studies of buyback programs, and there certainly has never been a program of the magnitude of the HUD $15 million program—which could help communities to buy back tens of thousands of guns. That is why HUD will make money available from the initiative to study the effects of buybacks, and identify promising practices to help make the programs more effective. However, it is also important to note that another important element of gun buyback programs is the impact they have on communities and their citizens. Gun buybacks give people an opportunity to get involved with law enforcement in local efforts to reduce violence, and they give residents hope that they can change their communities for the better.

Q: Weren't the guns retrieved in the last D.C. buybacks older guns and guns that wouldn't have been used in crimes?

A: The ATF reviewed the two gun buybacks conducted by the District last year and found that among the firearms most recovered were types of guns that are frequently used in crimes, illegally trafficked, or recovered by law enforcement agencies. This includes three of the most commonly recovered crime guns in America (the Raven .25 pistol, the Davis .380 pistol, and the Jennings .22 pistol). These same types of firearms are also consistently among the most frequently recovered firearms used in crimes in the District. In addition, handguns account for over 80% of all crime gun traces conducted nationally by the ATF, and 2,200 of the 2,912 guns turned into the District's buybacks were handguns. It only makes sense that by taking these types of weapons out of our nation's communities, we are reducing the likelihood of countless gun-related tragedies.

Q: Isn't it highly unlikely that a gun buyback would have prevented a tragic incident like this week's shooting at the zoo?

A: Well, there is an ongoing investigation into the zoo shooting and I believe that authorities do not yet have the gun used in that incident. Of course we may never know if one

Like the other media offices, the Press Office becomes involved after policy is made, not before. It generally becomes engaged in the process the day before a policy is scheduled to be presented to the public. Once engaged, the Press Office works in tandem with policy staff in preparing the information to be used to support press inquiries. These include fact sheets and press papers and question and answer sheets.

When an event will highlight a new or significant policy, the Press Office generally holds briefings with members of the policy staff who are likely to enter-

single action could have prevented the shooting. Still, this week's tragic incident serves as further proof that we must do more to keep guns out of the wrong hands—kids especially. Gun buybacks are just one way we can address this problem—and they work hand-in-hand with child safety locks for handguns, smart gun technology, and cracking down on illegal traffickers who supply guns to youth—are other ways which the President has also proposed. The President believes we must take action on all fronts in order to address the problem of gun violence in this nation. Today's announcement is simply one more tool the President wants to give local communities to support their gun violence reduction efforts.

Q: Do you really think removing even a few hundred thousand guns from circulation through the HUD program will make a difference when there are over 200 million privately owned guns in America?

A: We believe it will make a difference, although we agree that it certainly isn't a solution on its own. HUD's buyback program is just one more tool that we are giving communities and law enforcement to improve public safety and reduce gun violence. But Congress has an important opportunity to give communities even more tools to reduce gun violence, which is why they should pass common sense gun legislation that requires Brady background checks at gun shows, bans the importation of large capacity ammunition clips, and requires child safety locks for guns.

Q: If the HUD program is a $15 million initiative, why are only 85 communities participating? Why is so little money being spent out of the initiative so far ($2.7 million)?

A: These communities represent the first round of funding. Last week, HUD announced that Public Housing Authorities can use FY 2000 funds toward buybacks and we expect many more communities to seek funding in the second round. HUD has already begun to receive applications for the second round of buybacks.

Q: What HUD program is funding the buybacks?

A: Housing authorities commit HUD Public Housing Drug Elimination Grant (DEG) funds to the buyback and HUD provides 43 cents in additional funds for every dollar of DEG money committed to the buyback. For the District of Columbia, this breaks down to $70,000 in DEG funds and $30,000 in matching funds. Buybacks must be carried out in cooperation with local police or sheriffs and the guns must be destroyed unless it turns out they were stolen or are needed for a criminal investigation.

Source: Domestic Policy Council, the White House.

tain questions from the press corps. In the case of certain high-profile agencies and the White House, the Press Office may hold as many as two regular briefings every day. These briefings include a morning briefing by the press secretary's office, which is "on the record," but not on camera. The morning briefing usually focuses on breaking morning news and policy announcements that will take place later in the day. The afternoon briefing is "on camera" and is based on prepared question and answer (Q&A) sheets. Each day the policy staff prepare Q&A sheets on hot topics or on the policy announcement of the day.

Several points about the Q&A regarding a Gun Buyback Event should be noted. In the second Q&A exchange, the answer clearly responds to the question asked in the first two sentences. It states what types of guns were bought back, and that these guns are commonly used in crimes. Sometimes, however, the data needed to support a response like this are not available. When data are not available, the respondent must be prepared to provide a qualified response and should not avoid answering the question. For example, in the first Q&A exchange, the respondent does not have the data needed to respond to the question directly. He or she provides anecdotal evidence in response to the question, but then acknowledges that the actual data are not available.

In addition to answering the question, and either specifying data to support the case or acknowledging the need for additional information, the answers are short and concise. There are some good examples of concise responses and several examples of overly detailed responses. The fifth Q&A exchange is the most concisely written response to the question. It is short, factual, and to the point. The first Q&A, approximately 350 words, is simply too long and runs the risk that an administration spokesperson may forget or confuse part of the response when he or she is asked to repeat the administration's position. While some of the facts are useful, providing too much information can create confusion and could potentially open up additional lines of questioning. Finally, most of the responses to the questions are written in a style that is not laden with policy jargon and is generally approachable to a large audience.

In summary, there are four keys to writing good question and answers.

1. Make certain the answer to the question is in the first two sentences.
2. Provide evidence to support the answer.
3. Answers should be short, concise, and to the point. Anything over 200 words should be condensed.
4. Answers need to be written in terms that the general public can understand.

Following these guidelines as precisely as possible can promote clarity in communicating an idea, while minimizing the risks of being misdirected and not getting the primary message across.

Conclusion

A policy proposal that cannot be effectively marketed to the public and the press cannot be sustained over the long term. With the advent of the Internet and 24-hour cable television, the relationship between policy making and communications/media strategy and tactics has never been more important. In this chapter we have outlined some of the tools that policy makers and communications staffers use to present proposals. These tools are simple in concept, yet their importance cannot be underestimated. Despite ongoing advances in information and media technology, the role of speeches, fact sheets and press papers, and question and answer sessions will remain relevant.

Some argue that good policies speak for themselves while others believe that effective marketing can sell any policy, good or bad. We argue that the complexities of most policies make even those that are likely to achieve their objectives very difficult to understand without guidance. That is why it is important that policy makers communicate and market their ideas throughout the policy-making process. Such an approach will help ensure that proposals can be explained to the constituents they were intended to serve. This will increase the perception that the policy and the process are legitimate and reflect the concerns of their constituents. If a policy cannot be explained and its benefits are not clear, it will not be broadly supported. This does not mean the policy would have produced an unpopular result, as some critics might argue, but it does mean it is less likely to survive the political process and come to fruition.

Key Terms

Cognitive Bias: Unmotivated decision-making bias that results from an inability of individuals to process excessive or insufficient amounts of information. When faced with too much or too little information, individuals exhibiting a cognitive bias will tend to interpret information and events in ways that conform to what they expect to see given their beliefs about how the world works and their understanding of the specific context at hand.

Fact Sheet: Provides basic information about a presidential policy announcement for public consumption.

Fact Checking: Checking a public statement or release for factual errors. Sometimes a factual discrepancy is incredibly subtle. What appears to be factually accurate to a speechwriter may be a major error in fact to a policy maker.

Motivated Bias: Motivated bias results from the subconscious need of decision makers to see the world and interpret information in ways that match some underlying motivation. This motivation may come from desire on the part of the decision maker to a achieve a particular bureaucratic, political, or personal goal. In such circumstances, the policy decision is usually made first, and is followed by extensive justifications and rationalizations.

Press Paper: A fact sheet that is specifically targeted to the press and is designed to promote the president's policy objectives.

Spin: In policy circles, the marketing efforts used to promote support for a particular policy. Policy spin is factual evidence presented in a way to support a proposal or position. It is not meant to mislead but rather to inform the public in a way that puts a proposal in the best light.

Review Questions

1. What does John Timpane of the *Philadelphia Inquirer* argue is the first thing a good commentary or advocacy piece should do?

2. Describe the four rules to follow when preparing a speech announcing a new policy or set of policies.

3. What is a primary objective of a press paper or fact sheet? Who develops the first draft of a press paper or fact sheet?

4. What are the four keys to writing good questions and answers for government officials announcing new policy?

5. Name the three offices in the White House and federal agencies most involved in communicating and marketing policy. How do their roles differ?

CHAPTER 9

Welfare Reform During the Clinton Administration

Welfare Reform and the Political Process

The previous chapters presented the primary policy tools, techniques, and processes used by policy makers in the executive branch of the United States government; this chapter and the two that follow examine how they were applied in various situations. In each of the cases we present in this book, the effectiveness of the policy-making process was enhanced when the authority, responsibility, and accountability for a particular policy were centralized and all policy makers with a stake in the policy believed that the policy-making process provided an effective means to voice their concerns to the president or those responsible for policy development. When either of these conditions were not met, the policy-making process stalled and criticism of the policy increased.

This chapter analyzes how the Clinton administration used these tools, techniques, and processes to transform welfare reform from a campaign slogan to a fully developed policy proposal which served as the basis for the Personal Responsibility and Work Opportunity Reconciliation Act (PRWORA). During the administration's first two years, the welfare reform policy process was not centralized, nor were those involved in the process given a clear mandate. Indeed one of the primary lessons from the welfare reform experience is that a policy initiative that is managed *collectively*—without a specific unit being given decision-making authority and responsibility to shape the policy's development—is likely to stall. This is particularly likely when there is not a clear mandate from the president, and disagreements exist among the policy development team members regarding the president's objectives and the appropriate means to achieve those objectives.

The development of a welfare reform policy in the executive branch changed in 1994 in response to the midterm election victories by congressional Republicans that resulted in part from the inclusion of welfare reform in their policy platform. From that point on, the administration made welfare reform a priority. In contrast to the pre-1994 period, the president centralized authority, responsibility, and accountability for welfare reform policy exclusively in the Domestic Policy Council (DPC). In addition, the president and senior White House staff also became actively involved in sparring with Congress, using a variety of strategies to successfully modify the congressional proposals so that they converged with its welfare reform goals. With the centralization of authority and increased involvement of the president, the welfare reform process accelerated dramatically.

The tools and techniques described in earlier chapters were used throughout the entire welfare reform process. Policy-making memoranda, polling, SAPs, and LRMs served as the primary means of communication between policy makers before and after 1994. Prior to 1994, however, when the procedural legitimacy of the policy-making process was low, memoranda to the president and other tools were often devoted to expressing concerns about disagreements among policy makers about the president's priorities regarding welfare reform policy. After 1994 the foci of the memoranda and other policy tools were redirected toward aggressively creating and implementing a welfare reform policy that reflected executive priorities.

The development of a welfare reform policy during the first years of the Clinton administration demonstrates that when the policy-making process breaks down, policy makers tend to diverge from regular channels of communication, and progress in policy formation and adoption can be hampered. On the other hand, when participants have confidence that the process provides an effective means of voicing concerns support broadens, deviations from the process diminish, and policy initiatives are more likely to come to fruition. The purpose of this chapter is to review how the tools and techniques used in the policy-making process were utilized and to identify the conditions under which the policy process worked most efficiently. Since our concern in this is not assessing the merits of welfare reform, but rather the policy-making process that led to the enactment of PRWORA, the impact of welfare reform on the recipients, states, or national government will not be assessed.[1]

The Early Phase:
Decentralization, Debate, and Deadlock

On August 22, 1996, President Clinton fulfilled his campaign promise to "end welfare as we know it," by signing the PRWORA. Shortly after its passage, he also succeeded in restoring cuts to legal immigrants, thereby correcting what he saw as its primary limitation. The transformation of welfare reform from a campaign slogan

---

[1] Welfare caseloads fell by 51 percent between 1993 and 1999, and 1.3 million welfare recipients moved from welfare to work between 1997 and 1998 alone. For information see "Clinton-Gore Accomplishments Reforming Welfare by Promoting Work and Responsibility," White House press release, February 7, 1999, 2.

into a law was, however, much less efficiently accomplished than the convergence between the final policy outcome and President Clinton's campaign promises suggests. Let us begin at the beginning.

The degree of welfare reform proposed during the presidential campaign in 1992 marked a significant and uncharted change from the past. Although everyone understood President-elect Clinton's desire "to change welfare as we know it," the Clinton team did not agree about the urgency of welfare reform relative to health-care reform and other policy initiatives. Once in office, these debates expanded to include disagreements between members of his campaign team and his newly appointed advisers over how to interpret—and whether to implement—the president's campaign promises regarding welfare reform. These internal debates resulted in several actions early in the administration that undermined the potential for an early success at welfare reform. In particular, no financial support was provided for welfare reform, and the responsibility for policy development was delegated to a jointly administered interagency task force which was given only the minimal directive to "study" the problem.

The welfare reform process got off to a weak start early in 1992, when Secretary of the Treasury Lloyd Bentsen presented President Clinton with a five-year budget proposal that did not include any money for welfare or healthcare reform. Rather than providing new resources, the budget proposal required both policy initiatives to be self-financing. This financial constraint greatly complicated efforts to reach a consensus within the administration regarding the form welfare should take. It also undermined the efforts of those in the administration who wanted to make welfare reform a priority early in President Clinton's term. The resulting ambivalence toward welfare reform by some in the executive branch was reinforced by a belief that welfare reform would not be supported by the majority of Democrats in Congress—with the exception of Senator Moynihan, who strongly advocated pursuing welfare reform before healthcare reform.

These factors were compounded further by disagreements within the executive branch over how to interpret the president's objectives. For example, some people, including Assistant Secretary for Planning and Evaluation of the U.S. Department of Health and Human Services (HHS) David Ellwood, argued that welfare reform should be tested in a small number of states before pursuing a comprehensive change on a national scale. Others, such as Housing and Urban Development (HUD) Secretary Henry Cisneros, opposed placing time limits on welfare benefits. With no clear mandate and minimal direction, the president appointed a 27-member interagency task force to develop a welfare plan. The task force was jointly managed by then Deputy Assistant to the President for Domestic Policy Bruce Reed and David Ellwood, in collaboration with the assistant secretary for the Administration of Children and Family of the HHS, Mary Jo Bane. Bruce Reed was the administration's leading advocate of comprehensive reform. In contrast, both David Ellwood and Mary Jo Bane preferred pursuing more gradual and less comprehensive reform.

Between 1993 and 1994, there were disagreements between the DPC, HHS, and the Department of Labor regarding fundamental issues such as how to interpret the president's objectives regarding:

- The form and scope of welfare reform
- The degree of federal oversight versus freedom of states
- The issue of granting states waivers
- The rights of legal immigrants
- Whether to begin with a centrist or left-of-center policy
  and whether, how, and when to implement the policy changes.

Two of the most contentious issues involved the imposition of time limits on welfare recipients and the grant of **welfare waivers** that allowed states to pursue reforms independently of federal action. In general, the HHS pushed for a more liberal reform with more centralized control in the federal government, while the DPC preferred a **"new Democrat"** policy that granted states more authority. The HHS wanted to maintain oversight over state welfare policies and argued that waivers should be used sparingly and only after careful study. Some members of the HHS criticized the White House staff as being driven by expediency and politics, a desire for very quick access to information, and a bias toward giving increasing power to states. The White House staff, in comparison, wanted to use the waivers as a safety valve and saw them as a means to let states implement welfare reform even if no policy change was made formally.

In 1994, after welfare reform became more of a priority issue for the administration, it began granting waivers that allowed states to pursue welfare reform independent of congressional action, underscoring the administration's support for a politically popular issue. Granting waivers demonstrated the administration's ability and willingness to implement welfare reform at the state level regardless of whether or not it received congressional support. Before federal welfare reform was passed in 1996, 45 states and the District of Columbia had received federally approved welfare demonstration waivers. As a result, although their success varied, many of these states were actively engaged in limited welfare reform long before the national bill was passed.

Strain Toward Agreement

Unlike the process followed by the National Economic Council in 1993 which utilized formal meetings to resolve outstanding policy issues, disagreements among members of the welfare reform task force were typically resolved informally. When this failed, the chief of staff, and sometimes the president, played the role of arbiter to settle differences. Limited interaction with the chief of staff and the president to settle minor issues as well as major disagreements among task force members caused the policy-making process to grind down to a halt. Most of these issues could have been resolved within the working group if leadership and accountability had been placed in one entity instead of two. Ironically, joint leadership of the task force increased the perception among the members that their views were not being given a fair hearing by the president. As a result, group cohesion and effectiveness declined.

It is important to recognize that even when disagreements regarding a specific policy initiative exist, one of the primary goals of a policy-making committee like this task force is to strain toward an agreement that is acceptable to all participants (see Chapter 1). This generally requires the development of a **consensus document** or **consensus proposal**—that is, a proposal that the participants agree brings their viewpoints to the president's or chief decision maker's attention. Bruce Reed, for example, commonly used information and decision memoranda (see Chapter 5) to inform the president about progress on the welfare reform initiatives, to apprise him of disputes among members of the task force, and to seek clarification of his objectives and position.

When a consensus is not reached—or particular parties feel that their viewpoints are not being given a fair hearing before the president—the excluded parties often respond by raising public doubts or mobilizing public support against the policy in question. As we noted earlier, this can be achieved by leaking information to the press. This practice was common throughout the development of welfare reform policy. For example, members of the executive branch who felt that their opinions were not being addressed leaked information about a cabinet meeting on January 5, 1994 to the *New York Times*. In the article, they argued that the president was trying to devise a strategy to make it appear as though he were pushing for change in the welfare system, even though he was delaying action on the bill until healthcare reform had a chance to clear Congress.[2] The negative publicity created by this leak was compounded by published statements by Senator Moynihan, who was upset that the administration had placed a priority on health care reform rather than welfare reform. As detailed in the box on page 130, Jason DeParle of the *New York Times* reported that Senator Moynihan criticized President Clinton for raising the subject of welfare reform to appease the public "whenever he gets into trouble," while, at the same time, "appointing people who had no intention of doing it."[3]

In response to the publication of these leaks and criticisms that the administration was not acting on its welfare reform promises, Bruce Reed wrote a memorandum to apprise the president of the situation (including identifying reporters who are likely to write unfavorably and favorably about welfare reform), to highlight the danger of leaks—especially as related to new studies by the OMB and HHS regarding cost and financing estimates of the welfare reform plan—and to suggest ways to present and promote the president's plan.[4] He specifically suggested that the administration emphasize primary questions involving welfare reform—including where to find the money, how to get the states to come on board, and how to make the program work—and highlight the impact that phasing in reform would have on them. He argued that the forthcoming reports from the HHS and OMB would likely be leaked and that it was, therefore, essential that the administration present a good story to the press before additional negative stories are published. He even suggested that a specific reporter, Ronald Brownstein, be contacted. Three days later, Brownstein wrote a story for the *Los Angeles Times* that outlined and supported the administration's phase-in plan and highlighted the costs associated with

---

[2] Jason DeParle, "Clinton Puzzle: How to Delay Welfare Reform Yet Seem to Pursue It," *New York Times*, 5 January 1995, A13.

[3] Jason DeParle, "Moynihan Says President is Insincere about Reforming the Welfare System," *New York Times*, 8 January 1994, sec. 1, 8.

[4] Bruce Reed, "Memorandum for the President: Welfare Reform Damage Control," February 17, 1994.

Leaks to the *New York Times*

Excerpt from Jason DeParle, "Clinton Puzzle: How to Delay Welfare Reform Yet Seem to Pursue It," *New York Times*, 4 January 1994, A13

The Clinton Administration is trying to devise a strategy that would allow it to appear to be pushing for change in the welfare system, even while delaying action on a bill until the President's health care plan has a chance to clear Congress.

The effort to delay welfare legislation so it does not interfere with the Administration's primary goal of health care, while not acknowledged publicly, has been evident in a number of recent Administration actions and was discussed at a Cabinet meeting on Monday, officials said. They said the strategy would make it unlikely that a major welfare bill would pass Congress this year.

Mr. Clinton's pledge to impose strict work requirements on welfare recipients was one of his most popular campaign promises. But after almost a year in office, he has still not spelled out the details or developed a plan. The President has scarcely mentioned welfare in his recent remarks on domestic priorities. Next year's budget, now in preparation, contains no cost projections for a welfare plan. And Congressional leaders, warning that welfare is divisive, have urged him to work on health care first.

Clinton Describes Problem

At this week's Cabinet meeting, Mr. Clinton himself articulated his dilemma, people who were present said on the condition that they not be named.

The President argued that health care was so complex that it required the Administration's complete political and legislative attention. He said the country would not succeed in moving people off welfare until it passed universal health care, since many people stay on welfare for the health insurance. Mr. Clinton acknowledged that he was taking a political risk in appearing to delay taking action on a central campaign pledge. He worried that Republicans, who have introduced their own tough-sounding welfare bill, would accuse him of dragging his feet. "I think the President is concerned that the Republicans will portray him as a classic liberal, taxing and spending" on health care, while abandoning welfare, said an official who attended the meeting.

Political Motives Seen

Mr. Clinton complained to his aides that the Republican attacks were unfair, arguing that Republicans showed little concern about overhauling welfare when they controlled the White House. He accused Republicans of trying to exploit the issue for political gain.

A second official present at the meeting quoted the President as saying, "They didn't try to do anything about this," and now "they will say that I'm not serious about this and, in fact, I am." One strategy discussed at the meeting, the official said, was to introduce a bill but quietly to encourage Congress not to proceed until the health care debate was finished. "Introduce it, explain the general philosophy and principles, but don't have them take it up," the official said. Bob Boorstin, a White House spokesman, refused to comment on the Cabinet meeting. He said only that the Administration would send a bill to Congress this year. "I don't know what the chances are of a welfare reform bill passing in 1994," he said. "I'm not an oddsmaker." Others at the meeting concluded that without a major push by the Administration, welfare reform would languish. "There was a sense in the room that a bill probably wouldn't be passed this year," an Administration official said. . . .

Spin in the *Los Angeles Times* to Counter Leaks

Excerpts from Ronald Brownstein, "New Welfare Limits Could Be Aimed First at the Young," *Los Angeles Times*, 20 February 1994, A1.

A Clinton Administration task force is likely to recommend initially imposing the President's two-year limit for welfare benefits on young recipients exclusively, while leaving millions of older people to collect public assistance as usual, senior officials said.

The officials argue that phasing in the proposed limit in this manner would be more effective and less costly at the outset—and would send a clear message of changed expectations to the next generation of welfare recipients.

But the proposal also risks attack from critics who maintain such a gradual approach fails to fulfill Clinton's campaign promise to "end welfare as we know it."

Under the plan, which is emerging as the clear preference of a task force preparing the Administration's welfare reform recommendations, only new applicants and current welfare recipients born in 1971 or later would be required to work after two years on the rolls. Recipients who could not find jobs in the private sector would be given government jobs.

If the plan went into effect in 1995, the two-year limit would apply initially to all recipients 25 years old or younger. Each year, the time limit would automatically extend to new applicants one year older. By the year 2000, anyone 30 or younger would face the requirement to work after two years on the rolls.

The prevailing view in the task force apparently is to wait until the new system has been in operation several years before deciding whether to extend the work requirement to all other welfare recipients, though officials acknowledged that the decision could be reversed when it reaches Clinton's desk.

"I think the proper thing to do is to see how well the system has performed," said a senior Administration official. "Then in a few years' time you say: 'What additional resources are we going to need to (expand the requirement?)' and do it then."

Administration officials maintain that focusing resources on a relatively narrow group at first would increase the likelihood they could find jobs in the private sector and hold down the potentially enormous costs of creating public jobs for them. Those officials also argue that such a move is more likely to change the "welfare culture" and diminish dependency over the long run by targeting limited resources at one clearly delineated group, rather than diffusing efforts across the 5 million families now receiving public assistance.

"We think it is critical to break the cycle of welfare dependency by focusing on the next generation," said one ranking White House official. "It is important to send a clear unmistakable signal to a defined group of people.". . .

Another factor being considered by the Clinton task force is that a phased-in approach based on age would moderate the costs of welfare reform at a time when the Administration is struggling to pay for it by finding offsetting budget cuts.

Senior officials still say the welfare-reform plan could cost from $4 billion to $7 billion after five years, with an age-based approach likely to be nearer the $4-billion figure, sources said. Clinton has promised to forward his reform proposals to Congress this spring.

Preliminary estimates show that by 1999, about 2 million of the 4.7 million families expected to be on welfare at that time would have been phased into the work requirement.

continued

Spin in the *Los Angeles Times* to Counter Leaks *(continued)*

Under the Administration proposal, states would have the freedom to impose the two-year limit more broadly, as several have already requested.

In contrast to the Administration plan, a House Republican proposal would impose a two-year limit on all new welfare recipients who enter the system after the legislation is passed. The work requirement would be extended in 1999 to all welfare recipients who entered the system before the law went into effect. As a result, by 2001 anyone who had received welfare for at least two years would be required to work.

The House GOP approach wouldn't come cheap: The CBO calculated that by 1999 the GOP bill would cost the federal government $7.3 billion and state governments an additional $4.2 billion. Estimates were not available for the cost to states of the Administration task force's proposal.

Governors and state welfare administrators have already signaled that states will resist shouldering additional costs for welfare reform.

Cost is the most immediate problem. Because the government would provide day care, transportation and additional administrative oversight, requiring welfare recipients to work costs more than allowing them to remain at home. In a review of the House GOP proposal, the CBO calculated that requiring a welfare recipient to perform community service work would cost $6,300 a year more than providing benefits without work.

That reality has compelled the task force to seek ways to circumscribe the work requirement, at least at first. The President has ordered the welfare planners to produce a budget-neutral plan because, under legislative budget rules, new spending for a federal entitlement program can be paid for only with increased taxes or cuts in other entitlement programs.

Finding those cuts has been difficult. The task force has been examining proposals for capping grants given to states to provide emergency assistance to welfare recipients facing eviction or utility cutoffs, increasing efforts to root out fraud in the Earned Income Tax Credit for the working poor and limiting Social Security disability payments to drug addicts and alcoholics. The task force, however, has dropped a proposal to tax welfare benefits and food stamps the same way unemployment insurance is taxed. . . .

a congressional GOP alternative (without specifying the cost of the administration's proposal).[5] The resulting exchange of leaks, memoranda, and responses demonstrates how policy can be presented to the public with a negative spin to raise doubts and undermine support, or with a positive spin to increase or regain support for a specific initiative.

After extensive negotiations within the administration, President Clinton unveiled the Work and Responsibility Act. Most significantly, the bill placed a two-year time limit on individuals born after 1971, who were receiving assistance on the Aid to Families with Dependent Children (AFDC) program. People who could not find work were to be placed in federally subsidized jobs. To achieve this objective, the program called for $9.3 billion in additional federal funding over five years, and

---

[5] Ronald Brownstein, "New Welfare Limits Could Be Aimed First at the Young," *Los Angeles Times*, 20 February 1994, A1.

it strengthened regulations regarding paternity and child support. All but $2.1 billion in funding for this proposal would come from reductions in other federal entitlements. On June 24, 1993 the Clinton welfare bill was introduced in the Senate as S224 and in the House of Representatives as H.R. 4605.

The administration finally produced a bill, but it did not actively push for its passage and Congress chose to ignore the proposal. The inaction by the executive branch was the result of the ad hoc organization of the policy-making process, the lack of a clear mandate, and a perception of biases in the policy-making process that supported some views and shortchanged others. As a result, the bill that was produced did not gain widespread support. Once the president decided to make welfare reform a priority, the situation changed dramatically. In 1994, Clinton applied the hybrid organizational model that combined centralized management and multiple advocacy to welfare reform policy (see Chapter 1). Consequently, it succeeded in taking control of the welfare reform initiative and securing passage of a bill that ultimately met most of its concerns.

Phase II: Action, Response, and Resolution

The second phase of the welfare reform process began on November 8, 1994, when Republicans won a majority in both houses of Congress. As part of their campaign pledges, the newly elected members of Congress promised to fulfill the **"Contract with America"** by bringing action to the House and Senate floors on a variety of issues, including a conservative welfare reform proposal entitled the Personal Responsibility Act. The Republican victory served as an important catalyst for welfare reform in the Clinton administration in at least two ways. First, in post-elections polls run by *The Wall Street Journal*, voters cited welfare reform as their number one policy priority, surpassing other issues including healthcare reform, a balanced budget, and term limits.[6] Furthermore, the polls revealed that voters linked the existing AFDC welfare system to broader social problems—including the creation of an urban underclass, crime, social decay, loss of family values, and the rise of children having children. This outcome and the popular sentiment in support of welfare reform forced the Clinton administration to reassess the relative priority it had given to welfare reform. After 1994 the Clinton administration shelved comprehensive healthcare reform and made welfare reform a priority.

Second, the Personal Responsibility Act included in the Republican "Contract with America" made the Clinton administration's welfare reform proposal appear reasonable to Democrats in Congress. Unlike the Clinton proposal (the Personal Responsibility Act):

- Cut off all AFDC and housing benefits for illegitimate children whose mothers are under 18 and barred the children from ADFC for life.
- Recipients would have to work after two years of aid and would be permanently denied AFDC for life after five years.

---

[6] Mickey Kaus, "They Blew It," *The New Republic*, 5 December 1994, 14–18.

- AFDC, housing, and the Supplemental Security Income program were stripped of their entitlement status and placed under spending caps.
- Virtually all benefits for legal immigrants were denied.

Having recognized its mistake in not making welfare reform a priority, the Clinton administration was given—through the severity of the Republican alternative—a target which the president could justify vetoing and driving toward the center. With renewed vigor, the Clinton administration initiated a strategy to exploit differences between moderates and conservatives in the Republican ranks and between the National Governors' Association and Congress to regain the initiative in welfare reform. The Republican bill was approved as H.R. 4 by the House of Representatives in a 234–119 vote on March 24, 1995. The next day President Clinton used his weekly radio address to denounce the bill and launch the administration's counterattack.

The Centralization of Authority

The strategy behind the White House effort to reenergize welfare reform had several components. The first involved the centralization of authority and responsibility for welfare reform; the second involved the mobilization of senior policy makers and the redirection of the tools, techniques, and processes toward formulating, adopting, and implementing the president's welfare reform package. The process of centralization began when Bruce Reed of the DPC was given direct responsibility for welfare reform. This shift in authority to the DPC was helped by the departure of David Ellwood, who had to return to his academic responsibilities in order to maintain his university tenure. The resulting power shift was important because it meant that debate within the welfare reform task force could move beyond the question of what the president intended welfare reform to be, to questions of how to challenge the Republican proposal and promote the president's agenda. It also meant that welfare reform policy process was now run out of the White House.

The involvement of specific agencies and departments in this task force tended to shift over time as the welfare reform process evolved. Initially, welfare reform was centered in the DPC, HHS, and the INS. As the policy evolved, and particularly after it became law in 1996, the group was expanded to include the Department of the Treasury, the Department of Housing and Urban Development, and the Department of Transportation. The inclusion of these additional participants served two purposes. From a functional standpoint, this change reflected the expansion of issues involved in welfare reform. In addition, however, the inclusion of additional parties helped the White House spread information about its agenda and, thereby, facilitate the implementation of its objectives.

The Office of Management and Budget played an important management and evaluation role in the welfare reform process. While the A-19 Clearance Process (discussed in Chapter 7) was used only when legislation was involved, the OMB played an active role in reviewing both administration and congressional proposals. It paid particular attention to policies regarding legal immigrants and the impact of the proposals on children in poverty. For example, in November of 1995 it reported that the proposed policy changes that resulted from a House and Senate compromise between the Personal Responsibility Act approved by the House of Representatives (H.R. 4) on March 4, and the Welfare Reform Act approved by the Senate on September 18 (which included over 40 amendments to H.R. 4) would result in one million more children living under poverty. As a result of this assessment, President Clinton vowed to veto the budget reconciliation bill that contained the welfare reform provisions.

While the policy-making process was generally informal, the Domestic Policy Council was responsible for organizing key issues and bringing the various agencies and departments together. For example, rather than having the Department of Labor and the HHS discuss a particular issue regarding welfare reform with one another, the DPC would call a deputies' meeting that included both Labor and HHS to discuss the issues at hand. Meetings were held weekly when necessary, but they were stopped when their usefulness ceased. Participants in the process considered communication between the various parties to be open and congenial—ironically more so than when there was joint control.

Redirecting the Tools and Mobilizing Support

In addition to centralizing the authority, responsibility, and accountability for welfare reform in the DPC, the administration began a strategic effort to increase the role of senior administration personnel in promoting, and taking control of, the welfare reform debate. This effort began with the organization of a working session on welfare on January 28, 1995. It brought the president and the White House welfare reform task force together with members of the National Governors' Association (NGA), the House of Representatives, and the Senate, as well as mayors, county officials, and others in a forum to build a bipartisan partnership to develop a welfare program. The goal of the forum was to develop a means of promoting local control while not putting states at financial risk. The president also actively took part in the NGA's summer meeting, where on July 31 he announced his support for a compromise welfare proposal presented by Senate Majority Leader Robert Dole. He also announced that he had directed the HHS to provide "fast-track demonstration approval" to states with certain waiver requests.

Unfortunately, even when the policy-making process within the executive branch is operating smoothly and is perceived to be legitimate by those within it, opposition outside of the executive branch may keep the policy at hand from moving forward. Just as there is a strain toward agreement among members of the administration, there is a strain toward agreement within the Congress and also between the executive branch and Congress. Divisions between moderates and conservatives in the Senate made it difficult for Senator Dole to push the welfare bill through Congress. He did not succeed in doing so until September 19, and it was not until mid-October that House and Senate conferees convened to resolve the differences in the House and Senate bills.

As the debate in the Senate continued, support for Senator Dole's compromise by President Clinton and congressional Democrats began to fade. Support declined further following the release of a report by the OMB on November 8

Memorandum to the Chief of Staff Regarding the Status of Welfare Reform

December 18, 1995

MEMORANDUM FOR THE CHIEF OF STAFF

FROM: Bruce Reed

                Rahm Emanuel

SUBJECT: Welfare Reform Update

The Republicans have reached virtual agreement on a new welfare reform conference report. Their current plan is to bring it to the House floor on Wednesday and the Senate on Thursday. Unless Senate Democrats mount a filibuster or we find a way to engage in bipartisan negotiations, it could end up on the President's desk for veto before Christmas.

I. Summary

This latest conference report is designed to cause us maximum possible discomfort. It's not good enough to sign, but not enough to make it easy to explain our veto. It is actually better than the Senate bill on a few of our priorities (like child care), and because of add-backs and changes in the CBO baseline, the overall level of budget savings is lower than the Senate bill. But the new conference report still contains some obscure but important structural changes that we have strongly opposed, like two-tiered SSI benefits for disabled children and a block grant of certain foster care programs, as well as deep cuts in food stamps and benefits for legal immigrants.

So far, most Congressional Democrats are with us in opposing the current conference report. But the Blue Dogs may feel compelled to vote for it, and many Senate Democrats are concerned about how we make our case against the bill. Since the conference report has not yet been filed, Breaux is meeting with Roth tomorrow in a last-ditch effort to force bipartisan negotiations, and the Blue Dogs are meeting with Kasich and Shaw to insist on further improvements on welfare reform as part of the budget talks.

A. Overall Budget Savings: The original House bill saved $91 billion over 7 years, and the Senate bill $66 billion. The original conference report (vetoed as part of the reconciliation bill) was scored at $77 billion. The latest conference report saves $58 billion. Part of this reduction ($10 billion) is due to CBO's re-estimate of the baseline; most of the rest is due to add-backs in child care, child nutrition, child welfare, and SSI kids. In terms of budget cuts, the latest version is better than the Senate bill in some areas and worse in others—but because the overall number is lower, Republicans will argue that this bill is better than the Senate bill we endorsed. (CBO now estimates that the AFDC block grant in the conference bill will provide at least as much money over the 7 years as the entitlement.)

continued

suggesting that the Welfare Reform Act would result in one million more children living in poverty. Support finally evaporated when Congress linked the welfare reform proposal to contentious budget negotiations that ultimately led to a government shutdown. President Clinton vetoed the budget reconciliation bill containing the welfare provisions. In an attempt to embarrass the president, the House and

By comparison, the Coalition budget saves $46 billion on welfare, the Administration's Dec. 7th budget plan saves $39 billion, and the rough consensus from Democratic-wide negotiations this weekend was a savings target of $43 billion.

B. Child Care: The latest conference report is $1 billion better than the Senate bill on child care. That is still not as much as we think is necessary—the Coalition budget calls for $3+ billion—but we can no longer argue that the Republicans are cutting child care.

C. Child Nutrition: Lugar and Goodling agreed not to block grant school lunch, only to allow seven statewide demonstrations around the country. The level of child nutrition cuts in the conference report is now the same as in the Administration's budget.

D. Child Welfare: The conference report preserves the entitlement for maintenance payments, and no longer includes any big dollar cuts in child welfare. It does block grant foster care and adoption assistance (while maintaining baseline levels of spending), which we oppose—but they've made it harder for us to get much traction.

E. SSI Kids: This is the biggest political vulnerability of the new bill. It cuts SSI benefits by 25% for all but the most severely disabled kids—a cut of $3 billion more than the Senate (although $1 billion is returned to the states in a services block grant).

F. Food Stamps: The conference report cuts $26 billion, compared to $21 billion in the Senate and $19 billion in our current budget proposal. The state option to block grant food stamps is better than the Senate bill, but not as good as the original House proposal.

G. Immigrants: Again, the conference report cuts much more deeply than we would like—$15 billion on SSI for legal immigrants, compared to about $5 billion in our proposal and the Coalition's. Unfortunately, the Administration is almost alone among Democrats in fighting hard to reduce the size of the cuts in benefits for legal immigrants and in food stamps.

H. Medicaid: A recent version of the conference report ended the guarantee of health coverage for welfare mothers. If that provision remains in the bill, it may be our best argument for vetoing the bill. But the Republicans know that, and will probably fix it.

II. Strategy

The difference between our position and theirs is not enormous in budget terms—$58 billion vs. $43 billion. Our greatest challenge is persuading the Republicans that the long-term benefit of a bill becoming law outweighs the short-term advantage of forcing a veto. Breaux and the Coalition will approach the Republicans tomorrow with that message, as well as with the attached list of fixes which would force a bipartisan discussion and address most of our problems. If that effort fails, we should veto the bill on the grounds that Republicans are just playing budget politics rather than making a serious bipartisan effort at real reform.

Source: Domestic Policy Council, the White House

Senate resubmitted the welfare reform bill on its own. President Clinton vetoed the bill on January 9, 1996. He justified doing so by arguing that an acceptable bill must provide more funding for child care, health coverage for low-income families, requirements for state funding, and additional funding during times of economic downturn.

Shown on pages 136–137 is an information memorandum used during this period to inform the chief of staff of the policy debate in December of 1995. It underscores the political thinking of some of the president's key advisers at that time. It is an excellent example of a well-written information memorandum—except that it breaks the rule that information memoranda should not provide policy recommendations.

In the spring of 1996, the administration pursued a strategy of taking over the welfare reform initiative while emphasizing the inability of the 104th Congress to accomplish any significant policy goals. To demonstrate executive action, President Clinton used a meeting with the National Association of Counties in March as a platform to announce that he had approved waivers for 53 different welfare reform projects in 37 states, covering nearly 75 percent of all welfare recipients. The waivers were significant because they enabled states to act immediately, regardless of congressional action. Ultimately, waivers were granted to 45 states. In addition, the administration announced a series of executive actions to promote welfare reform. As we discussed in Chapter 4, the executive branch has several means of implementing policy directly. On May 4 President Clinton announced executive actions urging states to tighten eligibility of mothers on welfare. On June 18 he announced actions to strengthen child support enforcement through the implementation of a new federal system to track delinquent parents across state lines, he took executive action on teen pregnancy, and he took executive action on the earned income tax credit.

As a second step, the administration used speaking engagements by its senior members, radio addresses by the president and the State of the Union address as **bully pulpits** to publicize its actions and specify its position. For example, in the State of the Union address on January 23, President Clinton put the onus on Congress to send him a bipartisan bill and promised to "sign it immediately."[7] Health and Human Services Secretary Donna Shalala spelled out the administration's priorities while testifying before the Senate Finance Committee on February 28, 1996. She argued that the president would not support the National Governors' Association's welfare proposals unless they were modified to provide vouchers for children of parents removed from assistance, retained the entitlement status of child welfare services and food stamps, and included a fundamental revision of the issue of legal immigrants. On April 26, HHS Assistant Secretary Mary Jo Bane presented a new welfare bill from the administration to Congress, which she argued would promote work, encourage parental responsibility, and provide a safety net for children, all while saving $48 billion in seven years. Congressional Republicans responded by introducing a welfare reform bill modeled on the NGA proposal that made concessions to the president by promoting federal control of child protection and adoption programs and allowing legal immigrants who are not yet citizens to be eligible for cash welfare. In addition to these concessions, however, the congressional Republicans tied welfare reform to a bill that would give states control over Medicaid. President Clinton responded by calling the link to Medicaid a "poison pill." But then he surprised his Republican critics on May 18 when he used his radio address

---

[7] Jeffrey Katz, "Clinton's Changing Welfare Views," *Congressional Quarterly* (July 27, 1996), 2116.

to praise a new welfare plan proposed by Wisconsin that went beyond what they anticipated he would support. In an ironic twist of events, this action spurred the House of Representatives to take the unusual step of promoting a waiver by approving the "Wisconsin Only Bill." This allowed Wisconsin to put its plan into place, thus advancing the administration's goal of enabling states to take further action even though a bill had not moved through Congress.

The White House strategy succeeded. Freshman members of Congress urged their leadership to delink welfare from Medicaid, and on July 11 the Senate and House leadership announced their decision to split the welfare and Medicaid reform bills. White House spokesman Mike McCurry announced that, "We now stand on the verge of having a welfare proposal that can get bipartisan support and the president's signature." Although the president would seek some changes, they were not insurmountable obstacles to passage.[8] On July 16, as negotiations on the budget reconciliation package containing the Personal Responsibility and Work Opportunity Act began, President Clinton encouraged the process by announcing, "I think we have now reached a turning point, a breakthrough on welfare reform."[9] And, by August 1, the House and Senate conferrees had passed the final version of the bill.

The question at hand following the passage of the bill was whether the president would sign it. As it stood, the bill cut off welfare, Social Security, and food stamps to legal immigrants, and it did not provide child care necessities to mothers who had been on welfare and were cut off. The president valued all of these items highly. Bruce Reed fought hard to persuade the president to sign the bill, arguing that welfare reform was a process, not just a single piece of legislation and that it could be modified once passed. Dick Morris also pushed the president to sign the bill by citing recent polling results in which two identical samples of respondents were asked the same series of questions regarding support for spending on poor people and inner cities. In the first sample, the questions were asked without any bias; in the second sample, the question was asked with the caveat, "Please assume that Congress has passed and the President has signed a welfare reform bill requiring welfare recipients to work and setting up time limits for how long people can stay on welfare." The survey found that 65 percent of those who assumed welfare reform had passed supported spending on inner cities, while only half the others supported such spending.[10] Another public opinion survey indicated that vetoing the bill would transform a 15-point win for the president into a 3-point loss in a race with Dole for the presidency.[11] These polls clearly indicated strong public support for signing the bill. Liberal Democrats in the administration tried to counter the impact of these polls in a last-ditch appeal to convince the president to veto the bill.

---

[8] Ibid., 2116.

[9] Ibid., 2116.

[10] Dick Morris, *Behind the Oval Office: Getting Reelected Against All Odds* (Los Angeles: Renaissance Books, 1999), 303.

[11] Ibid., 300.

In order to make his decision, President Clinton called in senior advisers. Those who supported the bill included Vice President Gore and Bruce Reed; those who did not included Leon Panetta, George Stephanopoulos, and Donna Shalala. He asked each person in the room to voice any concerns, he listened to them, and then made his decision. On August 22, he signed the Personal Responsibility and Work Opportunity Act of 1996 into law and promised to seek changes to correct its greatest flaws. Not all members of the policy-making team supported his decision to sign the bill. In protest, Assistant Secretary for HHS Administration for Children and Families Mary Jo Bane and Acting Assistant Secretary of HHS Planning and Evaluation Peter Edelman resigned, citing concerns about the new welfare reform law.

Even with the passage of a bill, the administration's welfare reform goals were not yet achieved. After signing the bill, President Clinton began a strategy of publicizing the need for additional modification to the welfare policy and spurring Congress into action. These efforts began with the administration's use of the president's State of the Union address on February 4, 1997 to stress the importance of overturning the ban on aid to legal immigrants. President Clinton argued that, "To do otherwise is simply unworthy of a great nation of immigrants," and he called for an increase in spending, arguing that "no one can walk out of this chamber with a clear conscience unless you are prepared to finish the job."[12] He then used the fiscal 1998 budget proposal as a means of promoting an increase in spending to alter the restrictions regarding legal immigrants, Medicaid, food stamps, and the welfare-to-work component in the welfare reform law.

Borrowing strategy from the Republican Congress, President Clinton insisted that any budget deal would need to restore some welfare cuts. In contrast to the congressional failure to use a similar linkage to its advantage earlier—and largely because of the failure of Congress to negotiate a successful budget without closing down the government a year earlier—linking welfare reform to the increasingly bipartisan talks on balancing the budget helped to promote an agreement. The budget deal that was announced on May 2 restored $9.7 billion over five years for Social Security and Supplemental Security Income (SSI) benefits for a child with disabilities and Medicaid benefits to two-thirds of the legal immigrants who would have lost them. It also added $1.5 billion over five years to the food stamp program and provided $3 billion for state welfare-to-work programs.[13] Once the blueprint was established, budget reconciliation bills were negotiated by the House Ways and Means Committee, the House Education and the Workforce Committee, and the Senate Finance Committee, as well as by the House and Senate Agricultural committees which addressed food stamps provisions.

As the reconciliation bills were negotiated, the Clinton administration continued to use both its bully pulpit and Executive Orders to shape the outcome. In particular, Vice President Al Gore joined Senate Majority Leader Tom Daschle in publicly criticizing the House Ways and Means proposal to make certain legal

---

[12] "$13 billion in Welfare Cuts Restored," 1997 Congressional Quarterly Almanac (Washington, D.C.: Congressional Quarterly, Inc., 1997), 6–31, 6–32.

[13] Ibid.

immigrants ineligible even if they were disabled as an "extraordinary revocation" of the bipartisan budget blueprint. In addition, by executive action, President Clinton instructed the Labor Department to release guidelines applying a wide variety of federal laws, including the Fair Labor Standards Act, to recipients who were required to work under the new welfare law. This policy set federal minimum wages, overtime pay, and child labor and record-keeping requirements as well as requiring protection—such as unemployment insurance, the application of antidiscriminatory practices, and the Americans with Disabilities Act. Despite attempts by the Ways and Means Committee and the Education and the Workforce Committee to exempt welfare recipients from these provisions, pressure from the White House and the Senate succeeded in persuading committee members to capitulate.

On June 20 President Clinton sent a letter to Representative John Spratt, Jr., ranking member of the House Budget Committee, stating that he would veto a bill that did not follow the Senate version, restoring SSI and Medicaid benefits for legal immigrants. As a consequence, during final negotiations on the Senate floor, Frank Lautenberg of New Jersey offered an amendment to make immigrants who were legally in the United States as of August 22, 1996 eligible for SSI, regardless of when they become disabled. In the background of the bipartisan budget agreement, the amendment was passed by a voice vote with little discussion. In the House of Representatives, Republicans modified their minimum wage provisions. Ultimately, the revised bill met the administration's desire to extend SSI and Medicaid to legal immigrants, it provided funding to help states place long-term welfare recipients into the workforce, it continued Medicaid benefits for disabled children who had lost their SSI benefits, it increased spending on food stamps by $1.5 billion over five years, and it kept the policy that states must pay workfare recipients the federal minimum wage. As a consequence, the administration succeeded in using a budget reconciliation bill to correct what it saw as the greatest weakness of the welfare reform package. It succeeded in changing welfare as we knew it, and it even succeeded in modifying the final product so that it converged with the administration's priorities.

Conclusion: Making the Process Work

The development of a welfare reform policy during the early Clinton administration provides important insights into the nature of the policy-making process. In particular, it demonstrates that when the process is undirected or perceived to be ineffective or illegitimate, policy makers tend to diverge from regular channels of communication. In such circumstances, policy-making tools tend to be used to resolve disputes rather than to debate or promote policy options, and progress in policy formation, adoption, and implementation can be stalled. On the other hand, when the lines of authority and responsibility are clearly defined and participants have confidence that the process is an effective means of voicing concerns, support for the policy initiative will be broader and it is more likely that policy makers throughout the executive branch can be mobilized to promote its fruition.

In the welfare reform process, competing priorities—including healthcare reform, the crime bill, and balancing the budget—meant that even though President Clinton was personally engaged in welfare reform, he did not make welfare reform a clear priority in the first two years of his administration. As a result, rather than centralizing the authority and responsibility for guiding the policy-making process with a White House policy council, as he did with the economic plan, the president created a jointly administered task force co-led by an agency and the White House to study the problem. As a result, the process was bogged down in continual debate with no one accountable for bringing the process to closure. In the absence of clear accountability, the strain toward agreement among members of the task force was weak. The task force ultimately divided itself into two groups, reflecting the viewpoints of the two directors, orderly deputies meetings did not take place, memoranda to the president focused on policy minutiae and the resolution of disputes among members of the task force rather than more substantive policy matters, and some members of each group doubted that their viewpoints would gain a fair hearing with the president.

Ironically, joint leadership created a process that the participants considered unfair and illegitimate. As faith in the policy-making process broke down, members of the task force moved outside the process and used other means to communicate their viewpoints—such as communicating with the president directly or leaking information to the press. In essence, Senator Moynihan's criticism that the administration espoused an interest in welfare reform but was not getting anything done was correct; rather than being a result of a specific initiative to stall welfare reform, the lack of progress was due to a *breakdown of the process*. The tools and techniques described in the previous chapters can be used either to slow down the process or to keep it on track. When the tools are used to resolve disputes among policy makers rather than debate policy alternatives, they slow it down. In contrast, when they are used to advance a common agenda, they can keep the process working smoothly.

The second phase of welfare reform, in contrast, demonstrated how much more effectively the process can function when the policy initiative is given a mandate, when responsibility and authority are centralized in one entity, and when the policy tools and techniques are used to refine policy proposals and promote strategies aimed at bringing a particular policy to fruition. Once the DPC was given primary responsibility and authority for welfare reform, regular deputies' meetings were instituted, decision-making memoranda were used to evaluate policy alternatives and elucidate strategy, and other tools (including polling and the mobilization of the bully pulpit) were used to effectively publicize and promote the administration's objectives. It was much easier to achieve a consensus once authority and responsibility had been centralized in the DPC. In the end, all members of the task force and the senior White House staff did not agree with the president's decision to sign the Personal Responsibility and Work Opportunity Act of 1996. Despite this lack of agreement, however, the process enabled the participants to express their views and participate in the decision to sign and reform the Act. With a couple of minor exceptions, there was a consensus among the policy makers that the process, tools, and techniques worked effectively after 1994.

Key Terms

Bully Pulpit: The use of the prestige and unique access derived from someone's position—such as that of the president of the United States—to promote an agenda.

Consensus Proposal or Document: A document that the participants agree brings their viewpoints to the president's or chief decision maker's attention.

"Contract with America": A 1994 book prepared by the House Republican Leadership that outlined their legislative platform.

New Democrat: A term commonly applied to centrist and moderate Democrats who tried to reposition the Democratic party after the 1984 presidential election. President Bill Clinton closely associated himself with the New Democrat agenda during the 1992 presidential campaign.

SSI Benefits: Social Security and Supplemental Security Income (SSI) benefits for a child with disabilities.

Welfare Waivers: The pre-1996 welfare reform laws allowed states to petition the federal government for a waiver from Aid to Families with Dependent Children (AFDC) regulations in return for improving the welfare delivery systems to families in the petitioning state.

Review Questions

1. What are the primary lessons to be learned from the Clinton administration's efforts to reform welfare?

2. When was the Personal Responsibility and Work Opportunity Reconciliation Act signed into law by President Clinton?

3. What differentiates the early phase of the welfare reform policy process from Phase II?

CHAPTER 10

The Clinton Economic Plan

The Economic Plan and the Political Process

"It's the economy!" was the mantra of President Clinton and his staff during the 1992 campaign.[1] That slogan helped him win the election by directing public attention toward economic and domestic concerns—including an economic recession, historically high levels of people on welfare rolls, and a growing number of Americans with no health insurance—and away from military and international issues, where President George Bush had his greatest successes. Once in office, President Clinton made passage of his economic plan a top priority and fulfilled a campaign promise in creating a National Economic Council (NEC) to parallel the National Security Council (NSC) in importance and in structure. In comparison to the difficulties that characterized the first two years of policy making in welfare and healthcare reform (see Chapter 9), the development of the NEC and the 1993 economic plan are striking policy-making successes. We argue that the structure of the NEC and the policy-making processes it implemented helped to promote the development of the budget and the economic plan in the early Clinton White House. Indeed, as prominent scholars and practitioners have argued, the NEC and the budget process were "island(s) of effective White House process in the 'madhouse' of the early Clinton administration."[2]

---

[1] The success of this slogan also indicates how much budget matters have become part of the public arena. It is important to recognize that prior to the 1930s, most of the budget was devoted to executive departments and agencies. Since then, the portion going to public entitlement programs has risen dramatically as has public pressure on the OMB and the White House regarding budgetary priorities. For a discussion of the evolution of budgetary and economic policy making, see George C. Edwards III and Stephen J. Wayne, *Presidential Leadership: Politics and Policy Making*, 5th ed. (New York: St. Martin's/Worth Publishing, 1999), 433–472.

[2] I. M. Destler, *The National Economic Council: A Work in Progress*, Policy Analyses in International Economics, no. 46 (Washington, D.C.: Institute for International Economics, November 1996), 2; Jeffrey Birnbaum, *Madhouse: The Private Turmoil of Working for the President* (New York: New York Times Books, 1996); Jonathan Orszag, Peter Orszag, and Laura Tyson, "The Process of Economic Policy-Making During the Clinton Administration." Prepared for the conference on "American Economic Policy in the 1990s," Center for Business and Government, John F. Kennedy School of Government, Harvard University, Boston, Mass. June 27–30, 2001, 1–86.

This chapter analyzes how policy-making tools, techniques, and processes were used by members of the Clinton administration to develop an economic plan and budget that reflected its campaign promises and that would ultimately redefine economic strategy at the federal level. The evolution of President Clinton's 1993 economic plan into the 1994 budget can be divided into two phases.

During the first phase, the National Economic Council (NEC) was created and its role as the coordinating body responsible for developing the economic plan was legitimated. Throughout this period, there was a general perception among policy makers that the NEC and its Director Rubin were honest brokers who could provide access to the president.[3]

The second phase began after the president submitted the administration's budget to Congress. During this period, the size and frequency of meetings regarding the budget declined substantially. While the intensity of executive scrutiny of the budget process generally decreases at this point and does not return until Congress actually begins to vote on budget legislation, several key players, including the Treasury Department, felt excluded from what they perceived to be important ongoing budget debates. Consequently, the legitimacy of the process diminished and criticism of the economic plan from policy makers inside and outside of the executive branch increased. The Congress took advantage of this situation and succeeded in redefining the budget debate as one of tax increases and government spending. This put the Administration on the defensive and forced it to use a significant amount of its political capital to secure passage of its budget in the House and Senate. Unlike the inclusive and deliberative process managed by the NEC during the early development of the economic plan, efforts to secure its passage were managed in an economic **war room.** "War room" is the name for a rapid response operation that brings together representatives from every department into one room. While the war room was successful when used during the Clinton presidential campaign, it undercut the legitimacy of the administration's policy-making process and raised the political stakes of failure. (For further discussion, see pages 154–155)

The primary lesson from the economic policy-making process is that centralizing authority in the NEC was effective as long as there was a perception among policy stakeholders that it was an "honest broker" that could provide an effective and legitimate means for discussing ideas, developing consensuses, and expressing recommendations to the president regarding economic/budget, tax, and trade issues. The success in this regard set the economic/budget process apart from others, like healthcare, that were also given high priority status. Yet support of the economic/budget policy process was not uniform nor constant. When the NEC's role as an honest broker was questioned, or when policy makers felt excluded or unrepresented by the process, criticism of both the process and the policy grew.

---

[3] Although different in many other ways, the National Economic Council is similar to the Economic Policy Board established by President Gerald R. Ford in that both are examples of the multiple advocacy approach discussed in Chapter 1. For a comparison of the two, see Rudolph G. Penner, "The National Economic Council and the Economic Policy Board," in *Triumphs and Tragedies of the Modern Presidency: Sixty-Six Case Studies in Presidential Leadership*, ed. David Abshire (Westport, Conn.: Praeger, 2001), 140–142.

Phase I: The Economic Plan and the NEC

Economic and budgetary problems played a large role in President Bush's defeat in 1992. In addition to rising budget deficits of historic levels and the perceived need to request foreign assistance to pay for the cost of Operation Desert Storm and Operation Desert Shield, Congress had demonstrated a capability to reshape federal budget priorities with limited involvement of the executive branch by creating new revenue trends, altering entitlements, slashing defense, and capping domestic discretionary spending in 1990.[4] Seeking to monopolize on President Bush's weakness and avoid his economic pitfalls, Clinton focused on the economy throughout his campaign and began his economic planning well in advance of his inauguration. While volumes of memoranda were exchanged regarding various components of the budget, two events in particular defined the economic context in which the administration would have to act. The first was a domestic economic summit held December 14–15, 1992, with Alan Greenspan participating; the second was the release of projections by the CBO showing that the budget deficits would be much worse than President-elect Clinton's economic team had anticipated.[5] The domestic economic summit was crucial because it emphasized the link between deficit reduction, interest rates, and the investment and productivity growth that the Clinton administration wanted to pursue.

The Clinton economic team was skeptical of monetary policy and entered office with a plan to stimulate the economy through fiscal policy. Given this starting point, the domestic economic summit played a critical role in building a collective understanding of the link between fiscal and monetary policy. Despite the ongoing debate within the administration over a fiscal stimulus package, the December meeting set the foundation for two of President Clinton's major economic legacies: a recognition that there were real economic benefits to be gained from deficit reductions, and a gradual, difficult and fundamental shift from the use of Keynesian-style fiscal stimuli toward an increasing reliance on monetary policy and the manipulation of interest rates by the Federal Reserve to stimulate or slow the economy. In addition the public and congressional pressure to reduce the deficit was given further salience with the release of projections by the Congressional Budget Office (CBO) that showed a major deficit reduction package would be necessary to avoid reaching deficits of half a trillion dollars by the year 2000.

In light of the CBO announcements, Gene Sperling, a senior White House economic adviser who later chaired the NEC, sent a detailed information memorandum (see its Introduction on page 147) to President-elect Clinton on December 23, 1992, summarizing the core of a potential budget proposal and identifying some conflicting priorities that the administration would have to address in order to pursue the economic priorities it specified throughout the presidential campaign. (See Chapter 5 for a detailed discussion of memoranda.) Sperling's report summarized

---

[4] Lance LeLoup, "Budget Policy Transformation," in *Presidential Policymaking: An End of Century Assessment*, ed. Steven A. Shull (Armonk, N.Y.: M.E. Sharpe, 1999), 215.

[5] Congressional Budget Office, *The Economic and Budget Outlook, FY 1994–98* (January 1993), 38.

Introduction to Gene Sperling's Information Memorandum to the President-Elect

ECONOMIC OVERVIEW
Gene Sperling
December 23, 1992

INTRODUCTION

You have inherited a two-part challenge of historic proportions. On the one hand, the federal budget deficit threatens to keep capital costs high, drain savings needed to finance private sector investment, and prevent the United States from using fiscal and monetary policy to respond to future recessions. On the other hand, the United States also has a public investment deficit—particularly in lifetime learning and infrastructure. Either challenge by itself could be daunting but manageable. Both challenges together, with their contradictory elements (cutting the deficit, while increasing investment), amount to a formidable task.

While short-term and long-term decisions are linked together by a vision of investment-led growth and the need for a comprehensive strategy and message, it is still helpful to consider them separately.

The long-term challenge is to increase both public and private investment, so that the United States will enjoy faster productivity growth and a higher standard of living. We can't expect to finish this task or see all the results of a successful productivity-enhancing strategy, even within the next eight years. We can, however, make real progress. You have the capacity to get America back on track, and to create an ethic and understanding of the national imperative to invest in our people and our economic future.

Our short-term challenge is that we are not fully utilizing our current productive capacity. As a result, many Americans are unemployed, underemployed, and underpaid. Developing a short-term strategy involves an assessment of how the U.S. economy will perform over the next six to twelve months, instead of the next six to twelve years. Our capacity to ensure a stronger, investment-led recovery may be the economic challenge we face that will most affect the American people over your first term.

In the short-term, you must decide whether the economy needs a stimulus package, and if so, its size and shape. Furthermore, you have to decide how it should be linked thematically, strategically, and even legislatively with your long-term package.

For the long-term, this memo presents you with a Core Budget. The presentation of a Core Budget is designed to highlight the trade-offs you will have to consider in developing a five year budget. There are a number of unknowns, such as differing views on the feasibility of deep defense cuts or significant savings from improved management. The basic message of the Core Budget is that you can accomplish much of your investment agenda and achieve significant deficit reduction, without resorting to the most controversial options such as middle-class tax hikes or cuts in Social Security. However, if you want to pursue a more aggressive investment agenda, implement universal health care coverage, or reduce the deficit in half in five years, you will have to consider some of the more controversial budget deficit options.

Source: Office of the Presidential Transition, 1992.

the challenges associated with pursuing the president-elect's dual objectives of reducing the federal budget deficit on the one hand and reducing the country's "public investment deficit—particularly in life time learning and infrastructure"—on the other.[6] Indeed, the memorandum foreshadows many of the difficulties that the administration would have in pursuing the potentially contradictory goals of cutting the budget deficit while increasing investment without pursuing highly controversial options like middle-class tax hikes or social security.

Sperling's memorandum concluded by recommending that the president-elect make a major speech soon after the inauguration to demonstrate his commitment to tackle these difficult tradeoffs and to define the policy agenda by specifying administration priorities. In order to define these priorities, Robert Rubin and White House Chief of Staff–designate Thomas McLarty scheduled a meeting of President-elect Clinton's economic team on January 7 in Little Rock, Arkansas. This meeting defined the economic policy agenda and established budget priorities, including a decision to reduce the federal deficit by $145 billion.[7] In addition, it established the lead role of the nascent National Economic Council in the policy-making process and it set a tone that defined the management style Rubin and the NEC would use to effectively manage the first phase of budget development.[8]

Establishing the Management Role of the NEC

Rubin pursued a preemptive consultative management strategy in preparation for the January 7 meeting. He discussed the meeting's agenda with senior members of the economic team, he negotiated the particular points they intended to argue at the meeting, and then rehearsed their initial statements.[9] The meeting included senior players and many of their deputies, including the president-elect and the vice-president-elect, Lloyd Bentsen, Gene Sperling, Leon Panetta, Laura Tyson, Alice Rivilan, Alan Binder, and Lawrence Summers. During the meeting Rubin acted as both manager and facilitator. He defined the substance of the meeting broadly but kept it well structured. And, rather than presenting his own views, he emphasized his role in assuring the participants that they would have an opportunity to express their views and specify their priorities. As a result, despite differences in opinion regarding appropriate budgetary priorities, participants "uniformly found the process fair and productive. They knew how and where presidential policy was made, they knew they would be weighted in personally with their views, and they knew that Rubin would summarize them fairly."[10]

---

[6] Gene Sperling, "Economic Overview," Memorandum to the President (December 23, 1992), 1.

[7] I. M. Destler, The National Economic Council: A Work in Progress, Policy Analyses in International Economics, no. 46, (Washington, D.C.: Institute for International Economics, November 1996), 14.

[8] This meeting took place during the transition period before the NEC was formally established by an Executive Order.

[9] I. M. Destler, The National Economic Council: A Work in Progress, Policy Analyses in International Economics, no. 46, (Washington, D.C.: Institute for International Economics, November 1996), 14.

[10] Ibid., 14–15.

President Clinton's Economic Team

The Key Players
Secretary of the Treasury Lloyd Bentsen
Secretary of Labor Robert Reich
Office of Management and Budget:
   Leon Panetta, Director
   Alice Rivlin, Deputy Director
Council of Economic Advisers:
   Laura Tyson, Chair
   Alan Binder, member
   Joseph Stiglit, memberz
The National Economic Council:
   Robert Rubin, Director
   W. Bowman "Bo" Cutter, who managed the interagency process and international issues
   Gene Sperling, who led development of Clinton's campaign economic plan
   Sylvia Matthews, special assistant to Rubin and de facto NEC chief of staff

Rubin's strategy at the January 7 meeting was duplicated in the brokering role that he, Sperling, and W. Bowman Cutter created for NEC. As Cutter argued: " . . . the only way to achieve influence in the White House was to organize and manage a process through which issues get decided. If the process was perceived as fair and effective, agencies would accept it, come to use it, and perhaps even like it."[11] The legitimacy of the process rested on its ability to provide five primary services.[12] First, the NEC provided assurance that they would be able to participate in the process in basic ways: being invited to meetings, having their views heard, and being represented fairly. Second, the NEC provided a conduit for getting messages or issues of concern to the president. Third, the NEC was able to elicit a presidential decision or reading on an issue when it was needed. Fourth, it served as a source of economic information, including generating informational memoranda to the president on economic issues ranging from the political fallout of deficit reduction, to information about ongoing strikes, or the state of a local economy where the president was about to deliver speech. Finally, because economic policy was a principal focus for President Clinton, participating in economic policy decisions became important to most federal agencies. Many of these agencies sought direct access to the president in order to present their questions and solutions to him in the absence of contrary opinions and, when this was not possible, they often sought to coordinate amongst

---

[11] Ibid., 9.

[12] Interview with Mark Masur, October 24, 2000.

themselves to keep real choices away from the president so they could maximize their influence over parochial issues.[13]

Utilizing the NEC as a policy broker avoided unnecessary conflict with the Council of Economic Advisers (CEA), which was more focused on providing general economic analysis rather than policy development, and enabled Rubin to develop a mutually reinforcing working relationship with Laura Tyson at the CEA, who became director of the NEC in 1995. In order to avoid competition with other agencies that had process-oriented roles but whose chief responsibilities were the implementation of programs and policies—agencies like the Treasury Department, the NSC, the Office of the U.S. Trade Representative, and the Office of Management and Budget—Rubin made explicit efforts to identify himself as an advocate, representative, and guarantor of access to the president.[14] This latter role was particularly important because while the high degree of presidential involvement in the process meant that no single agency could dominate the process, it also meant that no agency could be left out. Rubin and the NEC became so adept at providing an honest forum for the discussion of ideas that it began to be used for issues that had only a partial connection to economic policy, such as the environment.

The NEC Process

As we spell out in Chapter 2, the NEC was established as a policy council with 19 members, including the president, vice president, ten cabinet secretaries and administrators of operating agencies, and six heads of staff in the White House and the Executive Office of the President. The core of the NEC consisted of the Assistant to the President for Economic Policy Robert Rubin and his staff. Between the January 7 meeting and the president's speech before a joint session of Congress on February 17, principals' meetings were held daily. The principals' meetings were led by Rubin and generally included the secretaries of Treasury, Labor, OMB, CEA, Commerce, and State, and the U.S. Trade Representative, and White House political and legislative people. Deputies' committee meetings, led by W. Bowman Cutter, met even more frequently. Cutter organized the NEC staff into "issue clusters"—including community development, international, markets and regulation, and science, technology and infrastructure that were intended to change as priorities shifted. The deputies' meetings served as primary forum for interagency discussion and were often characterized by brainstorming and policy debate.

Despite the distinction between principals and deputies, the general organization structure of the NEC was horizontal rather than vertical. Rubin and other senior members dealt directly with junior aides and encouraged them to speak out in the regular Monday evening staff meetings. He was seen by members of his staff and those in the broader policy community as an honest broker and a team player.

---

[13] I. M. Destler, *The National Economic Council: A Work in Progress*, Policy Analyses in International Economics, No. 46, (Washington, D.C.: Institute for International Economics, November 1996), 18.

[14] Ibid., 11.

Alan Cohen, who worked extensively on budgetary matters in the executive branch and at the Treasury Department, offered an often repeated comment from Rubin's staff that he possessed the rare capability of crediting people for their insights and praising people with interesting and insightful ideas.[15] One member of his staff described working in the NEC as follows. First, Rubin selected staffs who were knowledgeable about a wide range of issues and he tried to secure a large enough staff to cover all relevant issues for the administration. Second, he instilled a team mentality and used a consensus "no sharp elbows" approach to policy making. Third, rather than claiming credit for his staff's ideas, he acknowledged and encouraged the role of individual staff members. And fourth, he articulated a clear set of budgetary priorities, with budget discipline at the top.[16] Thus, while the objective of horizontal management was to create an institution that could react quickly to changing economic and political circumstances, it had the added benefit of breeding loyalty and respect for NEC.

The frequency and duration of the NEC policy meetings intensified in the three weeks prior to the February 17 address. The meetings took place in the Roosevelt Room of the White House and were often attended by President Clinton. The president was actively involved in the policy formation process and attempted to stimulate debates among the participants.[17] The meetings involved intense discussions and disagreements over a range of issues including investments and the stimulus package (supported by Reich, Sperling, and Commerce Secretary Ronald Brown) versus focusing on deficit reduction (supported by Bentsen, Panetta, and Rivlin), while others (including Director of White House Legislative Affairs Howard Paster and communications director George Stephanopoulos) argued against cuts that might diminish needed congressional support. In addition, unlike later policy processes, political advisers and consultants (including James Carville, Paul Begala, Stan Greenberg, and Mandy Grunwald, who had run the campaign's media strategy) were brought into the discussion. Both James Carville and Stan Greenberg argued that the president should do something "big" and "bold." Based on the results of survey data from focus groups (see Chapter 6), Greenberg argued, for example, that the public would support a broad deficit reduction program. Stephanopoulos and Begala opposed this strategy, arguing that the focus of the campaign had been on helping people rather than deficit cutting. Consistent with this viewpoint, the president agonized over budget cuts and taxes for the middle class and fought to promote investments promised in the campaign.

It is important to note the role of consultants during the early days of the White House. The majority of political consultants who had worked for Bill Clinton during the 1992 campaign had decided not to join the President's staff in 1993. These consultants saw the monetary advantage of keeping their private consulting operations intact and handling a number of clients besides the president. As a result, they were not involved in a number of the meetings and discussions that led to the development of the economic plan. Instead they were involved on an ad hoc

---

[15] Interview with Alan Cohen, October 17, 2000.

[16] Interview with Mark Mazur, October 24, 2000.

[17] Elizabeth Drew, *On the Edge* (New York: Simon and Schuster, 1994), 69.

basis, often giving their input at the end of the process rather than in the middle or beginning. This created problems for the policy councils. After weeks of negotiations between the agency members of the NEC, the political consultants would swoop in toward the end of the process and damage the consensus because they had not been included in prior discussions, either by their choice or the decision of the councils. Since they came into the game late, their objectives were often not fully informed by nor necessarily relevant to the focus of the policy. Later in President Clinton's first term, consultants were brought into the process earlier, and some, like Paul Begala, were actually hired onto the White House staff.

The outcome of the policy debates was an economic plan that focused on deficit reduction and $100 billion in new long-term investment in programs such as job training, rebuilding the nation's infrastructure, education, and promoting high technology (there was to be $60 billion in tax incentives and tax breaks for investment in high technology industries).[18] In addition, there were tax increases of $246 billion over five years (with the exception of the BTU [British thermal unit] energy tax, these increases mostly targeted couples earning $140,000 and above) and federal spending cuts of $247 billion. While the plan was criticized by Republicans who argued that the deficit reduction was too low and taxes were too high, the budget cuts, taxes, and investments proposed were compromises that reflected the collective judgment of the president and his economic team regarding what type of package would best fulfill the president's objectives and get through the Congress.[19]

Communicating and Marketing the Economic Plan

Recognizing that part of the program would be unpopular, and that the president would not initially be able to keep some of his campaign promises about the cuts, the economic team explored several funding options and employed a variety of strategies to market the plan and increase its viability (see Chapter 8 for a discussion of marketing techniques). For example, Panetta, Rivlin, Cutter, and Gore supported a cost-of-living freeze on Social Security, but Bentsen convinced the president that it would not be supported by Congress. Raising taxes on Social Security offered an alternative, but it would be unpopular. In order to increase the public's acceptance of the tax increases, the economic team decided to leak information that it was considering a cost-of-living adjustment (COLA) freeze for Social Security recipients. It intended to back down from the ensuing uproar and offer a Social Security tax increase as a more acceptable alternative.[20] In addition, in order to reduce the impact of negative stories in the press regarding tax increases, the economic team encouraged President Clinton to explain and justify his budget proposal—especially the lack of a middle-class tax cut—in an Oval Office address on February 15, two days before the presentation of his plan to Congress. Finally, to signal his endorsement of the economic plan, the

---

[18] Ibid., 73.

[19] Ibid., 74.

[20] Ibid., 69–70.

administration seated Federal Reserve Chairman Alan Greenspan between Hillary Clinton and Tipper Gore during the February 17 speech.[21]

Despite some modifications—including House and Senate Budget Committee decisions to cut the president's proposal by another $63 billion and freeze discretionary spending, which potentially threatened some of the president's investment plans—the House and Senate plans did not alter the president's basic emphasis of shifting from consumption to investment and deficit reduction.[22] On March 18, the House of Representatives approved the president's budget, by a vote of 243–183, with no Republican support.[23] The House also passed the president's stimulus program by a vote of 235–190. And, one week later, the Senate passed its own budget resolution, incorporating the president's program—also with no Republican support.

Phase II: Securing Passage of the Bill

Throughout the summer, opposition to the economic plan increased. Congressional opponents succeeded in shifting the message away from the promotion of investments and deficit reduction, to criticisms of the "tax and spend" strategies reflected in the energy tax and stimulus package. Although the NEC was not responsible for congressional politics, it failed to offer a solid rationale for the need for the stimulus, which proved to be unnecessary by the spring of 1993, nor did it anticipate the extent of opposition to the BTU energy tax. The deficit reduction bill was approved by the House Ways and Means Committee on May 13, but on May 27 the House passed the reconciliation bill only by six points, 219–213.[24] Faced with the prospect that the reconciliation bill might not be approved by the Senate, the Clinton administration altered its policy-making strategy. Rather than using the NEC as a facilitator and manager of meetings designed to air competing viewpoints and work out policy decisions, the administration adopted a war room strategy that it had developed during the 1992 campaign.

The war room strategy was effective during that campaign in responding quickly to changing circumstances and events. It was used multiple times during the early period of the Clinton administration, notably in the development of healthcare policy, and during the later phases of the 1993 economic plan. The war room strategy is, however, less representative than the typical NEC policy process. Rather than promoting a rational, calm, and consensus building process, it relies on the leadership of one relatively dictatorial person who can guide the operation to make rapid responses to situations. It also is inherently and intentionally reactive not proactive.

On page 154 is a memorandum from Paul Weinstein to senior Gore strategist Carter Eskew, during the 2000 presidential race describing how to set up a war room for the Gore campaign. The Gore campaign eventually created a war room

---

[21] Bob Woodward, *The Agenda: Inside the Clinton White House* (New York: Simon and Schuster, 1994), 139.

[22] Elizabeth Drew, *On the Edge* (New York: Simon and Schuster, 1994), 111.

[23] Ibid., 112.

[24] Ibid., 171.

The 1992 "War Room"

March 17, 2000

MEMORANDUM FOR CARTER ESKEW

CC: CHARLES BURSON   BILL KNAPP
                      LAURA QUINN   DAVID GINSBERG

FROM: PAUL WEINSTEIN

SUBJECT: **The 1992 "War Room"**

Per David's request, the following summarizes the operations of the "war room" during the 1992 campaign. In 1992, I served as one of Bruce Reed's deputies and as the policy staffer in the war room, where I was responsible for sign-off of all policy paper produced by the campaign. What I describe here is based on my first hand recollections.

Purpose

The purpose of the war room was to provide quick and coordinated rapid response to news events, attacks from the opposing campaign, and other situations that might arise during the course of the general election.

Size

The war room was staffed by roughly thirty individuals. Each office within the campaign—political, policy, opposition research, *Arkansas Record*, press, communications, scheduling, field, etc.—had a staffer in the room. The staffer was someone with decision-making authority, usually the head of the office or the deputy. Each office had a desk, with a computer, phone, modem in the room. At the center of this operation was James Carville, who served as the campaign's chief strategist. James literally sat in the center of the war room, he had a desk, a conference table and a couch. He and the director of war room operations, Ricki Seidman, coordinated the daily business of the room. Ricki had the final signoff on any paper produced by the war room staff. There was one staffer who served as the link to the campaign plane, and through her, and only through her, all paper was emailed or faxed to the point person on the plane.

The campaign's senior consultants also had a desk in the war room. Generally, the consultants spent roughly two to three days each week in Little Rock. The consultants who maintained desks in the war room included Stan Greenberg and Celinda Lake (pollster), Mandy Grunwald (media), Paul Begala (strategy), while others rotated in and out. The rest of the senior officials including Stephanopoulos, did not actually sit in the war room itself, but rather had offices down the hall. Across the hall from the war room sat the three policy offices—economic (Sperling), domestic (Wright), and foreign policy (Soderberg)—and the opposition research office. The close proximity of these offices to the war room was highly advantageous, since they helped produce the majority of campaign paper. Opposition research had roughly ten staffers and policy had about fifteen.

The war room also had two full-time writers/editors. These were not speechwriters, but rather individuals with excellent writing and communications skills who took the lead in drafting the documents with the considerable input and assistance of the policy and opposition research offices.

The war room had the best equipment available. There were three TV monitors in the center of the room which tracked news programs. VCRs were attached to all three TVs and were ready to record any important information. At the end of the day, a video news summary of the major network news shows was played for the staff. In addition, every staffer had his or her own personal computer (that was unusual at the time). The office had several printers, fax machines for ingoing and outgoing fascimiles, all the online research services (not much of an Internet existed). It also had the only direct email link to the campaign plane.

The plane served as an extension of the war room in some ways. A lead policy person, the press secretary, one of the consultants, and a speechwriter were always on the plane to serve as a link with the candidate. This link, and the interaction of all three with the war room was key to the success of the system, since these three individuals provided much of the "road feedback" on the documents that were being produced and what was needed. They also assisted in getting sign-off, when necessary, from the candidate.

Hours of Operation

The war room was operational 24 hours a day seven days a week from July of 1992 until election day. Sunday was the one exception, when staff were allowed to show up at noon. The day staff arrived at the office each morning at 7:00 am for Carville's morning meeting. It was during this meeting that the day's message and top priorities were set forth. At 7:00 pm, Carville would have a second meeting discussing the day's successes and failures, and previewing the next day's agenda. The day staff were required to stay until midnight. Two individuals served as the overnight staff. They would arrive at 8:00 pm and leave after the morning meeting. These two individuals were responsible for monitoring the overnight news programs and press, and any information about the Bush campaign. At the morning meeting they would report this information which was used to modify that day's message strategy.

Production of Documents

The main function of the war room was to produce rapid response documents. What triggered the production of such a document was usually either a news event or a Bush campaign attack. If we were responding to an attack from the opposition campaign, we tried to respond within one hour (the response process was actually timed by Seidman and Carville). Ricki Seidman would delegate a lead to draft the document usually from either the policy or the opposition research teams. They would work with one of the staff writers in putting together a document with the necessary information. If they needed any information from other offices, the staffer would go directly to the desk for that office in the war room. That person could provide the information, and give clearance for his or her office (at the beginning of the process Ricki would designate who in the war room needed to give clearance, since not every department needed sign-off). After a draft was produced, the consultants were given ten minutes to review. Then the info was sent to the plane, out to the regional press and field offices, to the DNC, and to all the major media outlets.

The war room, however, was responsible for producing more than just rapid response documents. It was also the sign-off point for any public document produced by the campaign, including issue papers, speeches, talking points, op-eds, etc.

The room, and Carville's conference table, served as the ad hoc meeting place for the consultants and other campaign officials.

The key feature that made the war room successful was that there was a representative of each of the main components of the campaign—from policy to opposition research to political—centrally located to produce and sign-off on documents immediately. Collectively, these staffers knew—or had immediate access to knowledge—about details and implications of the policy agenda of the candidate, the opposition's record and agenda, and other information critical to launch or respond to almost any criticism. Equally critical was the close proximity to the campaign's lead strategist to each core component of the campaign. This enabled the campaign to have a disciplined and timely message that was understood and reflected throughout the campaign.

Source: Private memorandum from Paul Weinstein to Carter Eskew, March 2000.

in the summer of 2000 and called it the "kitchen," due to its proximity to the kitchenette in the campaign headquarters.

In the 1993 budget process, the war room was managed by Deputy Treasury Secretary Roger Altman, with Ricki Seidman as his deputy. Members of the war room included the primary staff members of the NEC, Treasury, and Communications, as well as consultants including Begala, Greenberg, Grunwald, and Carville. The key objective of the economic team during this period was to secure sufficient votes in the House and the Senate to get the bill passed. To achieve this objective, the war room was directed to respond to any and all charges regarding the economic plan in the same news cycle. In addition, the economic team focused its efforts on those members of Congress whose votes were in question. For example, it worked to reassure the Black caucus that funds for investments and empowerment zones would be restored, and it reduced the energy tax to 4.3 cents a gallon to secure the vote of Max Baucus of Montana, who said that he would oppose any bill with a gas tax greater than that amount.[25] Once it became clear that Senator David Born would not support the bill, the team focused on securing the vote of at least one of the six Democratic senators who had opposed the bill in its early form—especially Senators Dennis DeConcini of Arizona, Richard Bryan of Nevada, Russ Feingold of Wisconsin, and Bob Kerrey of Nebraska.

As in the early phase of the process, the White House and the president played an active role. Clinton jogged with waivering senators, met with caucuses from the House of Representatives, met formally with senators, rallied the support of the business community, and made numerous phone calls. Ultimately, the Clinton administration narrowly achieved its objective: the House approved the bill by a vote of 218–216, and 51–50 in the Senate, with Al Gore breaking the tie. In the end, in light of the political climate, it was a significant achievement for President Clinton to harness Democratic votes for a deficit-reduction package in 1993. The final version of the bill reflected many, but certainly not all, of the initial aspects of the original economic plan; the best example was the defeat of the stimulus plan.

In terms of the policy-making process, it is important to understand that the role of the policy councils was still developing in 1993. This was the NEC's first test and it is generally considered a success, but the experience also showed that the institution was evolving. The creation of the NEC highlighted the historic trend of centralizing policy-making power in the White House. Furthermore, rather than controlling the policy apparatus through an ad hoc basis, the NEC provided a system for coordinating economic policy in a White House staff one-tenth the size of the smallest cabinet office on the council.

Although the NEC was a major step forward in the effort to create a legitimate policy-making process in the White House, it was undermined by the role of political consultants who freelanced around the process and by the use of campaign-style war rooms. War rooms were not effective policy-making operations. Rather than reflecting the give-and-take of competing opinions and ideas under the coordinating leadership of the NEC, policy changes in the war room were fought for and exchanged as needed to get the votes required for passage. The ultimate outcome was success, but the legitimacy of the process was undermined, and congressional support for the final product was weakened. It has been reported that the George W. Bush administration

---

[25] Ibid., 260–272.

has also made use of war rooms. For example, it created a type of war room to help secure passage of education reform legislation. Less use of the war room strategy, more coherence in the policy process, and greater consideration of Congress might have ensured that a more coordinated bill would have been adopted. However, compared to the healthcare plan, which was devised totally outside the policy-making apparatus, the 1993 economic plan was a major victory for the president and for those who believed in the role of the policy councils.

Conclusion and Lessons Learned

The purpose of this chapter is not to assess whether the economic plan of 1992 achieved its economic and political goals; rather it is to analyze how the various tools, techniques, and processes discussed earlier affected the outcome. It is clear from our discussion that the policy-making process was still evolving throughout 1993. Indeed, it would take another year and a change in the leadership of the White House staff before many of the processes and techniques we have discussed were fully embraced. Some of the delay was the result of a learning curve. A new, young staff trained in the combat environment of a campaign did not readily take to the more time-consuming and deliberate policy process required in government. Those who understood that the running of governments requires a system of consensus building eventually won out, but only after the weaknesses of the campaign style of governing became fully clear.

The NEC and the system of decision making it put into place was the exception, not the rule, during the early days of the administration. And even with all of Bob Rubin's influence, it took time for everyone in the executive branch to buy into the NEC's policy-making process. As this case study shows, the NEC had early success in putting together a sensible process, but the forays into policy making by political consultants, pollsters, and media advisers—who were not accountable to the system and worked outside of the government—occasionally held back the system. As a result, some of the economic policies put forth by the president had neither a sound economic rationale nor political support. This comment is not intended to negate the importance of political consultants. These individuals provide useful services. However, like any other form of information, the information consultants provide must be integrated into an accepted process. During the second term of the Clinton-Gore administration, consultants and the information they provided were included in the policy-making processes run by the NEC and DPC. Their information was used early in the process rather than at some last minute. The consultants also avoided—though not completely—end runs around the policy councils to the president directly.

Well-run policy-making processes do not guarantee good decisions. But a rational, inclusive policy-making system does help to ferret them out and make them more acceptable to a wide range of people. One need only to look at the 1994 Clinton healthcare plan, which was run outside the NEC and the DPC policy-making processes, to understand the dangers of ad hoc policy making. Despite some difficulties with certain aspects of the policy—especially the fiscal stimulus and the BTU tax—the Clinton-Gore administration created a broad and lasting consensus on three aspects of the national economy:

1. The need for more fiscal responsibility combined with a decline of reliance on Keynesian-style fiscal stimuli and an increase in the reliance on the Federal Reserve and its use of monetary policy to maintain national economic health (understanding the concert between fiscal and monetary policy was one of the great lessons learned by the Clinton administration)
2. The importance of free trade reflected in the pursuit of the North American Free Trade Agreement (NAFTA) and the inclusion of China in the World Trade Organization (WTO)
3. A recognition that incremental improvements and investments in education, Head Start, healthcare, and welfare reform were better than nothing.

While it did not succeed in developing a Marshall Plan–approach to solving social and economic problems, these changes had a profound effect on the nation's economy and the accepted role of the federal government in economic affairs.

Key Terms

Deputies' Committee Meetings: Interagency meetings in which individuals designated by the heads of participating agencies meet to discuss and prepare options on policy issues. These meetings differ from principals' meetings where decisions on policy issues are made.

War Room: A rapid response operation that brings together representatives from every department into one room. While effective for very short and defined periods of time, a war room strategy of policy making does not promote calm, rational decision making or consensus building. A war room is generally led by one relatively dictatorial person who can guide the operation to make rapid responses to situations. It is inherently and intentionally reactive, not proactive.

Review Questions

1. Name two events that defined the economic context in which the Clinton administration devised its 1993 economic plan. Why were they important? How did they affect the policy-making process?

2. What was the importance of the December 1992 memo on the "Core Budget" written by presidential adviser Gene Sperling?

3. What are the five primary services the NEC provides to others in the policy-making process?

4. Who were the key players on President Clinton's economic team in 1993?

5. What role did political consultants play in the policy debates over the 1993 economic plan?

6. What is a "war room"? What are its strengths and weaknesses?

CHAPTER 11

Desert Shield and Desert Storm

Security Crises and the Political Process

In the previous two chapters, we showed that centralizing authority, responsibility, and accountability for a particular policy in a policy council can enhance policy process legitimacy; it proved to be a turning point for welfare reform and a primary reason for the success of the NEC. At the same time, however, these cases suggest that the political benefits of centralization can be undermined if key stake holders believe that their views are not being expressed to the president or those responsible for policy development.[1] During the development of welfare reform and the 1993 economic plan, the level of political support for each policy was highest when stake holders felt that they were part of the process, and it declined when they questioned their ability to voice their opinions and concerns through the established channels.[2]

Policy-making processes developed during crises often differ from those used in noncrisis situations.[3] Especially in cases where there is a potential for military

---

[1] For a discussion of the trade-offs involved with empowering the president in foreign policy see Bert A. Rockman, "Reinventing What for Whom? President and Congress in the Making of Foreign Policy," *Presidential Studies Quarterly* 30, no. 1 (March 2000): 133–154.

[2] While Congress and the public generally accept presidential leadership in foreign affairs, they do not always support what the president has done. Examples range from President Wilson's efforts to promote the League of Nations, to President Nixon's overture to the People's Republic of China, to President Clinton's decision to stabilize the Mexican peso during a currency crisis in 1995.

[3] Political scientists have debated whether U.S. presidents receive more support from Congress in foreign than domestic affairs and can, therefore, expect to wield more influence in foreign than domestic policy making. See: Aaron Wildavsky, "The Two Presidencies," *Trans-Action* 4 (1966): 7–14; Lance T. LeLoup and Steven A. Shull, "Congress versus the Executive: The 'Two-Presidencies' Reconsidered," *Social Science Quarterly* 59 (1979): 504–719; Steven A. Shull, ed., *The Two Presidencies: A Quarter-Century Assessment* (Chicago: Nelson Hall, 1991), and Lee Sigelman, "A Reassessment of the Two Presidencies Thesis," *The Journal of Politics* 41 (1979): 1195–1205. Critics of this view include: George C. Edwards III, "The Two Presidencies: A Reevaluation," *American Politics Quarterly* 14 (1986): 247–263, and Richard Fleisher, Jon R. Bond, Glen S. Krutz, and Stephen Hanna, "The Demise of the Two Presidencies," *American Politics Quarterly* 28 (2000): 3–25.

action, policy making tends to be more centralized and the number of participants within and outside of the executive branch tends to be more limited than would otherwise be the case.[4] Consequently, one might expect the policy-making processes used to formulate responses to military actions like Iraq's invasion of Kuwait in 1990 to be different from those developed to address the welfare and budget issues presented in previous chapters.[5] Furthermore, one might expect stake holders within and outside of the executive branch to be more tolerant of a reduction in access to key decision makers than would otherwise be the case.[6] Policy making during Desert Shield and Desert Storm suggests, however, that procedural legitimacy is important in both crisis and noncrisis conditions.

The policy-making process used for formulating a response to Iraq's invasion and occupation of Kuwait on August 2, 1990 was highly centralized in a core group of decision makers known as the **"group of eight"** or the **"war council."** The core group included President George H. W. Bush, Vice President Dan Quayle, Chief of Staff John Sununu, National Security Adviser Brent Scowcroft, Secretary of Defense Richard Cheney, Chairman of the Joint Chiefs of Staff Colin Powell, Secretary of State James Baker, and Deputy Adviser on National Security Affairs Robert Gates.[7] The heavy reliance on a small group of core advisers is a common characteristic of decision making in crisis situations.[8] Indeed, Bush's reliance on his so-called war council during the Gulf War was similar to John Kennedy's use of his Executive Committee during the Cuban Missile Crisis, and Lyndon Johnson's use of the "Tuesday lunch group" during the Vietnam conflict.[9]

Prominent scholars have argued that in contrast to the management style he used in other policy arenas, there is little evidence that President Bush sought

---

[4] For a review of the decision-making and presidential decision-making literature in the area of national security, see William Newmann, "Causes of Change in National Security Processes: Carter, Reagan, and Bush Decision Making on Arms Control," *Presidential Studies Quarterly* 31, no. 1 (March 2001): 69–103.

[5] The rhetoric used by the president to define the issues at stake often plays a significant role in promoting and managing crisis situations. See for example Denise M. Bostdorff, "The Presidency and Promoted Crisis: Reagan, Grenada, and Issue Management," *Presidential Studies Quarterly* 21, no. 4 (Fall 1991): 737–750.

[6] The framers of the Constitution placed control over the initiation and authorization of war in Congress, however, war powers—particularly in crisis situations—have increasingly shifted to the executive. Despite efforts to restore congressional authority over the use of force in the 1970s, the executive branch has largely usurped the power to make war from Congress and it has done so without a significant challenge from the judiciary. See Louis Fisher, *Presidential War Power* (Lawrence, Kan.: University Press of Kansas, 1995).

[7] For a review of the role of the vice president during the crisis, see Paul G. Kengor, "The Role of the Vice President during the Crisis in the Persian Gulf," *Presidential Studies Quarterly* 24, no. 4 (Fall 1994): 783–807.

[8] Robert Art, "Bureaucratic Politics and American Foreign Policy," John Oneal, "The Rationality of Decisionmaking During International Crises," Jonathon Bendor and Thomas Hammond, "Rethinking Allison's Models," *American Political Science Review* (June 1992): 301–322; Andrew Bennett, "Models of Crisis Decision-making and the Experience in the 1990–1991 Gulf War," conference paper prepared for the Annual Meeting of the American Political Science Association, Chicago, September 1992, 3–4.

[9] James P. Pfiffner, "Presidential Policy-Making and the Gulf War," in *The Presidency and the Persian Gulf War*, eds. Marcia Lynn Whicker, James P. Pfiffner, and Raymond A. Moore (Westport, Conn.: Praeger Publishing, 1993), 7. For a reassessment of the groupthink dynamic during the Johnson administration, see Kevin V. Mulcahy, "Rethinking Groupthink: Walt Rostow and the National Security Process in the Johnson Administration," *Presidential Studies Quarterly* 25, no. 2 (Spring 1995): 237–250.

to promote debate among competing viewpoints when formulating his policy decisions during the Gulf War.[10] While the NSC served as the primary coordinating body for policy making and deliberation, members of the President's war council had privileged access and input into policy decisions.[11] Some scholars have argued that the homogeneity and solidarity of President Bush's inner circle were essential components of the success of the Persian Gulf war.[12] Yet, because the president did not rely on standard NSC procedures, even those in Bush's war council were occasionally surprised by important policy developments—including the decision to make the liberation of Kuwait a priority of U.S. policy, the decision to double U.S. troops in October of 1990, and the decision to end the containment strategy using sanctions and to rely instead on a military strategy in November of 1990.

The objective of this chapter is not to evaluate the policy decisions that President George H. W. Bush made during Desert Shield and Desert Storm. Rather, it is to examine how the tools, techniques, and processes discussed in the earlier sections operate in a highly centralized and relatively closed policy-making environment.

Responding to the Crisis

There were two turning points in the policy-making process during the Gulf Crisis: (1) the initial crisis response to the invasion of Kuwait in August of 1990 and (2) the noncrisis decision to double U.S. forces and pursue a military response in lieu of economic sanctions in October and November. We argue that a reliance on a highly centralized and relatively closed decision-making process in each situation reduced support for the chosen policies.

President George H. W. Bush centralized decision making during the Gulf Crisis in the National Security Council (NSC) and a small core group of top decision makers known as his war council. As in the previous cases (see Chapters 9 and 10) the principal decision makers relied heavily on the work of the policy councils' deputies' committee, which was responsible for drafting key memoranda and framing policy issues.[13] The NSC deputies committee was chaired by Brent Scowcroft's deputy at the NSC, Robert Gates, and it included staff from the Department of State, the Department of Defense (DOD), the Joint Chiefs of Staff (JCS), the

---

[10] James P. Pfiffner, "Presidential Policy-Making and the Gulf War," in *The Presidency and the Persian Gulf War,* eds. Marcia Lynn Whicker, James P. Pfiffner, and Raymond A. Moore (Westport, Conn.: Praeger Publishing, 1993), 7.

[11] Cecil V. Crabb and Kevin V. Mulcahy, "George Bush's Management Style and Operation Desert Storm," *Presidential Studies Quarterly* 25, no. 2 (Spring 1995): 256–259.

[12] Ibid., 250–265.

[13] Lauren Holland, "The U.S. Decision to Launch Operation Desert Storm: A Bureaucratic Politics Analysis," *Armed Forces and Society,* vol. 25, no. 2 (Winter 1999): 222.

Central Intelligence Agency (CIA), the Treasury Department, the attorney general's office, and occasionally other agencies.[14] While a general consensus existed among these policy makers regarding the need to respond to Iraq's invasion of Kuwait, there were substantial disagreements over how best to define the problem, what objectives should take priority, and how best to achieve them. In particular, there were major disputes over the objectives of U.S. involvement, the buildup of military forces, the likelihood and timing of military action versus the viability of the policy of containment using economic sanctions, and the need to secure congressional approval.

The first set of decisions—to commit U.S. troups to the defense of Saudi Arabia and the liberation of Kuwait—took place during a period of intense crisis and uncertainty from August 2 through August 5. Under severe time constraints, the administration was responding to a clear act of aggression against a U.S. ally that possessed a large quantity of strategic resources upon which other allies relied. Under crisis circumstances like these, the ability to consult with others is generally limited and the tendency for decision making to become centralized is strong. In contrast, the second set of decisions—to double U.S. forces and pursue a military option in lieu of relying on economic sanctions—was not made under the same restrictive conditions. These decisions were made in October and November without time or informational constraints that characterized the decisions made during the first week of August. Yet, they were also made using a highly centralized decision-making process, without reaching a consensus among executive branch players and without congressional consultation or permission. Indeed, the announcement of the troop increase was strategically delayed until after the November 6 elections. Failure to use a more representative policy-making process in both cases resulted in criticism and conflicting actions taken by key participants that complicated the process and potentially undermined the policy decisions.[15]

The Initial Response

On August 1, immediately following confirmation that an Iraqi invasion of Kuwait was underway, Brent Scowcroft convened an interagency deputies' committee directed by the NSC to assess the situation and develop an initial response.[16] The deputies' committee agreed to recommend a series of measures that could be quickly taken, including freezing Iraqi and Kuwaiti assets in the United

---

[14] Ibid.

[15] Robert Spitzer, "The Conflict Between Congress and the President Over War," in *The Presidency and the Persian Gulf War*, eds. Marcia Whicker, James Pfiffner, and Raymond Moore (Westport, Conn.: Greenwood Publishing, 1993): 34–35.

[16] George Bush and Brent Scowcroft, *A World Transformed* (New York: Knopf, 1998): 304.

States, moving a squadron of F-15s to Saudi Arabia (pending Saudi approval), and securing a condemnation of the invasion by the United Nations Security Council (UNSC). In response to these recommendations, White House counsel Bowden Gray wrote a set of Executive Orders (see the box) freezing the assets that the president signed the next morning. In addition, U.S. UN Ambassador Thomas Pickering negotiated with members of the Security Council which voted 14–0 in favor of UNSC Resolution 660, condemning Iraq's aggression, demanding that it withdraws its troops from Kuwait, and demanding that dispute is resolved through negotiations.[17]

Summary of Executive Orders

12722	2 August 1990. Froze Iraqi assets and prohibited transactions with Iraq.
12723	2 August 1990. Froze Kuwaiti assets and prohibited transactions with Kuwait.
12724	9 August 1990. Strengthened the previous orders freezing assets and prohibiting trade with Iraq.
12725	9 August 1990. Strengthened the previous orders freezing assets and prohibiting trade with Kuwait.
12727	22 August 1990. Ordered to active duty selected elements of the Reserves.
12728	22 August 1990. Allowed the president to suspend promotions, retirement, or separation of members from the Armed Services.
12734	14 November 1990. Allowed the president to redirect military construction funds to priority projects in the Gulf.
12742	8 January 1990. Gave the president the power to direct industry to produce necessary war-related goods over domestic products.
12743	18 January 1991. Allowed the president to call up the Reserves for up to 24 months if needed.
12744	21 January 1991. Designated the Persian Gulf region as a war zone for the purposes of the troops tax extensions and exemptions.
12750	14 February 1991. Designated the Persian Gulf region as the Persian Gulf Desert Shield area for tax purposes.
12751	15 February 1991. Authorized the secretary of Veterans Affairs to provide healthcare for wounded personnel from the Gulf Crisis.

Source: Andrew Leyden, *Gulf War Briefing Book: An After Action Report* (Grants Pass, Ore.: Hellgate Press, 1997), 107.

---

[17] Ibid., 414.

After its immediate actions on August 1 and 2, the administration's early policy response to Iraq's invasion was ostensibly developed between August 2 through August 5 in a series of NSC meetings. Yet, while the decision-making process remained formally centered in the National Security Council, actions by the president and individual members of the war council at key turning points in the evolution of U.S. policy suggest that the NSC did not play a role comparable to that of the NEC during the development of Clinton's economic plan. For example, impromptu remarks by the president on August 5 suggest that he was operating without the advice of the NSC. While it is often difficult to tell whether such remarks are mistakes or intentional indications of U.S. policy decisions, they can give the impression of disorder in the policy-making process, they can suggest that certain individuals have privileged access to the president, and they can send mixed signals about U.S. intentions or policies abroad.

For example, during the NSC meeting on August 4 at Camp David, policy debates centered around prioritizing U.S. objectives and determining what military options were appropriate. A consensus was reached that the first objective was keeping Saddam out of Saudi Arabia.[18] There were discussions about oil, ground troops, air power, Operations Plan 90-1002, and the security of Saudi Arabia, but no specific decision memorandum or options paper was or had been written that specified the administration's goals and their implications.[19] However, when returning from Camp David on August 5, reporters asked about the U.S. response and President Bush answered:[20]

> I am not going to discuss what we're doing in terms of moving forces, anything of that nature. But I view it very seriously, not just that by any threat to any other countries, as well as I view very seriously our determination to reverse this awful aggression. And please believe me, there are an awful lot of countries that are in total accord with what I've just said, and I salute them. They are staunch friends and allies, and we will be working with them all for collective action. This will not stand, this aggression against Kuwait.

The statement implies that U.S. objectives included reversing the Iraqi invasion of Kuwait in addition to deterring an attack against Saudi Arabia and defending Saudi Arabia if it was invaded. Such an interpretation implies objectives that go well beyond those discussed or debated during the NSC meetings that had taken place.[21] On August 8, President Bush attempted to qualify his statement, arguing that while the United States would seek the immediate, unconditional, and complete withdrawal of Iraqi forces from Kuwait, the U.S. military would be used only for the "military objec-

---

[18] George Bush and Brent Scowcroft, *A World Transformed* (New York: Knopf, 1998), 328.

[19] Bob Woodward, *The Commanders* (New York: Simon and Schuster, 1991), 259–260.

[20] George Bush and Brent Scowcroft, *A World Transformed* (New York: Knopf, 1998), 332–333.

[21] Ibid., 333; see also Woodward, *The Commanders* (New York: Simon and Schuster, 1991), 260.

tive" of defending Saudi Arabia and other friends in the Gulf. However, the decision had effectively been made and announced.[22] After several additional impromptu comments of this type, Bob Gates and Brent Scowcroft began joining Bush on his campaign stops to field questions related to the Gulf.[23]

In addition, failure to use a more accessible process frustrated several top policy makers some of whom then tried to sidestep the process to make their views heard. One example of this involves actions taken by Secretary of Defense Cheney when he became dissatisfied because, despite ostensibly being in charge of defense policy, he did not feel that his views or preferred options were given sufficient attention in the NSC meetings.

On August 2, during the first NSC principals' meeting following the invasion, CIA Director William Webster provided an intelligence briefing summarizing Iraqi actions, Robert Kimmitt summarized diplomatic actions in the United Nations Security Council, and Treasury Secretary Nicholas Brady presented an analysis of the potential oil profits that Iraq would receive from Kuwait production and the implications of a potential Iraqi incursion into Saudi Arabia.[24] The participants defined the issues at hand in terms of access to oil. They also identified the primary U.S. policy objectives as preventing Iraq from selling oil and blocking any effort it made to invade Saudi Arabia. CENTCOM Commander General Norman Schwarzkopf presented two military options for achieving these objectives. One involved retaliatory strikes by carrier-based aircraft, the other involved the execution of Operations Plan 90-1002 which had been designed earlier for the general defense of the Saudi peninsula.[25] The plan called for a massive ground and sea assault involving 100,000–200,000 troops and was expected to take several months to implement. No decision was made regarding these two options.[26]

According to Bob Woodward's account of the meeting, Secretary of Defense Cheney was dissatisfied because he believed that the NSC briefing failed to provide the president with a full range of military options—especially the use of air and sea power to conduct immediate or surgical strikes against Iraq.[27] Given what he saw as a failure of the NSC process, Secretary Cheney ordered Admiral Bill Owens and Air Force Colonel Garry Trexler to generate additional options involving the immediate use of sea and air power, including the potential use of

---

[22] Bob Woodward, *The Commanders* (New York: Simon and Schuster, 1991), 277.

[23] George Bush and Brent Scowcroft, *A World Transformed* (New York: Knopf, 1998), 389.

[24] Lauren Holland, "The U.S. Decision to Launch Operation Desert Storm: A Bureaucratic Policies Analysis," *Armed Forces and Society*, vol. 25, no. 2 (Winter 1999): 222.

[25] Bob Woodward, *The Commanders* (New York: Simon and Schuster, 1991): 228.

[26] House Armed Services Committee, *Defense for a New Era: Lessons of the Persian Gulf War* (US GPO, 1992), 84, cited in Andrew Bennett, "Models of Crisis Decision-Making and the American Experience in the 1990–1991 Gulf War," conference paper prepared for the Annual Meeting of the American Political Science Association, Chicago, September 1992.

[27] Bob Woodward, *The Commanders* (New York: Simon and Schuster, 1991), 234–236.

surgical air strikes—which JCS Chairman Powell opposed.[28] By thus **"pulsing the system"**—using informal ties to sample various services for options—Secretary Cheney bypassed the NSC process and sidestepped the Joint Chiefs of Staff and its competing viewpoint.[29]

We have argued that going outside the policy-making process undermines the procedural legitimacy of the process and increases the likelihood that those excluded will challenge the outcome regardless of the policy chosen. Consistent with this viewpoint, when he learned of their activities, JCS Chairman Powell chastised Owens for "freelancing out of this office."[30] He demanded that "all information and options for the services to the Secretary come through him and the Joint Chiefs" and he argued that all chiefs and services in the JCS were to act together by reaching a consensus rather than promoting individual service-based solutions. The fact that Powell and Cheney disagreed on the appropriate strategy for responding to Iraq is not particularly important. Instead, the primary lesson from this exchange is that when the process fails to provide a means for participants to express their viewpoints and engage in debates about options they feel are important, even very senior policy makers are likely to go outside existing channels.

The Delicate but Vital Matter of Inclusion

An inclusive process is essential even when the issue at hand involves military conflict. This sentiment is reflected in Colin Powell's assessment of the role of the NSC in the policy-making process during the Reagan administration. He argued:[31]

> We must make sure that all the relevant departments and agencies play their appropriate role in policy formulation. We must make sure that all pertinent facts and viewpoints are laid before the president. We must also make sure that no Cabinet official completes an "end run" around other NSC principals in pushing a policy line on which they too have legitimate concerns.

In the case of Iraq, maintaining political support for his policies was important because even though the policy-making process was highly centralized, President Bush remained dependent on others in the executive branch to promote and implement his policy decisions. For example, as much as President Bush and Secretary of Defense Dick Cheney tried to circumvent Powell's authority during the early deliberations over military options, they relied on him

---

[28] Ibid., 234–236, 239.

[29] Ibid., 235.

[30] Ibid., 238–239.

[31] Colin L. Powell, "The NSC System in the Last Two Years of the Reagan Administration," *Presidential Studies Quarterly, Proceedings* 6 (1989): 206. Cited in George C. Edwards III and Stephen J. Wayne, *Presidential Leadership: Politics and Policy Making* (New York: St. Martin's/Worth Publishing, 1999), 295.

to prepare the military force that would determine the success of the war against Iraq, just as Powell relied on General Schwartzkopf to implement the plan.[32] The president tried to overcome the legitimacy deficiencies of his policies throughout the conflict by securing the backing of the United Nations and the Desert Shield and Desert Storm coalition members. He also sought to rebuild his credibility with Congress by seeking congressional endorsement in support of UN Resolution 678 authorizing the use of force before taking offensive action. To achieve these objectives, Bush relied heavily on the efforts of *all* members of his administration to promote his policy and secure support for his policy from each of these groups.

On September 16, stories appeared in the *Washington Post* and the *Los Angeles Times* (reproduced in an accompanying box, pages 168–171) in which Air Force Chief General Michael Dugan leaked information about U.S. objectives and strategies in the Gulf.[33] In particular, the articles stated that the Joint Chiefs of Staff had decided that air power would be critical and that a single military service (the air force) would be the driving force in the U.S. response to Iraqi actions. In addition to promoting a policy-making and operational strategy that the chairman of the JCS disagreed with—and neither he, nor Cheney or Scowcroft was prepared to support—the article provided details about the deployment of U.S. forces in the region and assessed their readiness to enter battle. None of the central decision makers had been notified in advance that the stories were forthcoming. In response, with President Bush's clearance, Cheney relieved General Dugan of his command.

In this example, a stake holder felt that the NSC process had not given his agency's preferences (air power over ground forces) adequate consideration. As a consequence, he used the press to deliver his policy preference to the president. This backfired in two ways. First, Air Force Chief of Staff General Michael Dugan was removed from further participating in the process. Second, it provided potentially damaging information about U.S. forces on the ground.

This example highlights how mid-level policy officials can capitalize on disagreements at the highest levels in order to sabotage policy. Finally, this episode demonstrates that centralizing the process without providing a conduit for other stake holders to express their views and concerns can be counterproductive. Far from setting a rational, cohesive policy at the top level, the key advisers felt that the process gave the president a limited set of options. Furthermore, key stake holders were alienated or bypassed and, as a result, either inadvertently or intentionally, undermined the process.

---

[32] Lauren Holland, "The U.S. Decision to Launch Operation Desert Storm: A Bureaucratic Politics Analysis," *Armed Forces and Society*, vol. 25, no. 2 (Winter 1999): 221.

[33] Rick Atkinson, "U.S. to Rely on Air Strikes if War Erupts," *The Washington Post* (September 16, 1990), A1; "Top AF General Bounced: Dugan Told Press of Gulf Bomb Plans," *Los Angeles Times* (September 17, 1990), part P, 1, 6.

Policy Leak to the *Washington Post* and the Washington Response

Excerpt from Rick Atkinson, "U.S. to Rely on Air Strikes if War Erupts," *The Washington Post* (September 16, 1990), A1.

The Joint Chiefs of Staff have concluded that U.S. military air power—including a massive bombing campaign against Baghdad that specifically targets Iraqi President Saddam Hussein—is the only effective option to force Iraqi forces from Kuwait if war erupts, according to the Air Force chief of staff, Gen. Michael J. Dugan. "The cutting edge would be in downtown Baghdad. This [bombing] would not be nibbling at the edges," Dugan said in an interview. "If I want to hurt you, it would be at home, not out in the woods someplace."

Although U.S. ground and naval forces would play a substantive role in any military campaign, Iraq's huge army and tank force means "air power is the only answer that's available to our country" to avoid a bloody land war that would probably destroy Kuwait, Dugan said. That view, he added, is shared by the other chiefs and the commander of U.S. forces in the Persian Gulf region, Gen. H. Norman Schwartzkopf.

Consequently, the United States has in five weeks assembled in the gulf region a force of tactical air power roughly comparable to that deployed in Europe during the Cold War. Supplemented by Marine and Army aviators and three aircraft carriers, the Air Force has about 420 combat planes and 250 support aircraft operating from approximately 30 airfields in the area. Of more than 150,000 U.S. military personnel deployed as part of Operation Desert Shield, 30,000 belong to the Air Force.

Until two weeks ago, U.S. target planners had assembled a somewhat conventional list of Iraqi targets which included, in order of priority: Iraqi air defenses; airfields and warplanes; intermediate-range missile sites, including Scud ground-to-ground missiles; communications and command centers; chemical, nuclear and munitions plants; and Iraqi armor formations. Other targets, Dugan said, would include Iraqi power systems, roads, railroads and perhaps domestic petroleum production facilities—though not the oil fields.

"That's a nice list of targets, and I might be able to accept those, but that's not enough," Dugan said. He asked his planners to interview academics, journalists, "ex-military types" and Iraqi defectors to determine "what is unique about Iraqi culture that they put very high value on. What is it that psychologically would make an impact on the population and regime in Iraq?" The intent, he added, is to find "centers of gravity, where air power could make a difference early on.". . .

The Air Force also has identified three "culturally very important" sites in Iraq—possibly religious centers—that the U.S. bombers would avoid. "We're not mad at the Iraqi people, and when this is all over we don't want the Iraqi people to be mad at us and the rest of the allies we've brought together," Dugan said.

Air power gives "a special kind of psychological impact," he added, and hopefully would soon persuade Iraqis that "Saddam and his regime cannot protect them." Although the Air Force can guarantee tremendous devastation in Iraq, whether raining destruction would effect the withdrawal from Kuwait or Saddam's ouster is a political conclusion that the president and others must make, Dugan said. There also is no guarantee that bombers would be able to find Saddam.

The Air Force generals declined to comment on whether U.S. chemical or nuclear weapons have been moved to the gulf region for use against Iraq.

Part of the focus on air warfare is the consequence of unpalatable alternatives. The Pentagon has decided that it cannot and will not match Saddam's ground forces, much less assemble the 3-to-1 advantage considered necessary for an offensive campaign. Air power plays to a U.S. strength while avoiding a protracted armor offensive or extensive urban fighting in Kuwait City, several generals said.

Marine and Army ground forces could be used for diversions, flanking attacks and to block an Iraqi counterstrike on Saudi Arabia. If major ground warfare is to be avoided, then the air war cannot be restricted just to Iraqi targets in Kuwait or "obviously, air power cannot achieve the goal" of dislodging Iraq, Ferguson said. Ground forces may be needed to reoccupy Kuwait, Dugan added, but only after air power has so shattered enemy resistance that soldiers can "walk in and not have to fight" house-to-house.

Unlike some of the U.S. ground forces, which may take another two months to reach their gulf destinations, the Air Force is virtually in place and has sufficient forces to fight an all-out war. Some additional aerial tankers have yet to arrive, but adequate supplies of munitions are on hand except for flares and chaff used to deceive anti-aircraft missiles. To fill out their war reserve kits, squadrons deploying to the gulf did considerable "cannibalizing" from squadrons left behind, which in turn have borrowed from reserve and Guard units.

Although Schwartzkopf recently said he was concerned about the impending overhaul of Air Force transport jets, Dugan said: "I'm not aware of any significant problems with the airlift. Yeah, we're going to have to replace some engines, but we replace engines" periodically anyway. A more pressing problem is to find rested pilots, for which more reserves might be needed.

The generals expressed great satisfaction with the Air Force deployment under Desert Shield. The Saudis have spent many billions of dollars building runways, hangars, repair shops and hardened subterranean aircraft bunkers that are the "finest I've ever seen anywhere," Adams observed. A new, still-unopened airport in the eastern portion of the country is "bigger than Dulles and JFK [airport in New York] combined," said Maj. Gen. Philip G. Killey, director of the Air National Guard. Airmen have made good use of material from Harvest Falcon, goods stored in Egypt, Oman, Turkey and elsewhere.

In general, aircraft used for defensive purposes—such as tank killers and air defense jets—have been placed closer to the Iraqi border while offensive planes—such as ground attack fighter-bombers—are at bases farther back, one general said. That deployment likely would change if combat begins. Six aircraft battle-damage repair teams have been deployed to the region.

Excerpt from "Top AF General Bounced: Dugan Told Press of Gulf Bomb Plans," *Los Angeles Times* (September 17, 1990), part P, 1, 6.

Defense Secretary Dick Cheney fired Gen. Michael J. Dugan as Air Force chief of staff today after Dugan's public comments about contingency plans to unleash massive air raids on Iraq and target Saddam Hussein personally. Dugan, in the top Air Force job only three months, violated Pentagon rules by publicly discussing likely military targets inside Iraq and disclosing classified information about the size of U.S. forces in the gulf area, Cheney said.

"There are certain things we never talk about. We never discuss operational matters, such as the selection of specific targets for potential air strikes," Cheney told reporters. "We never talk about the targeting of specific individuals, who are officials in other governments.

(continued)

**Policy Leak to the *Washington Post* and the
Washington Response** *(continued)*

That is a violation of the executive order," the secretary said. "We never underestimate the
strength of opposing forces or reveal previously classified information about the size or dispo-
sition of U.S. forces. Nor do we ever demean the contributions of the other services," he
said. "Gen. Dugan's statements as reported in the press and as confirmed by him to me—
failed all of those tests," Cheney said.

Containment and the Decision to Double U.S. Ground Forces

The second major turning point in Gulf War policy involved the decisions to engage
in military action rather than relying on economic containment and to double U.S.
ground forces. As before, these decisions were made by a small number of individuals
through a very restricted policy-making process. As a result, these policy processes
faced many of the same problems experienced in the first phase of the conflict.

Despite a general consensus on the use of economic sanctions as an important
immediate response to the Iraqi invasion, disagreements persisted within and outside the executive branch regarding the ability to rely on economic containment
and the need for and the shape of military action. Brent Scowcroft and Dick
Cheney were consistent proponents of military action. Supporters for continuing
economic containment included Powell, Baker, Undersecretary of Defense for
Policy Paul Wolfowitz, Schwartzkopf, Lieutenant General George Lee Butler, as
well as Admiral William Crowe, Jr., and General David Jones, both former Joint
Chiefs of Staff, and most members of the UN coalition.[34] These competing viewpoints were expressed in a series of congressional testimonies, public statements,
and newspaper reports throughout the fall.

The choice between these alternatives was made by a small group of central policy makers with what has been described as little or no formal discussion of the benefits
or limitations of economic containment.[35] According to Bob Woodward's account,
during September and October of 1991, Chairman Powell expressed concern that the
NSC procedures and meetings had been casual about discussing the various positions
and alternatives and that clear decisions about options rarely emerged.[36] Given the
perceived limitation of the NSC process, Chairman Powell articulated his desire to de-

---

[34] Lauren Holland, "The U.S. Decision to Launch Operation Desert Storm: A Bureaucratic Politics
Analysis," *Armed Forces and Society*, vol. 25, no. 2 (Winter 1999): 223. For a discussion of sanctions in
U.S. policy see George Shambaugh, *States Firms and Power: Successful Sanctions in U..S. Foreign Policy*
(Albany, NY: SUNY Press, 1999).

[35] Ibid., 224.

[36] Bob Woodward, *The Commanders* (New York: Simon and Schuster, 1991), 301–302.

bate the options and express his preferences for pursuing economic containment versus military action in individual meetings with Cheney, Scowcroft, and Baker. Powell eventually succeeded in raising his concerns to the president, but he did so in a small meeting in the Oval Office with Cheney and Scowcroft rather than in the context of an NSC meeting. In the Oval Office meeting with the president, Powell reportedly specified the economic alternatives to military action, but he declined to express a personal preference for containment to a military option.[37]

The decisions to pursue offensive military action evolved gradually. The decision to increase the number of ground troops was reached through a series of discussions in October. This increased the likelihood of military action, as did the decision to assume an offensive position.[38] On October 10, a small group of decision makers including Powell, Cheney, Wolfowitz, and other members of the JCS met to review offensive war plans presented by Marine Major General Robert Johnston, General Schwartzkopf's chief of staff.[39] On General Schwartzkopf's instruction, Johnston argued that he needed roughly double the force level he currently had (in terms of the air force, navy, marines and army troops) to guarantee success, and that there was a window of opportunity between January 1 and February 15 that would be conducive to offensive action.[40] On October 11, Johnston repeated the briefing for President Bush in the **situation room.**

This was followed by a series of meetings in the military.[41] On October 17, Lieutenant General George Lee Butler, director of J-5, the JCS Planning and Policy Staff, sent Powell an options memorandum that identified four possibilities: (1) maintain the status quo to deter and defend; (2) prepare for long-term containment, increasing the pressure of sanctions that would have to be in place for six months to one year to be effective; (3) go to war; (4) or up the ante by adding sufficient forces for a credible offensive threat.[42] Butler recommended the second option, and advised against going to war. On October 21, Powell then traveled to Saudi Arabia to meet with Schwartzkopf and assess U.S. ground forces. Schwartzkopf reported that he was not persuaded that an offensive military operation was viable and that such an operation would require roughly double the current forces on the ground. Powell told Schwartzkopf that he would support the doubling of force levels, but that no decision about offensive action had been made.

On October 24, President Bush met with Cheney and indicated that he was leaning toward adding the forces necessary to carry out offensive operations, but that

---

[37] Ibid., 41–42, 302–303.

[38] Lauren Holland, "The U.S. Decision to Launch Operation Desert Storm: A Bureaucratic Politics Analysis," *Armed Forces and Society*, vol. 25, no. 2 (Winter 1999): 224.

[39] For a discussion of the negotiations over military strategy that took place at that meeting, see Bob Woodward, *The Commanders* (New York: Simon and Schuster, 1991), 304–307.

[40] Ibid., 306.

[41] For a discussion of these meetings and a bureaucratic politics perspective on the decision-making process, see Andrew Bennett, "Models of Crisis Decision-making and the Experience in the 1990–1991 Gulf War," conference paper prepared for the Annual Meeting of the American Political Science Association, Chicago, 1992.

[42] Bob Woodward, *The Commanders* (New York: Simon and Schuster, 1991), 308.

nothing could be announced until after the November 6 elections.[43] On October 25, during interviews on morning news programs on ABC, CBS, and NBC, Cheney suggested that troop increases were likely by arguing that, "We are not at the point yet where we want to stop adding forces . . . ," and that it was conceivable that the United States would increase its forces by as many as 10,000 troops.[44] According to Woodward's account, the announcement reflected a decision to increase troops and forgo economic containment that was made by Scowcroft, Sununu, and President Bush without a "full airing of views."[45] Indeed, Powell and Schwartzkopf both learned of the policy decision from the news reports, and General Schwartzkopf reportedly had to explain it to his Saudi Arabian contacts without any guidance from Washington.

On October 30, President Bush met with Baker, Cheney, Scowcroft, and Powell in the situation room to decide whether to switch to an offensive military option. In advance of the meeting, Brent Scowcroft wrote a memorandum to the president outlining his opinion and recommendation. In the memorandum, he argued:[46]

> Our basic objective at this point ought to be to regain momentum and take the initiative away from Saddam. This requires a two-track strategy: on the diplomatic side, a renewed push for full and unconditional Iraqi withdrawal as called for by Security Council Resolution 660; on the military side, accelerated preparations that provide a real alternative should diplomacy fail. One way of implementing this strategy would be giving an ultimatum to Saddam demanding that he withdraw fully from Kuwait (and release all hostages while permitting the legitimate government to return) by a certain date. I would argue that the date certainly should be around the end of the year, some five months since the attack and the imposition of sanctions.
>
> . . .
>
> I believe this general approach is preferable to sticking to sanctions. It does not appear that sanctions alone will accomplish what we seek in the foreseeable future. Meanwhile, the hostages remain hostage and Kuwait is being destroyed and resettled by others. The coalition shows signs of fraying at the edges because of disagreements over such issues as the use of force, the need for full Iraqi withdrawal, the restoration of the Sabahs, and the Palestinian issue.

According to Woodward's account, Powell was struck again by the informality of the discussions, the lack of organization to the proceedings as options were discussed, and the casual nature with which ideas were exchanged.[47] Powell succeeded in presenting Schwartzkopf's recommendation to double the U.S. military force and he received the president's approval for that action. At the same time, however, Powell felt that he had not been given permission to raise the issue of containment with the president again and that his advice in that regard would not

---

[43] Ibid., 311.

[44] Ibid., 312.

[45] Ibid., 312.

[46] George Bush and Brent Scowcroft, *A World Transformed* (New York: Knopf, 1998), 392.

[47] Bob Woodward, *The Commanders* (New York: Simon and Schuster, 1991), 318–320.

be welcomed. President Bush approved the increase in forces verbally during the meeting, and did so formally the next day, but he insisted that the decision not be released until the congressional elections had passed.

Echoing Powell's concern about the policy-making process, Brent Scowcroft noted that President Bush had come to the conclusion in early or mid-October that it was necessary to liberate Kuwait and that doing so would require using force.[48] He also noted that this was, ironically, only a general impression and did not result from a specific meeting or debate about going to war, setting out war aims, or setting out the strategic military objectives for the coalition and U.S. forces.

Similarly, upon reviewing the war plans, Undersecretary of Defense for Policy Paul Wolfowitz echoed Powell's concern about the lack of access and apparent lack of debate in the decision-making process. His assessment was that decisions were largely made in closed and frequent meetings between Bush, Baker, Cheney, Scowcroft, and Powell without the presence of staff or the participation of others outside of the group. As a result, he was "worried that the administration had transitioned to the decision on the offensive option without a lot of clear thought. There was little or no process where alternatives and implications were written down so they could be systematically weighted and argued."[49]

On November 8, at a news briefing, President Bush announced, "I have today directed the Secretary of Defense to increase the size of U.S. forces committed to Desert Storm to ensure that the coalition has an adequate offensive military option should that be necessary to achieve our common goals."[50] That announcement of escalation provoked congressional critics to demand a more meaningful congressional role.[51] As a result, securing congressional support became particularly important. After several days of debate, Congress gave its approval on January 12.[52] Once the announcement had been made, the administration set about to build congressional support, gain UN authorization for military action, and gain support from the coalition for the use of "all necessary means" to eject Saddam Hussein's forces from Kuwait if he did not pull out by the deadline of January 15, 1991. The UN resolution passed on November 29.

On January 15, 1991, President Bush met with members of his war council—including Quayle, Baker, Cheney, Scowcroft, Powell, Sununu, and Gates—to sign a top-secret National Security Directive authorizing the execution of Operation Desert Storm, provided that there was no last-minute diplomatic breakthrough, and that Congress had been properly notified.[53] At the same time, the president authorized Cheney to sign a formal Executive Order authorizing Schwartzkopf to execute Desert Storm pursuant to the warning order on December 29. Powell wrote the

---

[48] George Bush and Brent Scowcroft, *A World Transformed* (New York: Knopf, 1998), 382.

[49] Bob Woodward, *The Commanders* (New York: Simon and Schuster, 1991), 320–321.

[50] Ibid., 324.

[51] Robert Spitzer, "The Conflict Between Congress and the President over War," in Marcia Lynn Whicker, James P. Pfiffner, and Raymond Moore, *The Presidency and the Persian Gulf War* (Westport, Conn.: Praeger, 1993), 35.

[52] Public Law 102-1 (H.J. Res. 77), January 23, 1991.

[53] Bob Woodward, *The Commanders* (New York: Simon and Schuster, 1991), 366–367

Executive Order, both he and Cheney signed it, and they faxed it to Schwartzkopf. The Gulf War that ensued lasted 42 days. Kuwait was liberated.

Conclusion

While the NSC served as the primary coordinating body for policy making and deliberation throughout Desert Shield and Desert Storm, Bush established a de facto war council of individuals with privileged access to the president and input into policy decisions. Because the president did not rely primarily on NSC procedures, and because some members of Bush's team had privileged access, even those in Bush's war council were surprised by pivotal policy developments. Furthermore, those outside of the inner circle leaked information and engaged in behavior that undermined the administration's efforts. President Bush succeeded in gaining support for his policies from the United Nations, Desert Shield and Desert Storm coalition partners, and the U.S. Congress. He also succeeded in deterring an attack against Saudi Arabia and in liberating Kuwait. The success of these policy outcomes is laudable. It should not, however, minimize the lessons this case provides about the potential hazards of relying on a centralized policy-making process that does not provide a means for stake holders to express their views.

Key Terms

Group of Eight or the **War Council:** George Bush relied very heavily on a core group of decision makers known as the *group of eight* or the *war council* through Desert Storm and Desert Shield. The core group included President Bush, Vice President Dan Quayle, Chief of Staff John Sununu, National Security Adviser Brent Scowcroft, Secretary of Defense Dick Cheney, Chairman of the Joint Chiefs of Staff Colin Powell, Secretary of State James Baker, and Deputy Advisor on National Security Affairs Robert Gates.

Pulsing the System: The use of informal ties to sample various groups for options.

Situation Room: Located in the basement of the West Wing of the White House, it provides the president and the NSC direct access to all the communication channels of the State Department and the Department of Defense, as well as to some of the channels of the CIA.

Review Questions

1. Describe some of the impacts on the policy-making process that occurred when the perceived legitimacy of the process deteriorated during the Gulf crisis.

2. What was the "Group of Eight" and who were its members?

3. Describe the two military options presented by General Schwartzkopf during the first NSC principals' meeting following the August 2 invasion of Kuwait.

4. Why did Secretary Cheney relieve Air Force Chief General Michael Dugan from his command? What does this episode suggest about the policy-making process?

CHAPTER 12

Practice Scenarios

Practice Scenarios

The goal of this book is to introduce students and practitioners to the tools, techniques, and processes used to create and implement policy in the executive branch of the U.S. government. While the nature of policy making will shift depending on the issues at hand and the people involved, we have argued that the process of policy making will operate best when the authority, responsibility, and accountability for a particular policy are centralized and all policy makers with a stake in the policy believe that the policy-making process provides an effective means for expressing their concerns to the president or those responsible for policy development.

In many cases, the perceived legitimacy and effectiveness of the process of policy making are as important to members of the policy-making community than is a specific policy outcome. When the process is considered to be illegitimate or ineffective, policy makers will circumvent the process and use other means—such as leaking information to the media, ignoring the established chains of command, and/or using alternative means to contact the president or other key decision makers—to promote their objectives. Such activities undermine the policy-making process because they tend to present the president, or the decision makers responsible for the policy, and the public at large with a biased view of the issue at hand. Furthermore, they often spark similar retaliatory action by others who do not share their critic's views. The end result may be an ill-considered policy or political deadlock. To avoid these problems, it is vital for the student and practitioner of policy making to understand both the process itself and the tools and techniques that make it work. Combined, the tools, techniques and processes establish *systems* of decision making that enable the effective participation of all relevant policy makers. When these tools, techniques, and processes are applied appropriately, they can facilitate policy making; when they are ignored, the process tends to unravel.

In this chapter we present several scenarios that require action by the executive branch. The scenarios involve different sets of issues: a mix of security, economic, and political problems in the Taiwan Straits; economic and political problems associated with an economic recession in the United States; political problems associated with public demands for campaign finance reform; and environmental and trade concerns in the context of the United States-European trans-Atlantic agenda for the twenty-first century. While the reader may lack some of the issue-specific information needed to reach a final policy decision, there is sufficient information to design a policy-making process to acquire that information and develop potential policy responses to each of these issues.

The scenarios call for the involvement of different members of the executive branch and require different types of policy responses. The policy responses may incorporate a variety of diplomatic, economic, and military strategies and may require executive and/or legislative action. The key to successful policy making is to develop an effective and legitimate process for creating and implementing policy in response to an action-forcing event. Note the ten-step checklist on pages 178–179 for developing an effective and legitimate process. Each step is summarized with references to the earlier sections of this book to make it easier for students to reference information.

Scenario One: Taiwan Straits Crisis

The Republic of China on Taiwan (ROC) has been undergoing extensive democratic reforms while maintaining a strong military and robust free-market economy. It has the economic, military, and political systems of an independent state, but its sovereignty remains a matter of dispute from the perspective of the People's Republic of China (PRC). The issue has been diffused in the short term by a constructively ambiguous agreement to recognize "one China with two governments"—one in Beijing and one in Taipei. Taiwan has, however, continued to pursue recognition in international organizations, and domestic pressure to assert its independence is increasing. The issue is problematic for the United States, which has long-standing economic and political ties to Taiwan as well as increasingly important economic and geostrategic interactions with the PRC.

In a recent presidential election, Taiwanese citizens had an opportunity to voice their opinion concerning ROC membership in international organizations as well as national independence. The leading Kuomintang party (KMT) continued to pursue the objective of "one China with two governments." Its rival, the Democratic Progressive Party (DPP) argued that full recognition of Taiwan by the world community required a formal declaration of its independence from the People's Republic of China. After winning the election, the DPP announced that it had a mandate to declare Taiwan's independence. The People's Republic of China (PRC) opposes Taiwan's independence and its pursuit of recognition and membership in multilateral organizations. It also considers its relations with the Republic of China on Taiwan (ROC) to be a matter of domestic politics and opposes all international claims to the contrary.

Since the election a variety of domestic and international factors have recently heightened tensions, and the PRC has threatened to invade the ROC to stop its secession should it formally declare independence. U.S. intelligence indicates a buildup of military forces of unprecedented proportions is taking place along the coast in southern China. In addition, over the past week, the PRC has fired several missiles across the Taiwan Straits. Shipping from Taiwan's primary ports has been suspended, the Taiwan stock market has plummeted, and the Taiwanese government is considering suspending securities trading. The Taiwanese government has also put its defense forces on alert.

This morning, the National Security Adviser received an official request from the Taiwanese government asking for the following: (1) security guarantees that would include a commitment by U.S. forces to physically defend the island from an invasion; (2) increased patrols by U.S. naval forces of the Taiwanese Straits to demonstrate the U.S. commitment to Taiwanese security and to deter additional missile launches by the PRC; (3) the immediate shipment of advanced anti-missile and anti-submarine defense systems.

Assess whether this event constitutes an action-forcing event. If it does, develop a response following the ten-step policy process checklist in this chapter. When creating a policy-making process, consider the roles and views of some of the following stake holders:

Agencies

Secretary of Defense
Secretary of State
Chairman, Joint Chiefs of Staff
Director of the Central Intelligence Agency
Secretary of the Treasury
Secretary of Commerce
U.S. Trade Representative
U.S. Ambassador to the United Nations

White House Offices

National Security Council Director
White House Chief of Staff
National Economic Council Director
Chief of Staff to the Vice President
White House Director of Congressional Affairs
White House Communications Director
White House Political Director

Outside Advisers

Pollster

A Ten-Step Policy Process Checklist

Step 1:   Assess the context, issues, and implications of the action-forcing event. Given these factors, identify all necessary and appropriate participants to be included in developing a policy response. Identify a coordinating entity (e.g. the appropriate policy council) that will set up and manage the process. (Chapter 1: *Introduction: Why the Policy-making Process Matters*, Chapter 2: *The Policy Councils*, Chapter 3: *The White House Staff*)

Step 2:   Have the coordinating entity develop a specific time table for developing a policy response. The time table should specify precisely when the president or decision maker will need to have the policy options in hand so that he/she can determine which approach he/she will support. It should also specify how much time each agency, department or other policy-making body has to develop proposed policy options. In addition, the coordinating entity should establish a specific meeting schedule, determine how many sessions will be needed, what the topics of each meeting will be, and set deadlines for completion of all intermediary steps. (Chapter 2: *The Policy Councils*, Chapter 3: *The White House Staff*, Chapter 4: *Agencies and Policy Implementation*)

Step 3:   Have the coordinating entity identify which agencies are responsible for developing different policy responses and direct a series of interagency meetings at the deputy level. The first deputies' meeting should entail an overview of the problem and potential solutions from each participating agency's perspective. If there is an immediate consensus, the coordinating entity should identify one lead agency to work with the others in developing a single proposal for the principals. If there is no immediate consensus, the coordinating entity should identify those agencies that will be given primary responsibility for developing competing policy proposals. (Chapter 1: *Introduction: Why the Policy-making Process Matters*, Chapter 4: *Agencies and Policy Implementation*)

Step 4:   If there is a consensus, the lead agency should draft a complete decision memorandum for the agency principals. If there are competing proposals, then each agency should draft options that may be included in a later decision memorandum. (Chapter 5: *Policy-making Memoranda*)

Step 5:   If there are competing proposals, a second series of interagency meetings at the deputy level should be held. The coordinating entity should try to build a consensus around one or two of the competing options (or as few of the options as possible) without forcing any agency to retract their proposal. As the process develops, some proposals may be modified in a way to make them compatible, while some agencies are likely to drop competing proposals in light of debates within the working group. (Chapter 1: *Introduction: Why the Policy-making Process Matters*, Chapter 4: *Agencies and Policy Implementation*)

Step 6:   Once a consensus of one or more proposals has been developed by the inter-
            agency deputy-level working group, a draft decision memorandum should be pre-
            pared for the agency principals. Once the draft decision memorandum has been
            completed, the head of the coordinating entity will ask that public support for
            the various options be tested by polling before the decision memorandum is for-
            mally presented to the president or the chief decision makers. Draft polling ques-
            tions once a policy has been put forth. Consider what kinds of questions and
            sorts of polling techniques would accurately test the public support for the vari-
            ous options. The polling information is not officially entered into the memoran-
            dum, but will be considered by the principals while reviewing the deputy's pro-
            posal. (Chapter 6: *Polling and the Policy-making Process*)

Step 7:   If all of the department heads and agency principals accept the decision memo-
            randum, it can go forward to the president. If not, the coordinating entity will
            call for a series of principals' meetings to further narrow the options by seeking a
            consensus around one or more major proposals. Again, however, no agency
            should be prevented from putting forth a dissenting proposal in the final decision
            memorandum. (Chapter 5: *Policy-making Memoranda*)

Step 8:   The president or chief decision maker will either accept or reject the recommenda-
            tions or ask for more options and/or information. (Chapter 5: *Policy-making
            Memoranda*, Chapter 4: *Agencies and Policy Implementation*)

Step 9:   Assuming the president chooses one of the options proposed in the decision
            memorandum, the coordinating entity should direct the appropriate agencies
            or departments to implement the president's decision. If existing legislation
            is involved, or if the president has decided to submit new legislation, a
            Legislative Referral Memorandum (LRM) will be written by the OMB and
            an accompanying Statement of Administration Position (SAP) will be drafted
            by the relevant agency and circulated throughout the executive branch and
            then forwarded to Congress. If the president chooses to take regulatory or
            executive action to implement the policy, no SAP will be produced and
            the process will proceed through existing regulatory and legal channels.
            (Chapter 4: *Agencies and Policy Implementation*, Chapter 7: *LRMs, SAPs,
            and other Acronyms*)

Step 10:   Decide whether the president or a specific agency or department will take the
            lead in announcing the policy decision. The White House or designated agency
            or department will then prepare press paper/fact sheets, and possible questions
            and answers that will communicate and market the proposal to Congress and the
            public at large. (Chapter 4: *Agencies and Policy Implementation*, Chapter 8:
            Communicating and Marketing Policy)

Scenario Two: U.S. Economic Recession

Over the past six months many economists have begun to predict an economic downturn in the U.S. economy. After ten years of solid economic growth, historically low levels of unemployment, low inflation, and high productivity, this prediction is based on dramatically lower levels of consumer confidence and an increasingly volatile stock market. All this is occurring one year before the next presidential elections.

Last night, the Secretary of the Treasury was notified by analysts in the Treasury Department that, contrary to the previous month's projections, U.S. gross domestic product is no longer growing. In addition, the Department of Labor is planning to announce new data in three days that will show a significant increase in the unemployment rate, Congress is planning to hold hearings on the drop in consumer confidence, and the press corps is reporting that the Organization of Petroleum Exporting Countries (OPEC) is planning to raise the price of crude oil significantly at next month's meeting of oil ministers, raising the specter of rising inflation. Finally, public support for tax relief has dramatically increased, and the chairman of the House Ways and Means Committee has announced that he will draft tax cut legislation.

While economic conditions are worsening, there are still many indicators that the fundamentals of the economy are strong, especially over the long term. Budget surpluses are projected for the next ten years. The trade deficit has significantly decreased due to a weakening of the dollar relative to the Euro and the Yen. Interest rates remain low and the housing market is booming. Finally, the chairman of the Fed has stated he believes that the current economic outlook overall is positive, and he has indicated strong support for fiscal restraint.

Assess whether this event constitutes an action-forcing event. If it does, develop a response following the ten-step policy process checklist. When creating a policy-making process, consider the roles and views of some of the following stake holders:

Agencies

Director of the Office of Management and Budget
Secretary of the Treasury
Chairman of the Council of Economic Advisers
Secretary of Labor
Secretary of Commerce
U.S. Trade Representative

White House Offices

National Economic Council Director
White House Chief of Staff
Domestic Policy Council Director
Chief of Staff to the Vice President
White House Director of Congressional Affairs

White House Communications Director
White House Political Director
White House Public Liaison Director

Outside Advisers

Pollster
Media Consultant

Scenario Three: Campaign Finance Reform

During the last two Congresses, efforts to enact campaign finance reform legislation passed overwhelmingly in the House of Representatives, but failed by just a few votes in the Senate. As a result of recent general elections, supporters of campaign finance reform believe they now have a filibuster-proof majority in the Senate. In the past, the administration has remained neutral on this issue due to opposing views within the cabinet. Some people within the administration favor publicly financed campaigns as the only means to dramatically and fairly reduce the influence of special interests. Others believe that any bill that imposes limits on independent expenditures in support of candidates for federal office is a violation of the First Amendment and the right to free speech. Finally, additional groups argue that a ban of so-called soft money contributions—which are unregulated donations made by individuals and entities to candidates for the purpose of party building—is draconian. Fundraisers in both major parties are concerned, for different reasons, that constraints on soft money will hinder their ability to elect candidates.

Last night, the White House director of Congressional Affairs was notified by the majority leader that the Senate will take up campaign finance reform legislation next week. In addition, he is requesting that the administration issue a Statement of Administration Policy (SAP) on the bill. Specifically, the majority leader wants to know what kind of campaign finance reform legislation the president would sign and what kind he would veto. The growing likelihood that campaign finance reform will pass is increasing concern among certain key constituencies regarding the form it will take. For example, a number of labor unions, environmental and public health organizations, and several large corporations believe that the ban on soft money will decrease their political influence. While opposition to campaign finance reform grows among interest groups, public support in favor of this legislation has increased. According to a survey conducted last week by the president's pollster, 70 percent of Americans strongly support passage of the campaign finance reform.

Assess whether this event constitutes an action-forcing event. If it does, develop a response following the ten-step policy process checklist. When creating the policy-making process, consider the roles and views of some of the following stake holders:

Agencies

Attorney General/Department of Justice
Director of the Office of Management and Budget
Secretary of Treasury

White House Offices

White House Chief of Staff
Domestic Policy Council Director
Chief of Staff to the Vice President
White House Counsel
White House Director of Congressional Affairs
White House Communications Director
White House Director of Political Affairs
White House Director of Public Liaison
Staff Secretary

Outside Advisers

Pollster

Scenario Four: United States-European Environmental Negotiations

Environmentalists and the fishing industry in the United States have become increasingly concerned by the depletion of fish stocks throughout the Northern Atlantic. They have joined forces in a coalition calling for the United States to press Europe to address this problem in a way that can promote the growth of fishing stocks for future consumption.

In two days the president will be addressing an ongoing meeting between the United States and members of the European Union (EU) in Madrid to set a trans-Atlantic agenda for the twenty-first century. During the first two days of negotiations, two difficult issues were settled: burden sharing regarding the reconstruction of Afghanistan, and the establishment of a cooperative agreement aimed at eliminating trade barriers between the United States and the EU. The remaining issue involves the establishment of a multilateral agreement to manage the use of living resources in the Atlantic Ocean. The issue has become a matter of increasing international concern as fish stocks have declined and international competition over remaining commercial species has become more vicious.

The dispute has divided Europe, pitting Spain, Portugal, Italy, and France against the UK and Germany. The former group argues against multilateral management and supports increased privatization of the oceans, with no restrictions beyond extended exclusive economic zones (EEZs). They argue that extending the EEZs would not solve the problem. Furthermore Spain and its supporters argue that a multilateral management regime is destined to fail because the costs of monitoring and enforcement would be prohibitive. The British, the Germans and the U.S. argued that without a multilateral management regime the fishing industry will die in the next ten years.

Assess whether this event constitutes an action-forcing event. If it does, develop a response following the ten-step policy process checklist. When creating a policy-making process, consider the roles and views of some of the following stake holders:

Agencies

U.S. Trade Representative
Secretary of the Interior
Secretary of Commerce
Secretary of Agriculture
Secretary of State
Secretary of Treasury
Chairperson of the Council on Environmental Quality
Chairperson of the Council of Economic Advisers

White House Offices

White House Chief of Staff
Domestic Policy Council Director
National Economic Council Director
Chief of Staff to the Vice President
White House Director of Congressional Affairs

Index